The Reflexive Teaching Artist

The Reflexive Teaching Artist
Collected Wisdom from the Drama/Theatre Field

Kathryn Dawson and Daniel A. Kelin, II

intellect Bristol, UK / Chicago, USA

First published in the UK in 2014 by
Intellect, The Mill, Parnall Road, Fishponds, Bristol, BS16 3JG, UK

First published in the USA in 2014 by
Intellect, The University of Chicago Press, 1427 E. 60th Street,
Chicago, IL 60637, USA

Copyright © 2014 Intellect Ltd.

A catalogue record for this book is available from the
British Library.

Series: Theatre in Education
Series ISSN: 2049-3878
Cover designer: Stephanie Sarlos
Copy-editor: MPS Technologies
Production manager: Jessica Mitchell
Typesetting: Contentra Technologies

Print ISBN: 978-1-78320-221-8
ePDF ISBN: 978-1-78320-223-2
ePUB ISBN: 978-1-78320-222-5

Printed and bound by Hobbs, UK

To my past, current and future students—you are our future;
I feel honored to have witnessed one part of your journey.

Katie

To each of the Teaching Artists I have worked with in the
islands—I have learned so much from each of you.

Dan

Table of Contents

Acknowledgements

As over-reaching as it might seem, every single person I have encountered in the arts-education field has made me think about my own practice, often causing me depressing nights. But the light of morning always shined with new insights. This is especially true for all of the students and children I have worked with, and for, over the years. I only single out my co-author, Katie, for pushing hard enough at the precise right times that I went from reflecting to being reflexive. Thanks for the journey.

Daniel A. Kelin, II

* * * * * * * * * * * * * * * *

To my current and former colleagues at The University of Texas at Austin, Sharon Grady, Megan Alrutz, Roxanne Schroeder-Arce, Coleman Jennings, Lynn Hoare, Suzan Zeder and Joan Lazarus—thank you for supporting my efforts to create our very first teaching artist course and your belief in professionalizing the field. Special thanks to Brant Pope and Doug Dempster who gave me a new tenure-track position in teaching artist pedagogy and practice; your spirit of innovation and willingness to grow a faculty member from within will always be deeply appreciated.

To my dear friends and teaching-artist programming partners over the years: Jack Plotnick, Darlene Hunt and Meg Brogan, Julie Pearl, Gwenyth Reitz, Bridget Lee, and Lynn Hoare—thank you for joining me in the discovery of the power and potential of learning in and through arts. Special thanks goes to Stephanie Cawthon who taught me how to be a better educational researcher in theory and in practice; the action research model presented in this text is based on your excellent examples.

To Dan—my co-author, collaborator, critic and cheerleader—without your talent, tenacity and ability to meet deadlines this book would *never* have been completed. You taught me how to politely disagree and pushed me to rediscover my artistry. Oh how far we've traveled from that first conference hotel bar conversation! Thank you.

And, finally, to my parents and siblings who supported my every effort to be an artist and educator, and my family—my partner in all things, Bob, and my two children, Ruby and Lilah—thank you for understanding that even when I am away my heart is always and forever with you.

Kathryn Dawson

* * * * * * * * * * * * * * * *

To our many Teaching Artist contributors—thank you for meeting deadlines and remaining open to the conversation as we worked together to structure an innovative text for our field that truly honors the diversity of its practitioners and participants. Tremendous thanks goes to our early editors—Sarah Coleman and Shannon Baley—and our later critical friends— Cecily O'Neill, Eric Booth and Nick Jaffe—whose wisdom, eagle eyes and advice helped shape this text in significant ways. Special thanks to Jessica Mitchell at Intellect for your advice and enthusiasm.

Dan and Katie

Foreword

ERIC BOOTH

Know it or not, you just picked up the book that will take your best work as a Teaching Artist toward greater impact and satisfaction if you follow its lead. Reflection is the single-most stinted component of the arts learning spectrum; hell, it is the most stinted component of all institutional learning. And now we have a guidebook to add that essential oxygen to increase the organic combustion of learning—our own professional learning and our participants' learning. Not only that, Dawson and Kelin take reflection up a notch to reflexivity that moves the reflective learning into action. The book is brimming with useful discriminations you never made in your work before, invitations to apply new concepts to your own practice, and guidance for extending your practice into areas you haven't tried before. At least it did this for me, and I am a grizzled ancient of our young teaching artist field. While this book will be inspirational for new Teaching Artists, it is proudly the first book for advanced level Teaching Artists, guiding those of us who have been around to discover the next level of excellence, impact and satisfaction in our work. A sign of growing maturity for our field. Thank you, Katie and Dan.

John Dewey told us bluntly that if we do not reflect on our experiences we do not learn from them. Reflect on that! This reminds us that every time we fill a workshop to the brim with dynamic activities, we damage the possible learning takeaways for the participants if we do not include effective reflective opportunities throughout the process. Every time we fail to reflect on our own work in leading that workshop, including the habits and assumptions that led to the way we designed and led that workshop, we crimp our own potential. We need those pauses amid complex encounters to bend the experience back toward ourselves (the etymology of the word reflect, to bend back toward), so we can precipitate out those few things that are valuable to recall and retain. It is an entirely subjective process. Participants may need to mark a feeling for its unusualness or sense of veracity; they may have had a question or thought or memory they need to bookmark for later revisiting; they may be able to clarify a process they invented or a connection to some other part of life—who knows? We may need to note the discussion we led with eighth graders that didn't catch fire; the question we asked that led a high schooler in an unexpected direction; the way we weren't filled with genuine excitement when we worked with those 6-year-olds today.

The individual, student or Teaching Artist, knows what's important; yet she is less likely to own and activate that knowledge if we don't provide reflective invitations. This applies to our participants and to ourselves. The circumstances of our employment tend not to encourage reflective practice. And we live in a belligerently anti-reflective culture that consumeristically pushes for results and gratifications and "what have you got for me next?" Master Teaching Artists provide remedial work for this essential human capacity in our participants, and this book guides us to provide this masterfully for ourselves.

I am delighted that Dawson and Kelin chose to mention my Law of 80 percent in the early pages of this book—80 percent of what you teach is who you are. It is a deep truth of teaching artistry, of teaching in general (in formal and informal settings) and throughout life. Their book aims at the right target according to that Law. We ourselves must embody, radiate, revel in the values and pleasures of reflection to activate this in others. This book is a generous invitation to reflect within its pages in structured ways—the book itself functions like a good Teaching Artist. Follow the authors' lead and use the exercise machines they provide in this reflexive gym to gain full fitness to bring to your learners and your artist-self and your life. You are strengthening exactly the muscles of creative fitness in teaching artistry that tend to atrophy in our culture and our professional employment practices.

Reflective practice is an appropriate banner to follow for relentless improvement in any complex field, and Dawson and Kelin have raised the banner high and well. They present a set of fundamentals of teaching artist practice that guides our way. They have distilled the core of our practice into five areas—*intentionality, quality, artistic perspective, praxis* and *assessment*; these feel like a satisfying way to hold the collective wisdom our field has earned. In reading those sections, I repeatedly felt those moments of, "Yes, I know that from experience, but I didn't quite know I knew that." The case studies ground this conceptual framework in a way that great conversations with colleagues can. As much as Teaching Artists get excited about the 'architecture' of our practice, we need tangible examples: we want to talk about the buildings people have made, what happened inside them and what they learned in the process.

Dawson and Kelin lead us finally to two new ways of thinking about our practice—praxis and participatory action research. These are powerful ways to reframe the work we do. These are the ways advanced practitioners in any complex field think about their work. The best brain surgeons do not think like technicians delivering a service. They work within a context of praxis in which action unfolds within a network of experience, theory and experimentation. They work within a context of action research in which the improvisation of each surgery provides new data for the ongoing learning toward better performance—and the simple practices of data collection, analysis and sharing allows the surgeon and the field to advance. Teaching Artists are brain surgeons of embodied learning, and this book guides us toward new habits in our practice so we don't get stuck as mere deliverers of a service, but remain learners, researchers in practice.

On a personal note—I don't know how they did it. Katie and Dan are stupendously busy Teaching Artists, leading programs and maintaining a wide reach of deep commitments; a glance at their bios in this book barely hints at the scope of their activity. Yet somehow, they have managed to create this book for us. Through several drafts. Through working with the contributing writers. Through rigorous refinement of the conceptual skeleton of the book—which is an accomplishment in itself. Through the careful style they found that invites and informs, and includes activities, just as Teaching Artists always do. I especially enjoy the way they have allowed their voices to ring out individually on some occasions, and how clear they are when they speak as one. Thank you, Katie and Dan, for a standing stone that allows our field to step up to more powerful practice, which happens to be more rewarding for us and for our participants at the same time. This is how a profession grows—by two of its leaders pulling together the best of what they and their smart colleagues know, in a way that authentically invites the rest of us to follow with clarity and fresh enthusiasm.

CECILY O'NEILL

Writing from the dual perspectives of artist and educator, the authors of this book raise fundamental questions about the complex functions of the Teaching Artist and the possibility of artistry in teaching. They have a realistic appreciation of the challenges of mapping such a diverse field but approach their task with great skill and collegiality, inviting readers to reflect, identify and question their own purposes and practices. Their aims are to stimulate dialogue, strengthen individual and collective professionalism, encourage reflection and promote the experience, understanding and appreciation of theatre in schools and communities.

The authors accept that what you know and what you do as an educator and an artist is less important than who you are as a person. They invite their readers to reflect honestly on their personal and professional journeys through interactive exercises and offer their own candid reflections in return.

In seeking to establish the nature of collaborative learning environments the authors have identified five core concepts—*intentionality, quality, artistic perspective, praxis* and *assessment*—and offer these useful concepts as the beginning of a shared vocabulary for the field. Each of the concepts is explored through case studies that provide fascinating perspectives on Teaching Artists at work. These studies display impressive levels of insight, skill and sensitivity. They are enormously varied in context, and use dialogue and innovative technology to present their stories effectively. They demonstrate convincingly that engaging in drama and theatre can play a vital part in achieving a wide range of personal, educational, artistic and social objectives. Above all, the honesty with which all the practitioners reflect on their successes and failures will make these accounts invaluable to both beginners and experienced Teaching Artists.

The section on Artistic Perspectives is particularly fascinating. This is a concept that can be difficult to pinpoint clearly, especially in school contexts, where curricular demands may over-ride aesthetic considerations. The chapter highlights one of the many challenges facing the Teaching Artist—that of cultivating their own personal artistic growth while attempting to induct others into the art form. Ideally they should be able to develop and maintain their own skills as artists while extending their skills for delivering high-quality arts education experiences in diverse contexts and with varied communities. Effective Teaching Artists will

- Understand the possibilities and potential of their materials
- Animate these materials successfully
- Demonstrate their commitment to and excitement about the work
- Generate contexts in which failure is not relevant
- Use language that is inviting, exploratory and speculative
- Invite participants' contributions
- Cope with unpredictable responses
- Employ a range of appropriate strategies and approaches
- Raise interesting questions and promote different perspectives
- Suspend judgment and recover quickly from setbacks
- Embrace ambiguity and complexity

In the case studies reflecting on Artistic Perspectives, we are presented with moving accounts of work that reveal courageous Teaching Artists operating with all of the aforementioned skills and many more. Validating participants' experience and promoting each individual's skills and self-esteem requires considerable interpersonal skill and sensitivity. The Teaching Artist has to recognize the needs and interest of the individual while promoting and supporting the work of the whole group.

This aspirational and inspirational book presents an impressive array of research, reflection, theory and practice in a remarkable variety of contexts. With its understanding of a complex area of inquiry, its range of references and the depth of its scholarship, it will prove enormously useful to practitioners and academics alike. The book demonstrates that in the hands of gifted and reflexive practitioners, drama and theatre can bring about transformative learning. While there are dedicated, skilled and experienced Teaching Artists like those whose work is celebrated here, there is hope that drama and theatre will continue to make a positive impact on the lives of students, educators, schools and communities.

Prologue: The Teaching Artist Manifesto

It is the age of the Teaching Artist. National governments and urban US cities have begun to identify the arts as a tool for educational reform in our public schools (President's Committee on the Arts and the Humanities 2011; UNESCO 2006; UNESCO 2010; The Improve Group 2012).

It is the age of the Teaching Artist. Diverse organizations and institutions employ Teaching Artists through outreach and community-engaged programming.

It is the age of the Teaching Artist. Journals, websites, books and higher-education courses related to teaching artist pedagogy and practice in school and community settings continue to grow in number and diversity.

And yet ... Teaching artistry as a profession continues to struggle for recognition. Some school-arts specialists challenge whether Teaching Artists are *true* teachers while some professional artists challenge whether Teaching Artists are *true* artists. Even within the ranks of Teaching Artists there is a call for more definition and professionalism of the field.

And yet ... Teaching Artists remain under-theorized, underpaid and often misunderstood (Rabkin, Reynolds, Hedberg, and Shelby 2011).

HOW DO TEACHING ARTISTS NAVIGATE SUCH COMPLICATED TERRAIN?

By engaging in work through a clear sense of purpose, based on a deep understanding of who they are, why they do what they do, and how their work is in conversation with others.

Introduction

Your vocation, your life work, is 'where your deep gladness meets the world's deep need.'
(Buechner 1993: 95)

Written by two Teaching Artists for other Teaching Artists, this book includes the collective wisdom of 24 Teaching Artist professionals working in diverse settings and with a wide range of participants. For the purposes of this text, the pronoun *we* is used to signify both the authors' voice and *our* collective teaching-artist practice.

In this book we ask you, the reader, to consider:

Why am I a Teaching Artist? What is my vocation, my life's work, my calling? How can a reflective practice help me to become and/or remain an inspired, motivated Teaching Artist throughout my career? How can a reflective practice inspire a similar focus, energy and commitment in my collaborators and students?

- Focus: Reflective practice
- Enduring understanding: To improve we reflect
- Essential question: How does reflection enhance practice and purpose?

WHAT ARE WE WRITING ABOUT?

This book is a call to drama/theatre Teaching Artists to consider the power of reflective practice. Through our own reflection and the reflection of others we closely examine the practice of teaching in, through and about drama/theatre. We contend it is through the continued development of critically inquisitive, reflective practice that the greater field of drama/theatre education will build a stronger foundation for professionalism.

This text focuses specifically on the field of drama/theatre teaching artistry with the belief that what we present has application to other art and nonart practices. We choose to use the combined term (drama/theatre) since there are different histories and practices associated with each word. Some associate the term *drama* with the literature of the field (e.g. play scripts and other dramatic literature), others with the type of meaning making and interaction that occurs between participants and/or audience and performer (Nicholson 2009). Drama emphasizes the pedagogy, the *why* of the art form, with focus on the *how* of the process. The term *theatre* often references the particular skills and techniques related to creating and performing theatre in a variety of forms and contexts (Grady 2000; Saldaña 1998). Theatre emphasizes the practice, the *what* of the art form, with a focus on the *how* of the product. We also use the US spelling of *theater* (–er) to reference the space where theatre happens. We use the UK spelling of *theatre* (-re) to reference the practice. The wealth of published works available to read (or attempt to read, as it is admittedly a difficult task to keep up) is typically separated into two categories: theory/pedagogy and lesson plans/activities. This text attempts to live and think in the liminal space between these worlds, in ways that reach out in either direction.

To ground our pursuit we offer a series of foundational concepts as a reflective framework, illuminated by case studies from a wide range of teaching artist practice. The foundational concepts explored include: *intentionality, quality, artistic perspective, praxis* and *assessment*. In this text we will look closely at each concept to consider its purpose and offer questions to guide their practical application. We admit that this list of foundational concepts is the beginning of a conversation (or maybe debate?) rather than *the* definitive list. We believe that the concepts, collectively, contribute to exemplary work; they are a multicourse meal as opposed to a menu of singular choices. Seidel, Tishman, Winner, Hetland and Palmer's *Qualities of Quality: Understanding Excellence in Arts Education*; Booth's *The Music Teaching Artist's Bible: Becoming a Virtuoso Educator*; McKean's *A Teaching Artist at Work*; Hetland, Winner, Veenema and Sheridan's *Studio Thinking*, Greene's *Releasing the Imagination*; and Neelands' "Re-imaging the Reflective Practitioner: Towards a Philosophy of Critical Praxis" in *Research Methodologies for Drama Education*, among others, have influenced our writing. These works, and others like them, contribute to an ongoing discussion of quality within our field. As we posit here, and in chapters to follow, quality is informed by a number of factors. We will attempt to generalize these conditions but any given situation will be influenced by factors beyond prediction. In addition, we hope that what we write encourages further reflection by individuals and within the field. For this reason, this text offers brief activities as further engagement—questions to answer, charts to complete, a research process to follow—if you are interested in adding a kinesthetic engagement to your reflective process.

WHY DO WE HAVE OPINIONS ABOUT THIS TOPIC?

As stated before, there are two authors for this text: Katie and Dan. We've chosen to write together, in a single voice, although we have had diverse experiences and currently work in different contexts, located in different parts of the United States. In many ways our backgrounds represent the diversity of the drama/theatre teaching-artist field. Our combined resumes include work in schools; businesses; museums; arts organizations; universities;

professional theaters; children's television; and, urban, suburban and rural communities both domestically and internationally. Part of what drew us into the field and keeps us thinking, working and writing is a deep curiosity about the relationship between artistry and education. As a team of writers we celebrate both the education and artistry in our pedagogy and practice.

DAN:
From my vantage point as Education Director in a professional theater, through which I train and support Teaching Artists and work regularly as a Teaching Artist myself, I often consider teaching artist practice through the lens of an artist:

- Where does an artist begin?
- Where does an artist's process begin?
- How does an artist come to understand the process that best serves him?
- How does an artist develop understanding of and sensitivity to the achievements of his work?
- What is the balance between arts and instruction in any given moment during facilitation?
- How does a Teaching Artist quantify the impact of his work— on himself, his participants and places where he works?
- How does a Teaching Artist help guide young artists to understand and embrace their own aesthetic and artistry?
- What role does exemplary, professional theatre performance play in the education of young artists and nonartists?

KATIE:
As a university professor who supports pre-service and in-service teachers interested in shifting the learning culture of the classroom through the arts, I often consider teaching artist practice through the lens of an educator:

- How do we enter a new context with an understanding of the identities of the participants and systems of power that shape the space and place where we hope to work?
- What are the goals of our work together?
- How will we make decisions?
- What prior knowledge is necessary for our work to be successful?
- How can we consider and value our diverse, individual experiences within our collaboration?
- How can we reflect throughout our process and synthesize our collective understanding?

Through the negotiation of co-authorship, we have experienced how individual and joint reflection helps each of us challenge and consider the other's viewpoint, thereby deepening and enriching our own practice.

WHAT IS THE GOAL OF THIS BOOK?

This book invites the reader to become a reflexive Teaching Artist, someone who reflects on practice and engages in action based on the reflection, both personally and with others. We ask you, the reader, to consider the questions we pose along the way, to activate both reflective and reflexive thinking about your experience and the experiences of others. We encourage you to take notes in the here and now, thoroughly investigating your influences and beliefs and how you understand the purpose and efficacy of your own practice and our field at large. We challenge you to treat this text as a tool for practice. In Part 1: A Teaching Artist Reflects, Chapter 1 considers the term *Teaching Artist*—we define and examine the unique purpose and role that the Teaching Artist plays in twenty-first century American society and its current status in the educational and artistic landscape in the United States. We follow with activities that orient the individual within the world of teaching artistry through self-reflection. We invite you to recognize how your personal identity, beliefs and experiences shape your core values and influence your teaching artist identity and practice. Part 1, Chapter 2 examines the definition and purpose of *reflective* and *reflexive* practice. We consider the relationship between the terms and argue for their combined application in daily teaching-artist practice. We end with a brief activity that puts reflexivity into action. In Part 2: Collected Wisdom, Chapters 3 to 7 define our proposed conceptual framework for reflective practice: *Intentionality, Quality, Artistic Perspective, Assessment* and *Praxis*. Each foundational concept is personalized, contextualized and expanded upon through multiple examples from a wide variety of national and international drama/theatre Teaching Artists working in a range of professional contexts. The case studies privilege intention and inquiry, highlighting a deep commitment to connect the why, what and how of teaching-artist practice in an ongoing cycle. In Part 3: The Reflexive Practitioner, Chapter 8, we offer an invitation to the reader to apply key concepts of the book to their own practice through a step-by-step approach to participatory action research.

WHY IS THIS BOOK WRITTEN THIS WAY?

As Teaching Artists, and trainers and supporters of Teaching Artists, we have yearned for a text to share with our colleagues to inspire conversation and further professionalism of the field. Our goal here is to spur serious consideration of and conversation about 'big picture purpose.' Positioned as a call toward individual and collective reflexivity, we hope this book will reinvigorate beliefs and inspire a larger critical consciousness about each reader's particular calling to the field. We hope this text will encourage Teaching Artists of all levels of experience to continue a journey of self-education in order to enrich the experience of program participants, colleagues and collaborators. Mostly, we hope this book will contribute to an ongoing conversation about the elemental aspects of our field offering further clarity, purpose, agency and voice to those engaged in the daily work of the Teaching Artist.

It is the Age of the Teaching Artist. We invite you to improve the professionalism of our collective practice through ongoing and purposeful reflection.

PART 1

A Teaching Artist Reflects

Chapter 1

The Teaching Artist

A Teaching Artist is a practicing professional artist with the complementary skills, curiosities and sensibilities of an educator, who can effectively engage a wide range of people in learning experiences in, through, and about the arts.

(Booth 2010: 2)

Today, Teaching Artist has become the term used to describe the wide range of activities for those individuals who both practice their art form and engage in teaching others the knowledge and processes they employ as artists.

(McKean 2006: xii)

As drama/theatre Teaching Artists, we, the co-authors, shamelessly embrace the field. We recognize its great joys, its shortcomings, its highly engaging nature, its lack of clearly defined criteria and the related disagreements among professionals of drama/theatre and education. We also acknowledge the impressive spectrum of work included under the umbrella of drama/theatre teaching-artist practice.

In this chapter, we explore the definition and context of teaching-artist practice and pedagogy to give the reader a way to understand and define their own place and purpose in the field. Since reflection is central to our premise for the book—ask and reflect, think and rethink, question personal understanding and redefine possibilities—we will organize our reflection through guiding questions and conclude with brief activities for further self-reflection and synthesis.

WHO IS A TEACHING ARTIST?

Artists who teach. Teaching with great artistry. Teaching about art or through art or with art or using art to teach, explore and/or reflect on nonart topics. All of these descriptions could apply to the definition of Teaching Artist. Therefore we contend that to have purpose and credibility a Teaching Artist should be experienced and knowledgeable about both teaching *and* art.

Sounds overly simple, but it underlines our journey with this book. The *art* of teaching. The Teaching of art. Teaching *artfully*. Art-inspired teaching. Art-full teaching. The art of teaching is to inspire. Inspired by their own art experiences, the Teaching Artist facilitates experiences that inspire, guiding students to discover their own inspirations.

WHAT IS A TEACHING ARTIST?

Drama/Theatre Teaching Artists work in a wide range of settings (e.g. professional theaters, arts organizations, schools, communities, universities, business, prisons, museums, etc.) in urban centers, communities and villages across the globe. Teaching Artists work with a range of populations who represent a variety of ages, gender orientations, sexual orientations, cultures, ethnicities and races, abilities, and socioeconomic statuses. Some focus on a specific population and/or location (e.g. preschool students) while still others practice a specific form of theatre with a variety of populations (e.g. youth theatre, such as devising and/or directing original or scripted performances with youth of all ages). Some are housed in a specific arts organization and/or a professional theatre. Others are employed independently, situated on a roster or are instructional staff for multiple arts organizations or they facilitate their residency or workshop practice through their own business. Still others are employed full or part-time by a school or university but use the title of Teaching Artist to illuminate a particular approach to education in and through the arts as a desired way of working. In this text we will characterize teaching artist practice as *work* located in specific settings: school, communities and professional theatre. Although these categories are fluid for many in the profession, the mission or intention and funding for practice is often facilitated through one or more of these larger entry points, and this shapes the approach or type of work they are asked to do.

WHY TEACHING ARTISTS?

Teaching Artists often serve as a bridge to the arts or an artistic process. In the continuing debate about who has access to art, who is engaged by art and/or who feels most welcome in art institutions, Teaching Artists are a valuable asset. The more experience an individual has with art, the more she understands how art works as a form of expression and as a medium in which she can learn to express herself. However, art access for young people is dwindling, particularly in public schools. There is less of an opportunity for students to experience and understand the power of art and art making. A drama/theatre Teaching Artist in schools, the community and in professional theatre has the potential to be the conduit for a complement of experiences that inspire a desire to encounter, practice, investigate, understand and appreciate theatre.

WHO AND WHAT SUPPORTS AND SHAPES THE TEACHING ARTIST PROFESSION?

Teaching Artists in schools

Since the days of the Settlement House in the early twentieth century in the United States, teaching artist practice has been shaped by the way society has viewed creativity and the education of its people, particularly its young people. Now, in the twenty-first century, globalization and innovative technology has shifted the ways we educate (Nicholson 2011). The field of drama/theatre has also changed in significant ways. New media and technologies have impacted some of the ways performance is created and shared with others. Educational reformers have adopted art-based terms—creativity, imagination, innovation and collaboration—as the Partnership for 21st Century Skills (2011). The US Government May 2011 report from the President's Committee on the Arts and Humanities recommends arts education and arts integration as an effective and cost-efficient way to address teachers' and students' needs in schools. It specifically names Teaching Artists as a source of innovation and a sea change in the field.

The field of drama/theatre teaching artistry has yet to fully benefit from the increased interest in the profession. Nick Rabkin's (and others) 2011 research study of over 3500 Teaching Artists, program managers, teachers, principals and other key stakeholders was predicated on the supposition that "arts education and Teaching Artists in particular are hidden, underdeveloped, and underutilized resources in our national effort to improve schools" (2011: 27–28). Nevertheless, the results of their study confirmed that Teaching Artists are "bringing innovative pedagogy and curriculum to schools. And [the] broad belief that there is something in the nature of arts learning itself that has a particular power to drive student development" (Rabkin 2011: 6–7).

As research opens more possibilities to the place of art and applied or integrated art in the classroom, the Teaching Artist can and should play an important role in shifting instructional practice and the learning culture of the classroom. In many parts of the country, Teaching Artists collaborate with schools and teachers to plan, facilitate and evaluate the impact of learning in, through and about the arts. However, this requires that Teaching Artists have adequate training in instructional pedagogy and the skills to link and co-support academic and artistic learning objectives. Teaching Artists need to understand and be able to articulate the potential impact of their work and how to advocate for their place at the instructional table. They need to use the tools of the theatre artist (e.g. voice, body, imagination, among others) and dispositions, or habits, of the artistic process (e.g. engage and persist, envision, express, observe, reflect, improvise) and be able to connect this type of thinking and doing with moments in the instructional cycle (e.g. create, collaborate, analyze/synthesize, translate). When this happens, the drama/theatre learning experience becomes a crucial link in the education of the whole child.

Despite the renewed focus on the benefits and outcomes for learning in, through and about the arts, the professional, arts education community still struggles to agree on an appropriate definition and role for Teaching Artists in the educational environment. How does the current political and ideological climate of arts education, arts integration and education impact Teaching Artists? As increased research on the positive impact of Teaching Artists in schools is published, some members of the certified, arts specialist community are re-engaging with long-held concerns that more Teaching Artists mean less certified arts specialists in schools. Consequently, there is a growing need for Teaching Artists individually and collectively to re/name and re/claim their contribution within the fields of arts and education.

Teaching Artists in communities

Teaching Artists regularly create community programs that bring together participants from a range of settings to achieve specific goals through structured arts and arts-based interactions. One indicator of the diverse application of drama/theatre is the multitude of community settings in which Teaching Artists volunteer or are employed to work. Prisons, retirement centers, museums, health organizations, businesses, houses of worship, homeless shelters and the political arena are among the places that not only benefit from but seek out the skill set of the Teaching Artist. The diversity of work within community settings has the potential to strengthen the place of theatre within our communities and society, as participants develop a greater appreciation of and investment in the place theatre plays in their lives. Helen Nicholson (2005) writes, "The application of drama to different institutional or community settings illuminates fundamental questions about the role and significance of *all* theatre practice to society, and about how theatre-making articulates and challenges contemporary concerns" (4–5).

Within this community setting, practitioners have defined themselves using a variety of titles. In some cases this has contributed to a tension in the relationship between the Teaching Artist and the Community Artist. Eric Booth considered these issues in his 2010 *Teaching Artist Journal* reflection on the first international conference on teaching artistry:

> Teaching Artists [...] seek to empower the encounters with artworks, and community artists seek to enhance the quality of community life. To clarify the difference [...] community artists might say that teaching artists have swallowed the values of elite arts institutions and are agents for institutional preferences and priorities; teaching artists might say that community artists are willing to settle for mediocre art, without rigorous attention to quality, when excellence is what delivers arts' power. [... However] I have noticed in recent years that these two traditionally-separate approaches are merging in the US.
>
> (Booth December 2010)

Titles aside, a beneficial aspect of a community-oriented application of drama/theatre is the common focus on issues beyond K-12 education. This may include an investigation of social/emotional learning, culture, identity, politics or other larger questions of society. Drama/theatre learning experiences—whatever the application, focus or setting—provide ample opportunities for participants to carefully reflect on their actions, beliefs, life experiences and connections to their community and society. The influential work of community-based practitioner and artist Augusto Boal, for example, exemplifies the wide-ranging impact of Teaching Artists working in and with communities to discover their own voice and to focus their energy toward social and/or political change.

Teaching Artists in professional theaters

Professional theaters often provide a setting for the training and development of artists to perpetuate the professionalism and quality of live performance while seeking effective and affective ways to engage with its audiences. No formal overview exists that specifically focuses on the growth of Teaching Artists within a professional theater setting, but it might be argued that this specific area of practice developed nearly concurrently with work in the schools and community settings. Three particular programs of the last century significantly impacted the role of Teaching Artists in a professional theater setting. The Works Progress Administration's (WPA) Federal One program put tens of thousands of unemployed artists to work in such projects as the Federal

Theatre Project and the Negro Theatre Project and this resulted in impacts on art and education that continue to this day. The Comprehensive Employment Act (CETA) put artists to work through funded local initiatives. The National Endowment for the Arts (NEA), responsible for the Artists-in-the-School model still in use, financially supported field trips to plays and productions that traveled to communities. While these performances did not necessarily include direct interaction with the audience, the artists were considered teaching artists of a sort and many organizations marketed the work as educational.

Professional theaters employ Teaching Artists in educational departments located within the theaters "drawn from their own member rosters and artistic personnel [… L]arger companies tend to employ educational administrators and staff, many of whom also serve as teaching artists" (Anderson and Risner 2012: 4). It is difficult to generalize these programs since education programs may be focused on youth performing, adults performing for children and youth, training programs for adults and/or youth, informational programming related to the theater's productions, or programs built in collaboration with other community organizations and/or schools. This is also where pre-professional theatre training happens for young people and/or early career artists hoping to make theatre a career. Often these educational programs are considered outreach for the theater with the goal of increasing revenue for stage productions or developing future audiences. In this space the Teaching Artist serves as a bridge with the community, providing direct access to, experience with and understanding of theatre performance in a professional setting.

The title, the setting or the purpose?

Certainly, the intertwined practice of art and education has wide-ranging applications. In theory and in practice, the Teaching Artist is limited only by imagination. However, there is an ongoing debate around terminology that defines practitioners who teach in, through and about drama/theatre. *Are you a drama educator, artist educator, teaching artist, actor educator, community artist, artist teacher or something else?* Given the relative youth of the field, it is no wonder that titles continue to appear and evolve. We, the authors, use the term *Teaching Artist*, as the combination of terms suggests that the practitioner needs to be skilled and/or conversant in both teaching and artistry. As Daichendt (2013), Booth (2010), McKean (2006) and others make clear, a Teaching Artist lives in the rich, overlapping space between the work of the artist and the educator.

As we consider teaching artist practice throughout a range of settings and purposes, there are multiple entry points of inquiry. What specific skills and knowledge/s does each of these locations require from the Teaching Artist? How does the designation of Teaching Artist, as a *chosen* profession, support a further sense of professionalism and a need for a type of 'specialized knowledge' in each of these locations? How do unique funding streams impact how we conceptualize and implement our teaching artist practice, whether we work in schools, community or professional theatre settings? Part of the challenge of teaching artist practice is its potential to contribute to so many different contexts each with its own unique characteristics, systems and needs.

WHAT IS THE TEACHING ARTIST SPECTRUM?

As stated, the term 'Teaching Artist' is a hybrid of two rich disciplines: education and the arts. Each is associated with particular skills and understandings, and practiced by people of all ages and orientations. It can be useful to think of the *work* of the Teaching Artist sitting at the center of a spectrum to avoid an unnecessary and unproductive either/or binary.

EDUCATOR   *<Teaching Artist Work>*   **ARTIST**

Figure 1: The Teaching Artist Spectrum.

Where to place each teaching artist lesson, workshop, project or program on this continuum is informed by multiple factors. Ideally, though, *Teaching Artist Work* sits in a middle space on the *Teaching Artist Spectrum*. The specific context (which includes funding sources and location) and participant population can shift the needle toward one end of the spectrum or the other. For example, the particular context of funding and location (e.g. a three-day in-school process drama residency for fifth graders is supported through a grant related to a safer-schools initiative) might suggest that educational goals are prioritized in the conceptualization and evaluation of the program. However, this does not mean that the Teaching Artist is any less committed to the artistic goals of process-centered educational drama in their facilitation of the program model. So although the stakeholders within a project may choose to shift priorities to focus on the educational side of the spectrum, the Teaching Artist may still prioritize the artistic skill of role-play in the implementation of the work. Or a professional theatre that supports Teaching Artists facilitating the creation of an original documentary theatre production with youth might seem to be located more toward the artistic point on the spectrum. However, if the program is designed for young people on the autism spectrum, the Teaching Artist will need to consider the unique educational goals of the participants, and this shifts her intentions back toward center.

Since the teaching artist's work exists in a liminal space between the joint identities of artist and educator, the term *drama/theatre learning experience* is used in this text as a way to center the practice in the middle of the spectrum. We hope this term will capture an acknowledgment of the educational and artistic skills required of the profession. We want to place an equal emphasis on the learning process within, through and about the drama/theatre art form, along with the recognition that a variety of factors may shift each experience on the continuum.

READER REFLECTION

We promised this would be an interactive text. Here we offer your first opportunity to stop and reflect on your practice.

REFLECTIVE MOMENT: 'WHERE DOES MY PRACTICE SIT ON THE *TEACHING ARTIST SPECTRUM?*'

Think about a recent teaching artist experience. This might be a lesson, a workshop, a short- or long-term residency, a class, a production or some other activity that you classify as a drama/theatre learning experience where you served as a Teaching Artist. If you are a new Teaching Artist, considering this field for the first time, identify an experience you had as a participant or consider the type of experience you hope to lead in the future.

Got your example? Write a very brief description here (or call it out if you aren't one for pencil or paper or are working on your feet in a group).

My example:

Now map your drama/theatre learning experience on the *Teaching Artist Spectrum (TAS)* on the next page with a dot on the line. Draw a line up from your dot and label the experience. Or, for all the kinesthetic learners out there, why not imagine an actual line on the floor (don't forget your two end points) and place yourself on it. Even better do this with collaborating partners. Where does each of you place the project on the *TAS?* Whether on paper or on your feet make this choice quick; it's a gut reaction.

EDUCATOR	ARTIST

Now consider, why did you place yourself on this spot along the line? Write down your thoughts or if you are on your feet with colleagues, tell someone else.

Why?

If you are working with a group, give time for people to shift their opinion based on what others say. Now pick another drama/theatre learning experience, where would you place this practice on the *TAS*? Repeat until full.

Why am I a Teaching Artist?

Part of the work of a Teaching Artist is determined by necessity: "This is the available work so this is what I am doing." However, even within a project that is defined by outside contexts we still have autonomy to shape our experience. And, in an ideal world, our teaching artist practice is determined by a deep intrinsic need to work in a specific way, in a specific place, with specific people. With that in mind, why do *you* work as a Teaching Artist? What do you bring to the practice and how do you benefit from what you do? What influences the choices you make as a Teaching Artist? Specifically, how do your beliefs about theatre/drama and how people learn with and from each other shape what you do and how you do it? Many have written about the way our past experience shapes our current attitudes and actions. Russian educational theorist Lev Vygotsky's (1978) theories of social constructivism stress the temporary nature of what we know; we are constantly reconstructing our understanding based on our experiences, which are mediated through culture and society. In simple terms, our outside world and experience shapes our understanding of who we are and what we know.

Who am I and why does it matter?

While we are great believers in practice being at the heart of what we do, practice alone won't actually move us forward. We need to be evaluators of our work, but we also need philosophers and anthropologists, as well as drama specialists who are not necessarily practitioners who can help us.

(Blei 2012: 9)

Eric Booth (2010) suggests that 80 percent of a Teaching Artist's success is based on who they are. He invites the reader to remember his or her favorite teacher. What was the quality that made this person so memorable? Success as a Teaching Artist, Booth writes, comes less from the materials shared or the "perfect" lesson plan, but the "quality of who [we are] as humans" (5). So how do we become our best selves? Taking the time to reflect on identity, experience, and core values are central to becoming a Teaching Artist who is intentional, present, rigorous and constantly improving. It is a good start toward becoming your best (a.k.a. *most memorable and inspirational*) Teaching Artist self. Understanding how to engage in work that honors and furthers personal beliefs and curiosity about art and education is a strong step in the direction of quality. Most importantly, understanding what you hoped to accomplish and why enables you to celebrate what worked and the tools to figure out what went wrong, when it so often does, backed by the confidence to try again.

What defines me as an artist and an educator?

We begin our reflection from the easiest vantage point—the visible and invisible markers that shape our lives. We draw on our lived experiences (e.g. as a Latino, as a male, as someone raised in an upper-middle class household) to portray the imagined experiences of others. As Teaching Artists, we bring who we are into the classroom. Sharon Grady (2000) argues for a deep interrogation of personal identity markers (race, ethnicity, class, gender, sexual orientation and ability) particularly as they relate to hegemony or what is privileged by society. She suggests that the bias in our language and action when we teach (e.g. articulating that a romantic relationship means a man and woman; that gender is fixed; that everyone is able to jump, see or hear; that we all celebrate Christmas) can inadvertently alienate a student who sees herself differently than the most common identities of power in the United States. Grady argues toward a pluralistic approach—an instruction that honors and values the rich multiplicity of identities in our world. This deep awareness of context, both yours and your participants, can help further define who you are.

What identity markers shape your experience of the world?

If white, straight, Christian, able-bodied, upper-class men are often presumed to function from a status with more power in the United States, where does your identity place your level of privilege and/or access in relation to these assumptions? What sort of power (acknowledged and not) do you bring into the room when you teach? How does an awareness of your power in relation to the identity markers of others impact how you relate to your students, your colleagues and your employer? Think about the types of things you teach. What sorts of knowledge and experience does your teaching privilege? By taking time to reflect on 'who we are' and 'what we do,' we can develop a better sense of who and how we want to be with others.

Reflective moment: Inspirations and Influences list

Take a moment to consider your past experiences as learner. What experiences in your life have influenced who you are today? These might be people who are important to you: a mentor, relative, teacher or friend; training you've received; or individuals or a community you taught or learned with or from. This might be other artists or Teaching Artists, or a philosopher or theorist whom you have read or studied. This might be a set of beliefs or a type of theory that shapes how you work or live in the world. As authors, we will take on each of the offered assessment tasks as a model and an example of how we reflect on our own experiences.

Example: Dan's Inspirations and Influences list

Among the influences on my practice	
Laurel and Hardy	Their sense of timing, their honesty, their work ethic, their collaborative spirit and their great respect for each other. (When told that Laurel gets paid more, Hardy famously noted, "Well, he works harder.")
Chinese Beijing Opera	The discipline I learned has served me in all my work as an artist, teaching or otherwise. I discovered the ability to work within a highly strict structure, yet still find the possibility for immense creativity.
Maxine Greene	Her deeply held belief about how the aesthetic of art should permeate our sense of being human.

Robert Wilson	I am mesmerized by his palette of theatrical images, his intense investigation of the smallest of moments in time and space and the simplicity he finds in his enormous vistas.
Constructivism	As a learner I have always had to understand purpose to then make meaning out of whatever experience I was involved in. As a Teaching Artist, I consider my students to be collaborators and co-investigators in the learning journey.
Laurie Anderson	Her vocal stylings, her use of repetition, the way she entices the listener to attend closely to her verbal images that play off and in tandem with each other. There is a kind of mystery that keeps the listener entranced.
Postmodernism	Individual interpretation is a necessary aspect of understanding; each experience, each idea, means something different to each of us, which means creative endeavors can and should reflect the individuals involved. 'No one size fits all.'
Preschool	No one thinks like a preschooler. My favorite avant-garde story was told to me by a 4-year-old. Listening to their ability to combine the random events of their life is a lesson in risk and creativity.
Kieran Egan	Mystery. That's all I'll say. Mystery.
Pacific Islands	Life lived on a tiny dot of earth changes relationships, communication, time and understanding of how large the world is.

Example: Dan's reflection

I found this to be quite quick and easy, as I think about these kinds of influences regularly. In fact, I seek them out. I'm always on the lookout for attitudes, approaches or moments that capture my attention or make me think twice about an event or moment. As I look over my list, I realize I am influenced by the rhythms and reasons as much as the forms and structures of the performing arts. How we interact with each other, influenced by the engaging style of performance, is as useful to me as what I teach about theatre. I also notice how much I focus on the smallest aspects of my work, that the momentary decisions and choices I make contribute to the overall experience as much as what I teach.

I am attracted by the unconventional. I seek experiences that challenge me and make me look at previous experiences and understanding in fascinating and eye-opening ways. I like to work through problematic tasks, particularly those that I know will end up revealing themselves in unexpected ends. This is why, I believe, I find myself using mystery with students, as it grabs their attention and makes them desire to participate. Most significantly I see how influenced I am by the attitudes and approaches of others, making me realize how my own attitude as a Teaching Artist could have a strong impact on my colleagues and students.

Now it's your turn!

Reflective moment: Inspirations and Influences list

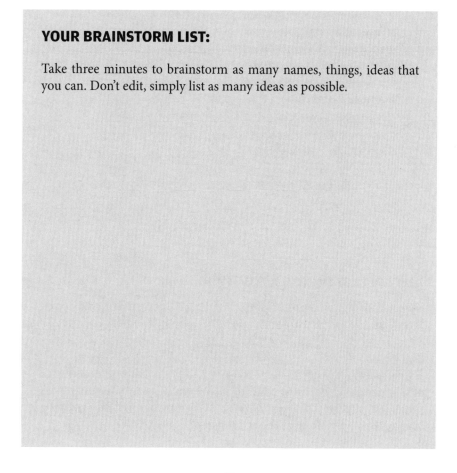

YOUR BRAINSTORM LIST:

Take three minutes to brainstorm as many names, things, ideas that you can. Don't edit, simply list as many ideas as possible.

YOUR TOP TEN LIST:

From your list, pick ten or less that you feel influence you the most. Write the answers in the left column. Then write two–three sentences about how or why each influences you.

INFLUENCE	HOW IT INFLUENCES ME

REFLECTING ON THE ACTIVITY:

What did you notice about yourself during this exercise? Which parts were easy? Which hard?

Note which of your influences were people, a type of training or experience, a theory, or something else. Consider why your influences were drawn primarily from this area. Why do you think more of your examples were from this type of category?

How has your life been shaped by your spheres of influence? In what ways do you engage these various influences and how often?

When you work with a particular population how do their experiences inform their spheres of influence?

What influences shape and inform your choices as a Teaching Artist? Why?

YOUR REFLECTION:

What are my core values?

Merriam-Webster defines a value as "something (as a principal or quality) intrinsically valuable or desirable." The idea of *intrinsic* is most important here as it suggests that what we value is essential and that it naturally belongs to each individual. It is quite literally core to who we are and what we do. Core values are big ideas. They hold weight and power. They are a result of both our complex identities (age, race/ethnicity, gender, sexual orientation, ability) and our experiences. Values function as our compass rose; they offer gut, heart and mind guidance for our daily actions and decisions. They are individual and mutable. One person's core values may not be another's core values. Some core values we hold today may look different to some of our core values tomorrow because we had new experiences. Or some core values may remain the same because they are core to who we are as human beings; they are forever, held fast, impenetrable to time or experience.

Teaching Artists often work with metaphor and representation, teaching others to connect body and soul with opinion and expression (see Chapter 5: Artistic Perspective). Teaching Artists are often invited into a school or community to facilitate a new understanding for participants through conversation, interrogation, collaboration and the creative process. As artists and educators, Teaching Artists have the opportunity to work more explicitly from a set of core principals. Naming your core values can help you understand how you function, or want to function, as a Teaching Artist in the world. Look again at your ten influences and why they are important to you. How does each of these ideas shape a value that is core to who you are?

Reflective moment: Core values activity

The next activity was adapted from an exercise facilitated by Steve Barberio at the 2008 American Alliance of Theatre and Education Leadership Institute. It is based on his work with Servant Leadership at the James P. Shannon Institute.

Example: Katie's core values

In this activity, Katie identifies her top ten values. She then focuses her list to the top five of her top ten. Finally, she synthesizes it to her top two–three core values.

What I value most	Top 10	Top 5	Top 2–3
1. Achievement: Sense of accomplishment	X		
2. Innovation: Creation of new methods and practices, creativity	X	X	
3. Adventure: Exploration, risks, excitement, fun	X		
4. Personal freedom: Independence, making my own choices			
5. Authenticity: Being frank and genuinely myself			
6. Excellence: Pursuit of high quality, being good at something important to me	X		

7. Service: Dedicated to helping others	X		
8. Spirituality: Meaning of life, religious belief			
9. Power: Having influence and authority			
10. Responsibility: Ownership of actions			
11. Learning: Commitment to personal growth and pursuit of knowledge	X	X	X
12. Meaningful work: A relevant and purposeful job	X	X	X
13. Respect: Showing regard for others	X		
14. Family: Happy and congenial living situation	X	X	X
15. Integrity: Acting consistently in adherence to one's beliefs and values	X		
16. Wisdom: Understanding, insight			
17. Justice: Fair and equitable treatment for all people	X	X	
18. Recognition: Being well-known, having prestige			
19. Security: Having a secure and stable future			
20. Tradition: Honoring history and past practices			

Example: Katie's reflection

What this exercise showed me was how hard it is to edit my list down to three ideas; I value ALL of these things. Where I landed today is my consideration of how I struggle with life–work balance. As a professor at a major university who has a partner and two small children, I am often pulled in multiple directions. My children need me, my students need me and my husband probably needs me but we are often too busy juggling kids and work to say this to each other. I wonder how to balance multiple core values in my life.

I also realize how important it is for me to remain a life-long learner who is engaged in meaningful work. As someone who works at a university but spends a major portion of her time working outside the academy as a Teaching Artist in schools and communities, I realize how much I value what I learn from the teachers and students whom I work with across the state of Texas. I strive as an artist and educator to make work with and for people that is meaningful. I have a deep attention to how meaning is made within artistic and educational processes.

Reflective moment: Core values

Read through the following list. What do you value most? Put an 'X' in the first column next to the top ten values that are important in your life. Next, look back over the top ten and put an 'X' in the top five column to signify which are the five most important. Finally, put an 'X' in the top two–three column to identify those values of supreme importance in your life.

What I value most	Top 10	Top 5	Top 2–3
1. Achievement: sense of accomplishment			
2. Innovation: creation of new methods and practices, creativity			
3. Adventure: exploration, risks, excitement, fun			
4. Personal freedom: independence, making my own choices			
5. Authenticity: being frank and genuinely myself			
6. Excellence: pursuit of high quality, being good at something important to me			
7. Service: dedicated to helping others			
8. Spirituality: meaning of life, religious belief			
9. Power: having influence and authority			
10. Responsibility: ownership of actions			
11. Learning: commitment to personal growth and pursuit of knowledge			
12. Meaningful work: a relevant and purposeful job			
13. Respect: showing regard for others			
14. Family: happy and congenial living situation			
15. Integrity: acting consistently in adherence to one's beliefs and values			
16. Wisdom: understanding, insight			
17. Justice: fair and equitable treatment for all people			
18. Recognition: being well-known, having prestige			
19. Security: having a secure and stable future			
20. Tradition: honoring history and past practices			

REFLECTING ON THE ACTIVITY

How did that go? What did you notice about yourself during the process? Was this process uncomfortable? Easy? Were you honest?

How and where did words get negotiated as you had to make fewer and fewer selections? Were you surprised by what did not make the final list?

Take a look at your final two or three core values and consider how these values impact your practice as a Teaching Artist. Where do these values shape how you make decisions about where you work, with whom you work, why you work and in what way/s?

REFLECTION:

Connecting values to intention to practice

Consider again how values are shaped by influences and identity markers to define the Teaching Artist. McKean (2006) suggests that, "[h]ow teachers use past experiences and knowledge to inform their present and future situations are part of the professional stories each teacher brings to the act of teaching" (9). For example, if part of Katie's core values relates to meaningful connections and her position as a learner, than Katie might ask:

How can I model and position myself as a learner in my teaching artist work? How can I create learning environments where I authentically co-construct new understanding in, and through, art with participants? How can I make authentic, meaningful connections in each lesson and project between what we are exploring and the participants' lived experiences? How can I privilege reflection throughout each lesson and project as essential to the creation of new understanding? Keep track of your final selected core values. We will return to this material in Part 3 of this text.

FINAL THOUGHTS ...

The Teaching Artist lives within the space between artist and educator and benefits from each set of skills. The journey for each individual Teaching Artist involves recognition of the influences that shape core values, and the core values that shape intention and choice within daily teaching-artist practice. The next chapter deepens our engagement with reflective practice as we offer a more complex definition of this concept through the unpacking of the terms 'reflection' and 'reflexivity,' and considers how to develop our own reflexive skills within reflective practice.

Chapter 2

Reflective Practice

The outcomes of reflection may include a new way of doing something, the clarification of an issue, the development of a skill or the resolution of a problem. A new cognitive map may emerge, or a new set of ideas may be identified. The changes may be quite small or they may be large. The synthesis, validation and appropriation of knowledge are outcomes as well as being part of the reflective process. [A] significant skill in learning may be developed through an understanding of one's own learning style and needs.

(Boud, Keogh and Walker 1985: 34)

'Reflection'—*re* meaning 'back' and *flectere* meaning 'to bend'—is from the Greek meaning light 'bending back' on itself from reflective surfaces. In Ovid's *Echo and Narcissus*, Narcissus 'bent back' so far he became directly absorbed into his own reflection. In *Hamlet*, William Shakespeare defined reflection through intention, "The purpose of playing, whose end, both at the first and now, was and is, to hold as 'twere the mirror up to nature." While Narcissus warns us of the trap of self-absorption, the Bard suggests that reflective practice is the tool of the artist, mentally 'bending back' to reflect on our work and the work with our collaborators, students and audiences.

Reflection permeates an artist's work. From an initial imaginative spark of inspiration, to the deliberate choice of interpretation and purpose, to the ongoing desire for revision and rethinking, to the final decision of completion, to the reception of the experience or the work—reflection feeds each choice in the artistic process. The Teaching Artist, as with the artist, engages participants in a personalized, critical, reflective practice, in order to consider anew the ideas explored through art-making and in a work of art. She challenges participants within the practice to make connections to their lives and experiences. This is one of the tenets of art: inquire for insight.

John Dewey (1933) recognized that to learn we must reflect on our experience. An experience, posed Dewey, encompasses both action and interrogation of the action. A democratic and emancipatory process, reflective practice encourages a collaborative partnership between teacher and learner, artist and audience. The experience benefits from the negotiation between the collaborators about their ongoing endeavor. The process empowers the learner, encouraging ownership, self-directed learning and the freedom to take risks. Such work empowers the Teaching Artist to consider choices beyond the normative to construct experiences that are reflective of and responsive to participants. It frees the Teaching Artist to ask, "what if ..." instead of, "This is ..." It frees the student from asking, "Is this right?" and encourages statements like, "How about this ..."

Through this chapter we define and examine reflection and reflexivity within reflective practice. We consider how and why learning occurs in reflective practice and how to consider reflexivity about and within personal practice. We encourage and challenge Teaching Artists to embrace various applications of reflection to improve and strengthen personal practice, student learning, and the field in general. We end, as before, with activities to kick-start the reader's foray into investigation and introspection.

Re·flec·tion (ri-flek-*shuhn*) noun. 1. The act of reflecting or the state of being reflected. 2. A fixing of the thoughts on something; careful consideration. 3. A thought occurring in consideration or meditation. *A focus on choices, actions and endeavors, reflection makes sense of experience.*	**Re·flex·ive** (ri-'flek-siv). adj. 1. Directed back on itself. 2. Grammar. Of, relating to, or being a verb having an identical subject and direct object. *A focus on the individual, reflexivity questions beliefs, assumptions and habits.*

Figure 2: Reflection and Reflexivity.

WHAT IS *REFLECTION?*

Reflection is central to learning in a variety of ways. When a Teaching Artist works with participants to collaboratively shape her process through a discussion of common goals and desired impact, she learns. As he unpacks an experience to understand what happened, examining it from as many perspectives as possible, he learns. When a Teaching Artist considers how to apply the experience to a repeated or new action, she learns. Greater than thinking simply about what she is doing, more than ending a session with "What did you learn today?", reflection requires investigation and interrogation. For learning to truly be beneficial it should stem from intentional dialogue with self or others throughout a process. Then, the learner can consciously and purposefully apply the past and present to new situations or experiences. Through this inquiry process, a Teaching Artist develops an awareness of the available choices in any situation and begins to recognize how to achieve the results he most desires. This is called Reflective Practice. Donald Schön (1987) divided reflection into three, interwoven parts. In this text, we connect Schön's theories in relation to five core concepts as a way to consider more fully the possibility of reflection in all aspects of teaching artist work.

Knowing-in-Action

Knowing-in-Action consists of a Teaching Artist's constructed knowledge and skills, built through training, inspiration, imitation, experience, influences and environment, the combination of which informs choices and actions. This is the *what*, *how* and *why* of daily action. In this book, we articulate these as Teaching Artist *intention, quality* and *artistic perspective.*

Reflection-on-Action

Reflection-on-Action occurs post-experience when an artist thinks back on the *knowing* to assess efficacy and improve on choices. Often an unscheduled, undefined process, Reflection-on-Action benefits from conscious contemplation and revision. For students, this process can be paired with an activity, rehearsal or experience. In this text we articulate this type of reflection as a part of teaching-artist *praxis* and *assessment.*

Reflection-in-Action

Reflection-in-Action happens 'in-the-moment' when the unexpected or surprising transpires in the midst of an experience. These are the moments we strive to stay awake and attentive to within our instruction and artistic process. Sometimes called 'teachable moments,' these are unplanned discoveries that occur through a genuine response to ideas and/or action within an artistic process that lead us to the next step in our dramatic process. In this text we articulate this type of thinking as another element of teaching-artist *praxis* and *assessment.*

WHAT DOES REFLECTIVE PRACTICE LOOK LIKE?

In its basic form, a reflective session consists of three considerations in which participants describe what happened, analyze and interpret the experience based on the observations, and relate their understanding to a larger instructional goal or personal understanding of the world and their experience. Rolfe, Freshwater and Jasper (2001) describe this process as an

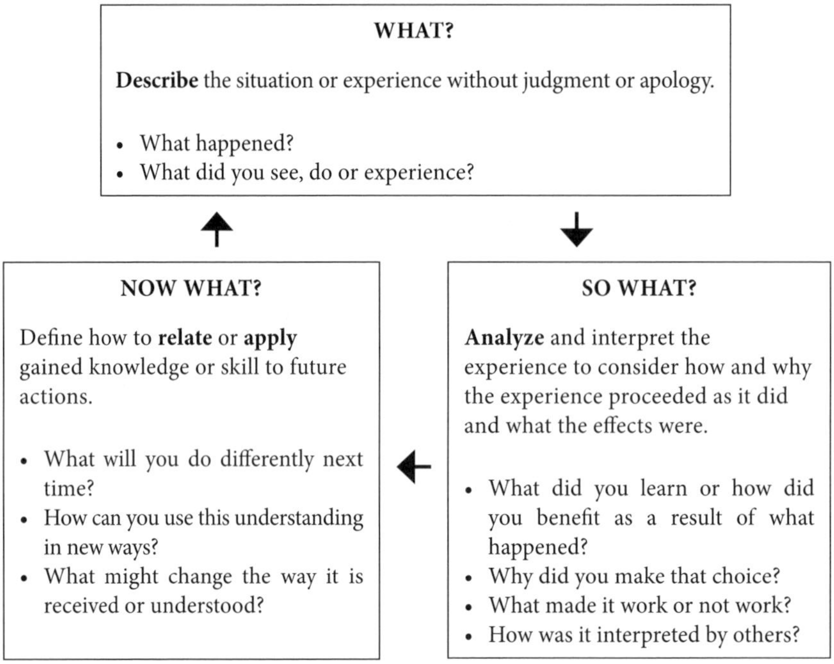

WHAT?

Describe the situation or experience without judgment or apology.

- What happened?
- What did you see, do or experience?

↑ ↓

NOW WHAT?	**SO WHAT?**
Define how to **relate** or **apply** gained knowledge or skill to future actions.	**Analyze** and interpret the experience to consider how and why the experience proceeded as it did and what the effects were.
- What will you do differently next time? - How can you use this understanding in new ways? - What might change the way it is received or understood?	- What did you learn or how did you benefit as a result of what happened? - Why did you make that choice? - What made it work or not work? - How was it interpreted by others?

←

Figure 3: Reflective Cycle chart adapted from Rolfe, Freshwater and Jasper (2001).

ongoing, reiterative cycle of inquiry and learning that asks *what, so what* and *now what*.

By naming what has happened and why, reflection improves our capacity to transfer our learning from one situation to another, making larger connections between our intention and the impact of our actions, which develops our capacity to apply *reflexivity* within our reflective practice.

WHAT IS *REFLEXIVITY*?

Reflexivity is introspection, which demands a more intense scrutiny than reflection as well as willingness to revise, update or even upend personal beliefs and assumptions. Reflexive thought invites us to closely consider what informs who we are as individuals. Reflexive thought invites us to critically examine how beliefs and values, actions and attitudes, our very intuitions shape choice, influence collaborators and students, and significantly influence the results of our and our students' experiences. The reflexive individual entertains *what could be* and even considers *what challenges all that I have known, believed or practiced*. A reflexive thinker seeks to understand how he interrelates with others, how open he is to considering choices and ideas that are in opposition to his own, and how responsive he is to the momentary and evolving needs of others. A reflexive thinker turns the lens on herself, interrogating how those deep-seated aspects of who she is determines how she will react to any given experience or situation.

Reflexivity helps young learners develop into reflective practitioners. It is the capacity for reflexive interrogation that will be the foundation for future achievement. The reflexive individual understands how to thoroughly investigate choices and alternatives and when to challenge her choices to improve both her practice and the experience of colleagues and collaborators.

Let's consider two types of reflexivity. In the first, a Teaching Artist puts his sights on his beliefs and assumptions about his work—the *why* of the work. The Teaching Artist can consider why certain drama or theatre strategies are effective tools for learning, why participants receive pro-social benefits from the drama learning experience, or why he believes more young people should have access to drama/theatre learning experiences. This is sometimes called *epistemic reflexivity*. In the second, a Teaching Artist targets her instructional design—the *how* of the work. The Teaching Artist can closely examine the kinds of activities, strategies, lesson plans, or training methods that she uses and how effectively students engage in and benefit from those choices. Essential to this examination is how clearly students exhibit the desired outcome of the experience and what assumptions about the experience succeeded and which did not hold up to expectations. This is referred to as *methodological reflexivity*.

Reflexive dialogue can also be embedded within an artistic experience. Artists such as Christo and Augusto Boal propose and stage events that stimulate conversations about a particular artwork as well as what defines art. Art itself is a reflexive practice, they contend. Built into an art experience, reflexivity increases personal engagement with the art while challenging participants to consider carefully their reactions to the art and the subject of the artistic experience. Engaging participants in this manner, in deep interrogation, increases ownership and appreciation of how art functions within our lives and society and simultaneously enhances reflexive practice. Reflexivity, then, rewards us with greater levels of understanding, renewed inspiration and significant insight.

WHAT IS THE ROLE OF *REFLEXIVITY* WITHIN REFLECTIVE PRACTICE?

Ideally, our work cultivates our students' as well as our own capacity to engage in reflection and reflexivity. Argyris and Schön write about the relationship between both reflection and reflexivity and how they both inform a third type of learning in their trilogy of looped learning (1974, 1978). Reflective practice occurs in the initial loop; we reflect to make work more efficient and effective when we ask ourselves: *Are we doing things right?* Inherent in this reflection is the determination of 'right' (see Chapter 4: Quality) and the application of this criterion to the action. In evaluation terms this often looks like a summative reflection where we consider the *results* of each *action*. Reflexivity occurs in the second loop, as underlying patterns of thinking and behavior are identified to reshape and strengthen thoughts and actions. We reflect here on the larger impulses and beliefs that shape the actions in Single-Loop Learning. In evaluation terms this is the formative assessment where the personal *assumptions* that drive the action that gives us certain results are considered. As we see in the chart below, the second loop feeds back into and contributes to the success of the first loop. Triple-Loop Learning builds on the knowledge of the first two loops. In the third loop the focus is on meta-cognition through an understanding of how to learn. The focus is on the larger process of naming how we learn; what was the process used; and, how can we apply this type of learning to other contexts or situations in the future. The focus is on developing our ability to regularly and effectively carry out reflexive practice and how to apply or transfer the learning to a new situation.

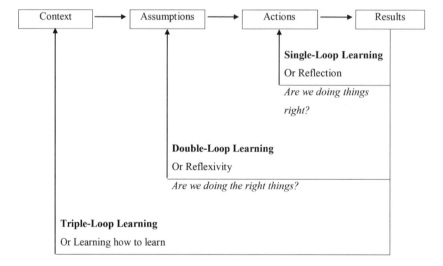

How do we decide what is right?

Figure 4: Triple-Loop Learning, adapted from www.thorsten.org, based on a diagram published by Masterful Coaching, www.masterfulcoaching.com.

READER REFLECTION

We ask that you, the reader, now consider how you might apply Triple-Loop Learning to your past experience. In this next activity, we invite you to interrogate a past moment using Triple-Loop Learning as a tool toward developing your own reflexivity with your reflective practice. In order to complete this exercise, consider an experience in which you served as the facilitator or teacher or as a participant.

Reflective moment: Triple-Loop Learning activity

1. Single-Loop: Describe a moment from a drama learning experience that caused you to consider, question or shift your beliefs about your own practice.
2. Double-Loop: Analyze the experience and discuss how the experience impacted your current beliefs.
3. Triple-Loop: Relate the learning to the choices you made (or hope to make) based on the experience. How did you apply or hope to apply your learning as new thinking about your work?

Example: Katie's reflexive moment

Single-Loop: Describe a moment in a drama learning experience that caused you to question your beliefs about your practice. Sixty miles south of the Arctic Circle sits a tiny Alaskan Native village. The mostly Koyukon Athabascan community lives in isolated 'bush' country—to reach the village one must either fly, or arrive by dog sled or snow machine, or on boat during the four months when the Yukon River flows. Historically, pedagogy in bush Alaska has been founded on hierarchies based on the assimilation and uprooting of the native population. In 2001, the third year of an annual two-week drama residency in the community, my Teaching Artist partner and I (both white women from the lower 48 states) brought a documentary filmmaker to work with the community. We decided that the high-school students should interview the elders of their tribe as part of class project. We arranged a day for interviews and invited respected tribe members (the students' relatives) to the school. We told the youth that their task was to interview the elders about the elders' lives. An hour before the elders were due to arrive, the students said they wouldn't make the film; they were "tired of the old people telling them what to do."

In this moment I realized that I had completely missed the point of my work in and with this community. The village has one of the highest suicide rates for young men in the world. I had been brought to the community to help activate and energize the learning environment. Although my desire was to connect students to their cultural history, I was still another white outsider telling them what I thought they should do. My co-teacher and I made a quick decision. We pulled the youth together and explained our mistake. We acknowledged that we hadn't asked them what they wanted to do in this process. We also explained that the elders were coming, soon, and we weren't sure what to do. A lively discussion broke out; eventually, the teens decided that they wanted to interview the elders, but it would be about them. The teens would be the topic of conversation. They wanted their voices in the movie too. We filmed as the teens asked their grandparents, aunts and uncles what they thought of the teenagers in the village and then filmed the students as they discussed the same question. The result was a complicated snapshot of a community in transition. "Growing Pains," tells the story of Native Alaskan teenagers who love to trap beaver, go to fish camp, use e-mail and listen to rap music. It features the words of teens and adults who struggle to prepare for a rapidly changing future without losing their skills and understanding of the past.

Double-Loop: Analyze the experience and discuss how this moment impacted your current beliefs. This experience taught me to consider the context and intentions of my participants. In my desire to honor cultural history, I repeated past mistakes and reinforced a cycle of disempowerment for the young people in the community. Through the students' choice to challenge my decisions I was forced to admit that I had not considered their needs. By admitting my mistake and asking for help, I was able to engage the students in the re-conception of the project. However, I still wonder, even now, if my privilege and power as a white teacher forced a community to tell a story they may not have been ready to tell. How relevant was this task for the community? As an outsider, was it appropriate for me to determine what story this community should share?

Triple-Loop: Relate the learning to what choices you made or will make based on this experience. How has this learning impacted your future thinking? This moment of learning marked a major shift in how I choose to engage with communities. Now, when I develop a new partnership, I work to discover the needs of a range of stakeholders. I recognize the larger intentions of the systems that fund my work (the school, the city, the state) as well as the individual participants' goals for the project. Most importantly I consider why I am engaging with the project; what drives my choices of content and approach. I work to share my intentions clearly and to stay open to shifting my goals to support the larger intentions of the stakeholders' needs.

Reflective moment: Triple-Loop Learning

SINGLE-LOOP
Describe a moment in a drama learning experience that caused you to question your beliefs about your practice.

DOUBLE-LOOP
Analyze the experience and discuss how this moment impacted your current beliefs.

TRIPLE-LOOP
Relate the learning to what choices you made or will make based on this experience. How has this learning impacted your future thinking?

HOW DO WE USE *REFLECTION* AND *REFLEXIVITY* IN DRAMA/THEATRE LEARNING EXPERIENCES?

Within our field of drama/theatre education, reflection and reflexivity can and should play a significant role in enhancing learners' educational experiences. Reflection and reflexivity should exist as both a tool for and a topic of drama learning experiences. As a tool, the Teaching Artist uses reflective questions in order to prompt participants' investigation of choices, experiences, insights and learning throughout the artistic process. The Teaching Artist models how and when reflection best serves the learner, helping participants develop their own capacity for effective self-questioning and reflexivity. This, in turn, further supports the participants' ownership of and responsibility for their own growth and discovery.

The prevailing challenge is that much of modern education, even within the arts, is based on 'imitate this, memorize that' practices that do not promote the development of imaginative, critical thinkers, skilled learners or performers; instead it produces merely short-term show pieces of preordained achievement. Without engaging in reflection or developing the capacity for reflexive thought, learning is short-lived; the learner often lacks the ability to transfer understanding or skill to future efforts. Students run the risk of being, as Shakespeare might say, "full of sound and fury, signifying nothing." A Teaching Artist must avoid structures based on the regurgitation of information or line readings from the leader. Without contemplating what they do, how they do it and why it is effective, their achievements may be merely coincidental and short-lived, devoid of true artistic understanding. The chapter on Artistic Perspective found later in this book suggests ways that a Teaching Artist can build understanding and appreciation of theatre even as they create it.

As a topic of drama/theatre learning experiences, reflection and reflexivity can also shape how we view our work and the work of others. We need plenty of reflective and enriching encounters with art both as practitioners *and* as viewers in order to develop connections with, understanding and appreciation of, and opinions about theatre and drama. We need opportunities to see, play and do, as well as time to discuss, argue, theorize, respond, consider, analyze and reassess. Too often when we view drama/theatre work we promote the reactive, as opposed to the reflective. We ask, "Did you like it?" and "Was it good?" More meaningful and ultimately more beneficial questions follow a taxonomy such as Bloom, Engelhart, Furst, Hill and Krathwohl's (1956), or the revision by Anderson et al. (2000), where questions focus more on the process:

What did they do? How did they work? Why did we/you receive or interpret the meaning in this way?

These reflective questions can also be asked to the performers:

What will you do next time? Why? How did what you do affect your partners? Why did the others react in the manner you describe? When and where might you apply what you learned here? How might your revisions change the reactions of others?

Cultivating the reflective and reflexive skills of an individual ultimately contributes to a more informed, thoughtful, open-minded person who considers multiple perspectives, analyzes available information and makes purposeful, well-thought-out choices that reflect both her beliefs as well as her understanding of what she has yet to learn. Beneficial learning— a combination of understanding and applying, reflecting and doing— culminates when an individual develops the ability to apply learning in a unique or distinctive manner, demonstrating both the skill of application and an understanding of how to employ that skill effectively.

FINAL THOUGHTS ...

Being a reflexive practitioner is not easy. It requires the willingness to embrace defeat, to recognize the need for growth and help, and to listen to and accept new ideas, which may challenge a Teaching Artist's current understanding. Simultaneously, reflexivity rewards the practitioner with inspiration and a reinvigorated sense of purpose. Reflective practice and reflexivity are about becoming one's best advocate for improvement and continued learning. Finding a place for both reflection and reflexivity is essential for the long-term life of the Teaching Artist and teaching artist profession.

The next part of this book features stories from the field: Teaching Artists from a range of locations open up their work and share how reflexive thinking has shaped their practice. The case studies are organized by five core concepts for reflective and reflexive practice. We selected these core concepts based on the belief that drama/theatre learning experiences are shaped by our *intentions*, infused with a clear agreement between facilitator and participants of the way *quality* and *artistic perspective* will shape the process. We argue for criteria that allow us to *assess* both our work together as well as the work of others. This reflection shapes our next action, beginning an ongoing cycle of *praxis*.

PART 2

Collected Wisdom

THE FIVE CORE CONCEPTS

> Reflective practice at its best is neither just a set of operational techniques nor a clearly identifiable group of academic skills, but rather a critical stance. Good reflective practice takes practitioners beyond mere competence towards a willingness and desire to subject their own taken for granted and their own activities to serious scrutiny. Competence is not enough. The reflective practitioner has to become, if not an agent provocateur, an educational critic who is willing to pursue self and peer appraisal almost to their limits.
>
> (Johnston and Badley 1996: 10)

In this portion of the book, we identify five core concepts and related lines of inquiry that provide a foundational approach to reflexivity within reflective teaching-artist practice. Each chapter that follows defines and examines a specific core concept in detail followed by a series of case studies, which interrogate the concept in practice. The case studies share reflection from Teaching Artists with diverse identity markers and experience, working in a variety of contexts, with a range of populations.

Our list of concepts that contribute to reflective practice and effective learning in, through and about drama and theatre is not an exhaustive list. However, through conversation and contemplation, we identified five core concepts that we believe are essential to reflective practice for Teaching Artists from all segments of the field. Each component uses reflection and reflexivity to engage with the artistic and educational requirements of effective teaching artist pedagogy and practice. In combination they represent the rigorous heart and spirit of what a Teaching Artist does best—they support a collaborative learning environment where participants and facilitators work to make meaning and discover relevance for each individual participant as well as for the collective whole. The core concepts are:

- Intentionality
- Quality

- Artistic perspective
- Assessment
- Praxis

Though presented individually, the core concepts are most effective when considered and examined collectively. Within this shared scope, they deserve equal consideration in the construction and realization of a drama/theatre learning experience. Although one concept may drive our actions more distinctly at any given time, together these concepts frame and feed the growth of our work. They clarify how we engage our participants in, through and about creative processes. They help us define high standards for achievement. In addition, they challenge us to consistently consider each choice carefully and with connected purpose. This codified criteria is our effort toward a shared vocabulary with each other and the field. By defining what we do and why we do it, we find we are better able to create this same space of reflection for and with our participants.

Paulo Freire (1993) states, "Human beings are not built in silence, but in word, in work, in action-reflection" (88). Consequently, the case studies in this text move beyond simple programmatic description; they are purposeful models of revealing reflexivity. We tasked our contributing writers to look inward in this manner, considering when, how and why they faced new understanding about their own pursuits and beliefs. Our hope is that the reader will gain insight into how a reflexive attitude grows from the core values of each writer, which in turn feeds their Teaching Artist identity and improves their instructional and programmatic design. To advance both individual practice as well as our field in general, it is fundamentally important for Teaching Artists to engage in similar practice—regularly, transparently, collaboratively and, ideally, with an eye toward sharing learning through formal courses, trainings, writing, roundtables, informal discussions and coffee shop conversations.

So browse around, follow a straight or meandering path of exploration through any or all of the core concepts and related case studies. Consider the types of questions each writer asks of themselves throughout their reflexive journey. Hopefully the introspection of Teaching Artist peers will inspire and encourage a parallel reflective process. Ideally the reader will use her journey through this book to launch into her own action research, as presented in the final section of this text.

Chapter 3

Intentionality

In the face of this plurality I suggest that it is an intentionality which all the various groups have in common. They share a belief in the power of the theatre form to address something beyond the form itself. [...] The intentions of course vary. They could be to inform, to cleanse, to unify, to instruct, to raise awareness.

(Ackroyd 2000: 1)

The online American Heritage Dictionary defines *intention* as, "A course of action that one intends to follow; an aim that guides action; an objective." This book argues that intentionality is a core component of reflective practice because a Teaching Artist with clear intentions (or intentionality) makes choices that reflect an understanding of the multiple objectives that inform his or her work. There are many reasons why a drama/theatre Teaching Artist chooses to engage in a specific program with a specific population through a specific practice. We suggest that teaching artist work should be developed and implemented with purpose—through an acknowledgment and understanding of the needs and goals of all participants (including the facilitator) as well as of the complicated systems that surround the program or project (the arts organization, school, funder, public policies, etc.).

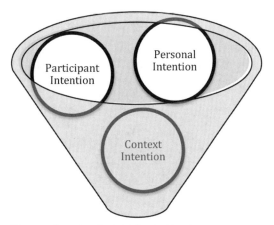

Figure 5: Intentionality in Reflective Practice.

Intentionality suggests that we examine and make visible the external and internal influences that shape our choices. The collected wisdom shared in this section highlights three key ways to work toward intentionality as part of reflective practice as a Teaching Artist. First, we consider how experience as an artist and educator shapes *personal intention*. Second, we explore ways to honor and support *participant intention* as part of reflective practice. Specifically, we acknowledge that participants have their own localized understanding of their situation and experience that is central to the drama/theatre exploration. We also acknowledge that participant intention in some cases requires a singular 'group' mindset or intention to be most successful. Finally, we consider the importance of acknowledging and reflecting upon the larger objectives of the *context intention* by naming and recognizing the impact of the systems within which a Teaching Artist might work. When intentionality is a part of reflective practice, the facilitator creates space and a place for all participants to consider, share and reflect on how past experience shapes new action.

Consider for a moment
As you prepare to engage in a new teaching artist project, what questions do you ask of yourself and your participants, your employers and collaborators?

PERSONAL INTENTION: WHY DO YOU DO WHAT YOU DO?

What drives me? What am I curious about? What core values, learning theories, or philosophies inform my approach? Which established practices or methods inform my practice?

Much of the first two chapters of this book were written to engage the reader in a process of self-reflection. Through the exploration of the relationship between core values and influences, training and experience, the reflective Teaching Artist begins the difficult task of articulating personal intention. Personal intention is shaped by a consideration of why we, as Teaching Artists, do the work we do in the way we do it.

As an intentional Teaching Artist, it can be productive to acknowledge the personal intention(s) that drive each project or program. Teaching artist work is a job. It is a job that often involves multiple projects that occur concurrently in multiple places with multiple constituents. Ideally, being a drama/theatre Teaching Artist comes with a living wage, which allows the individual to eat, pay the rent and do more of other things they want to do in their life. Sometimes the Teaching Artist takes on a task for growth and experience, stating a personal goal. They decide: "I really want to learn how to work with this community or stretch myself in a new way." The Teaching Artist does the project because they care deeply about the population or the process they hope to facilitate. These opportunities often feel the most rewarding because in this scenario the Teaching Artist is able to look past common challenges to the larger intention or goal of the experience.

On less altruistic occasions, the Teaching Artist might take on a project because it was an assigned task and it pays, or there is a hope that the job will lead to something else within the organization. When work tasks lie outside the Teaching Artist's deeper calling or mission, the job can feel overwhelming and frustrating. In this case, the Teaching Artist might still try to ask: "How can I find agency and empowerment in this task by stretching myself in a new way that supports my core beliefs?" Other times the job is one that has been done many times before. The repetition of the work (or the curriculum, location and/or population) causes the Teaching Artist to be less engaged or excited about the task. In these moments, it becomes even more important to reflect on personal intentionality, asking such questions as:

> What can I gain from this process? Can I revise a lesson plan and try out a new skill or approach? Or will I work with a group that I know well so I can help them grow and develop in a new way?

For example, the Teaching Artist might consider that she has worked in an afterschool theatre program for three semesters. She understands the curriculum and generally understands the population and the system that informs the program design and goals. Instead of feeling bored or taking on a 'been there/done that' attitude, the Teaching Artist might say:

> I know what I'm doing ... so now, I have the space to focus on how I facilitate questions in this residency as part of commitment to *social justice* in the classroom. Or I can try out those exercises I saw modeled at our last Teaching Artist training to further develop my artistic skills and *learning*. Or I can focus on activating the classroom behavior contract to think more about *equity* or *responsibility* in my teaching to make sure every voice in the room feels valued and heard.

By returning to her core values, the Teaching Artist can reframe the experience into an opportunity to engage in the type of drama/theatre learning she hopes to do.

Striving for personal intention even when it is not obvious or easy to access ensures that the Teaching Artist will continue to grow and develop as an educator, artist and person. Requiring personal intentionality for *every* project is a rigorous, reflective practice that demands tenacity and commitment but has the potential to increase job satisfaction tremendously. Each time a project begins, a Teaching Artist has another opportunity to personally reflect on the task ahead.

> **Consider an upcoming project, lesson or workshop**
> What do I want to accomplish in this experience, and how will I achieve my goals?

PARTICIPANT INTENTION: WHAT DO MY PARTICIPANTS WANT AND NEED FROM THIS EXPERIENCE?

At its most powerful, personal intention expands to support reciprocity. As the Teaching Artist works to understand and share her own intentions in a project and process, she also strives to provide opportunities for participants to understand and share their individual and collective goals and intentions. The facilitator and participant intention are weighed equally and communicated through a transparent process. At the beginning of a new drama/theatre learning project, many of the activities and strategies used to create ensemble can also generate a discussion about intention. Simple name games can include processing language, which encourages individual reflection (e.g. "What choices helped you play this game successfully?") and group consciousness (e.g. "How can the skills used in this activity—listening, focus, clear choices—help us succeed in our play-building process?"). By creating space and a place to reflect upon and co-construct an understanding of what a success looks like (changes in skills, attitude and knowledge), the facilitator and participants create a common vocabulary and intention for their collaborative process.

For example, a facilitator working with a group of students or community members who can comfortably express their opinions in written form can assess group goals and opinions through a *poster dialogue* (Dawson 2009: 23). In this collaborative, kinesthetic conversation, all participants are given a marker to silently complete prompts written on a number of newsprint papers. A Teaching Artist beginning a shadow puppet exploration of a collection of stories from the Indonesian Wayang Kulit tradition might use poster dialogue statements related to the drama skill being explored such as: *A question I have about shadow puppets is…*; *One thing I hope to learn about shadow puppets is….* She may also ask questions related to the chosen stories: *A good story…*; *Courage means…*; *We share stories to…* as a way to have participants consider the larger themes of the stories and the cultural tradition of Indonesian Wayang Kulit Puppetry, in addition to establishing goals for the artistic product prior to beginning the artistic process.

Once a language for individual and group goal setting has been established, the intentional Teaching Artist can return to the same type of reflection throughout their process. Participant intentionality often makes visible the relationships between individual and group goals and in some cases merges them together. For example, a middle-school youth theatre company sharing a devised performance may take 20 minutes before their first performance to breathe and focus as a group. Each member is invited to share one goal he or she has for the evening's performance. After each student shares his or her intention, the entire ensemble says, "We hear you and will help you to make it happen." The group understands that each individual goal is now the groups' task to support. This ritualized claiming of intention (i.e. your intention is my intention; we will make it happen together) is a further reminder that the best performances are a collective, reciprocal endeavor.

Consider an upcoming project, lesson or workshop
How will I invite participants to reflect on and share what they hope to accomplish through our process? How can we synthesize our individual needs into larger group goals?

CONTEXT INTENTION: HOW DOES CONTEXT SHAPE YOUR PRACTICE?

Intentional practice recognizes the impact of identity and location (physical as well as larger systems of power) that inextricably shape Teaching Artist decisions. The reflective Teaching Artists asks: "How does context inform what I do and how and why I do it?" The work of the Teaching Artist is inherently interdisciplinary. The name itself is a hybrid of education and arts practice. As discussed earlier in this text, the work of the Teaching Artist occurs in a variety of places and spaces with participants of every identity marker. Each location a Teaching Artist works in is shaped by complicated histories and material conditions that mark the individuals with whom they partner and teach.

For example, public schools, which are the location for most of the Teaching Artist work currently occurring in the US, have a long history of educational policy, rules and regulations, which deeply impact the work of Teaching Artists. The nationwide focus on benchmarks, frameworks and standards has shifted America's classrooms in extraordinary ways, from statewide tests to a narrowed curricular focus that primarily prepares students for the tests.

For drama/theatre Teaching Artists working in US public schools *context intentionality* suggests that Teaching Artists understand what schools locally, statewide and nationally are demanding of their students and teachers. If art-integrated work is to be done during the school day, the intentional Teaching Artist may be required to connect the goals of the classroom and campus to their tasks. Most Teaching Artists in schools are familiar with state and/or national standards and have aligned their work with these standards in a clear, articulated manner. Community sites outside of schools may also have dictums that shape how a teaching artist program should occur. It is essential, therefore, that wherever a Teaching Artist works, he takes the time to understand the complex ecosystem that facilitates decisions in the specific location. These rules or policies may come from the location itself or from larger governing bodies, like city, state or national officials.

> **Consider an upcoming project, lesson or workshop**
> What does the host organization, the funder and other key stakeholders on this project hope that we accomplish? How do their guidelines shape what and how I do what I do?

HOW DOES INTENTIONALITY SUPPORT REFLECTIVE TEACHING ARTIST PRACTICE?

The following case studies offer reflection and wisdom on the negotiation between personal, participant and contextual intention within drama/theatre learning experiences in a variety of contexts. Each essay shows the interdependency of intention. Often they suggest that personal intention is based on a desire to listen to, support and engage with the intentions of participants and the context. Our first essay, by Sarah Myers, uses the language of civic practice to describe the relationship between personal and participant intention during a university residency within a local Somali American community. Roxanne Schroeder-Arce examines the evolution of her personal intention as a white woman working in, and with, Spanish-speaking communities as an act of critical cultural engagement and border crossing. Amanda Hashagen interrogates the tensions between agency and ownership in a devising model facilitated with young women in the juvenile justice system where contextual intention deeply informs the artistic process. Lisa M. Barker reflects on a shift from an audition-based model to open participation policy in an undergraduate playmaking program for local schools. Barker analyzes her attempt to align the unique needs of the context with personal and participant intention. In the final essay, Michelle Dahlenburg navigates the challenges and potential benefits of a Teaching Artist working within a city planning process where personal and contextual intentions clashed. Through a reconnection with her core values, Dahlenburg makes new discoveries and reclaims personal agency even within a difficult process.

Intentionality
Case Studies

Sarah Myers

LEARNING TO LISTEN: LESSONS FOR TEACHING ARTISTS FROM A MINNEAPOLIS MOSQUE

In 2011, I received a grant from Augsburg College in Minneapolis, where I teach, to work with women and girls from the Somali community in the nearby Cedar-Riverside neighborhood to create an original piece of theatre inspired by personal narrative. Armed with my background in critical ethnography informed by the work of Dwight Conquergood and D. Soyini Madison, critical pedagogy inspired by Paulo Freire and bell hooks, and many years running various youth theatre programs focused on gender and identity, I wanted to share my skills as a Teaching Artist outside the confines of the college classroom, while learning from and about the vibrant community around me.

This was the official narrative of my intentionality—and not an untrue one. But official narratives often lack the complexity of what actually motivates us as Teaching Artists; they don't take contradictions and nuances into consideration. I'd like to move past my own official narrative to examine the forces influencing and inspiring me in this particular project—from my religious and cultural identity, to the physical setting of the work, to my desire to get everything 'right.' By thinking beyond my official narrative, I hope to consider how being a Teaching Artist can be an act of deep listening and, in effect, a civic practice.

Investing in intentionality

As I slowly got to know Cedar-Riverside community members over many months—through Augsburg's Center for Citizenship and Learning, Bedlam

Theatre, and eventually the Health Commons at Dar Ul-Quba Mosque—what started as an effort to create an original production transformed into a weekly voice workshop. The workshop took place at the Dar Ul-Quba Health Commons, a drop-in center focused on health education, massage, group activities and connecting people to community resources. As a joint venture of Fairview Medical Center and the Augsburg College Nursing Department, the Health Commons has Somali and Oromo interpreters on site and serves as a place where community members can meet with and learn from health-care providers and each other. Informal classes focus on everything from gardening and nutrition to parenting and community organizing, and the workshops I led became part of the myriad offerings.

Before the workshops even began, I tried to stay as intentional about my practice as possible. I worked closely for nearly eight months with Rabia Mohammad (former youth program director at Dar Ul-Quba) and, later, Hiba Sharif (an AmeriCorps VISTA volunteer now employed by Fairview) and Katie Clark (Augsburg Nursing faculty member) to figure out exactly whom to serve, when, why and how. We all agreed that a workshop series (rather than a performance) at the Health Commons could focus on women in the Cedar-Riverside community who had the desire to speak more easily in public, but who felt inhibited for various reasons. A workshop would also fit in with the Health Commons' other offerings, be easy to carry out in the comfortable multipurpose room of the mosque where we met, and allow for flexibility in planning, as the group of participants would inevitably shift from week to week. I went on to recruit Augsburg student Aminah Hussein— a trilingual Theater minor enrolled in voice classes—as an intern, knowing it would be important to have the voice of a dynamic Somali American woman as co-facilitator. I encouraged Aminah to lead whenever she felt comfortable, and I asked her to translate if and when it was necessary. In turn, we had many conversations—in the car on the way to and from the Commons, at Dar Ul-Quba itself, and even through text messages—about religion, culture, gender and performance.

As the workshops began, there was a consistent crowd of (mostly young) women joining us to breathe and stretch, try out performance exercises, and discuss how and why certain voices are silenced in society. Our sessions seemed to fit well with the relaxing, restorative culture of the Commons; we often left with a calm glow. I say *we* here, as I think my early work at the Health Commons had as much to do with my own pleasure, as it did the participants' growth. I don't doubt that several of the young women benefitted from the work, and the casual approach made sense for a group that shifted weekly and didn't have a concrete goal in mind, but I started to feel like I might not actually be doing enough, helping enough, teaching enough. My feelings were no doubt related to the fact that, try as I might to focus on process, I had internalized the expectations of a product-focused project. I had also adopted the barely conscious, deeply problematic belief that my own pleasure and growth shouldn't be significant in my role as a Teaching Artist—which were, in fact, indicators of my laziness and/or failure.

Intentionality and identity

As Teaching Artists we often don't talk enough about our identity markers as motivators in our work, and we rarely discuss how our search for comfort and kinship fuels us to take on projects in the first place. We may name our privileges and acknowledge our power as Teaching Artists once we're immersed in the work, but this acknowledgment doesn't necessarily address intentionality—and it doesn't always make space for unexpected alliances and cross-cultural commonalities.

If I'm going to veer from my 'official narrative,' I have to admit that I was motivated in my work at the Health Commons as much by my desire to find allies as the intention to share skills and learn about local culture. As a Jewish woman, I am a religious and cultural outsider at Augsburg (a college of the Evangelical Lutheran Church in America)—both like and unlike the increasing number of Muslim students of Somali ancestry who call the college home. While Augsburg is progressive in its politics and often open to diverse perspectives and difficult dialogues, the fact remains that there are only a handful of self-identified Jewish faculty members and just one full-time Muslim staff member on the whole campus, despite the growing number of Muslim students. While our cultural differences are deep, and I carry more societal privilege than Augsburg's Somali American students as a white, middle-class professor, what we share is the fact that the college does not recognize our holy days, that we carry a burden of religious representation, and that the material of our everyday lives is seen as 'interfaith' whether we want it to be or not.

Conversations about religion and culture took on a new tone at Dar Ul-Quba. While the Health Commons is run by a mix of white and Somali staff, Dar Ul-Quba itself is a markedly Muslim space. When Aminah told me about her meditation classes grounded in Islamic prayer or the goals she set for herself during Ramadan, it was not against the backdrop of a Lutheran college, where she played the role of religious Other. And when she asked me about Judaism, it was with genuine interest, specific questions and a desire for interfaith understanding on our own (non-Lutheran) terms.

Part of my motivation in being a Teaching Artist is that I can work in contexts that transform the ways that stories are told, rather than those that re-inscribe power structures. Being at Dar Ul-Quba prompts me to listen deeply and differently to all the narratives that surround me. But identification across difference is a tricky terrain to navigate—it can easily turn into essentialism or *over*identification without a nuanced understanding of power and privilege. How do we learn from listening, forge connections across difference, and find similarities in unexpected places without projecting our own identities onto other people? How, in Helen Nicholson's words, do we find, "points of connection between acts of altruism and self-interest, and [recognize] that they operate as a continuum rather than binary opposites" (2005: 31)? Is it possible to enjoy my time at the Health Commons while also doing work that has concrete benefits for the community? And how can I combat my feelings of failure by acknowledging that listening and learning take time?

Learning to listen deeper

In June, once the academic school year ended, I transitioned my attention to a new group of women at the Health Commons who had already been chosen as part of a Cedar-Riverside leadership group. These women, decades older than the ones with whom I had previously worked, were scheduled to give a presentation to funders from the Blue Cross Foundation as part of a "Growing up Healthy" grant focused on children and communities. Their objective was to convey their recommendations about where grant funds should go in the neighborhood, and they had collectively decided to focus on a hub where young children could gather to play while parents exchanged advice and support. Hiba, Katie and I discussed ways I could help the group prepare for their presentation, and with a more concrete goal in mind, I was secretly eager to fight my fears of not doing enough.

When I started working with this new group of women, I began with the same breathing and stretching exercises, the same conversations about why and if people were comfortable speaking in large groups that I had used with relative success with the younger women. Many of them seemed interested and amused, but when I returned the following week, introducing a gibberish activity adapted from Viola Spolin, one woman, Fatima, asked what this had to do with 'public speaking.' I talked about nonverbal communication, how much we say with our eyes and bodies—and then I asked if she'd rather do something else, if she thought I was taking the wrong approach. "We already know what you're teaching us," Fatima said, "and we didn't go to school to learn it." At first, I was horrified. My worst nightmare is treating anyone as though my academic credentials somehow give me greater clout or insight, as though the only real learning takes place inside the academy. My mind started spinning: *I took the wrong approach, I started the wrong way. I failed.* But then I realized that I was thinking only about *me*—my philosophy, my intentionality, my perceived failure—not the woman who was standing right in front of me. So I stopped spinning for a moment and tried to really listen.

Fatima explained that the gibberish activity was similar to communicating with deaf people in Somalia—and that everyone could do it, unlike in the United States. The participants (none of them hearing impaired) started showing me all sorts of signs. Lively conversations in Somali erupted around the room. An older woman pulled me aside to tell me about a deaf neighbor who had reported her rebellious adolescent behavior to her father when she assumed he wouldn't be able to cross the language barrier. Aminah suggested that older women who had lived much of their lives in Somalia tended to communicate more easily than more Americanized younger women who were often steeped in self-consciousness. Luul, another of the group members, talked about schooling in Somalia *requiring* confidence: "If you couldn't speak in front of a class, you'd fail," she said. I asked if I could pose a question. "Ask whatever you like! Questions are how we learn," said Luul, and then she launched into a story about a white woman at the hospital where she worked asking if she had hair. This prompted another lively conversation about non-Muslim women's insensitivity about *hijab*.

I started to realize that my presence that afternoon was a catalyst for conversation among the women—an opportunity to turn the tables and laugh at the bizarre and offensive questions people who look like me often ask. My lack of knowledge about deaf Somali culture also allowed these women to exert their expertise and honor the importance of lived experience. And Luul's "whatever you like," followed by the story about the ignorant white woman, put her in a position of authority and implicitly told me that "whatever you like" didn't actually mean *anything*. My intention before and during this entire interaction was to listen—and what I came to learn was that real listening, in this case, entailed receiving a certain amount of pent-up frustration, annoyance and anger. Listening was about standing in for any number of ignorant white people without getting defensive or obsessing over my own 'failures' in critical pedagogy and ethnography. Listening was about learning not to focus on myself.

Listening in that moment also allowed me to reflect back on the listening that was part of the workshop planning process as well. While I had made cultural sensitivity a priority from the get-go, I had relied so heavily on the opinions of *young* Somali American women (ages 20 to 26) that I did not adequately consider how their ideas and experiences might differ considerably from those of older women in the community with very different experiences of identity-making. My carefully constructed intentionality missed the mark in this case, but somehow it also catalyzed an important conversation—and made me rethink what listening means for Teaching Artists.

Teaching Artist as civic actor

In his July 2012 post on *HowlRound*, Michael Rohd makes a plea for a conscious investment in civic practice, "activity where a theater artist employs the assets of his/her craft in response to the needs of nonarts partners as determined through ongoing, relationship-based dialogue." He points to theatre artists' experiences with everything from collaborative decision-making to public-event planning as skills those outside the field could benefit from. At the core of all this practical experience is listening, and, as Rohd argues, "we can radically alter our role in our communities if we employ it with greater intentionality and generosity" (2012).

Helping women in the leadership group prepare for their presentation might be considered a civic practice. It certainly fulfilled a concrete community need and wasn't about dramatic performance or even applied drama. Further, it was active, deep listening that helped me start to fulfill my civic responsibility as a Teaching Artist—to become a sounding board, a student, a stand-in, as well as someone with practical presentation skills to share. After all, as Nicholson argues, "citizenship is not simply a collection of legal rights and obligations, which are not easily changed, but it is also a more fluid and pliable set of social practices" (2005: 22).

In one of our last meetings before their final presentation, I told the leadership group that they didn't need me as a coach anymore. "There's always more to learn ... Can you sew?" Hodan, one of the senior group members, asked, half-jokingly. I hadn't yet considered sewing (or building, or design, for that matter) as part of the civic practice equation, yet many theatre artists are competent, if not proficient, in these areas. "Yes?" I replied, and all the women turned my way: *Really? You can sew?* Creating clothing is an integral part of Somali culture, I was told, but few of the women in the group knew how to use a sewing machine. While I had been thinking that our next step might be a Theatre of the Oppressed workshop or town hall meeting, I was clearly still not listening hard enough. After the final presentation, several of the women, deft organizers all, approached to let me know they had located sewing machines and were ready to start classes whenever I was. "After Ramadan," I said, "Let's begin again."

Roxanne Schroeder-Arce

STORIES OF MY LIFE: A TEACHING ARTIST REFLECTS ON CULTURAL CONSCIOUSNESS

As I drove down Cesar Chavez Street in East Austin for the first time, I was immediately immersed in the story of the community. Mexican restaurants lined the streets; colorful piñatas hung outside Raquel's Party Land store; a quaint church stood in the midst of humble homes. Walking to the entryway of the school, I noted mature trees and gravel where grass wanted to be. This was a school, like many in the United States, which serves a Mexican American community, yet often missed opportunities to reflect its rich, undeniable culture. The Open Hearts/Open Minds program was developed in collaboration with the University of Texas at Austin and Metz Elementary School in East Austin, Texas in the 1990s. The Metz student population was, and is, primarily Latino/a and many students are English Language Learners. The objective of the program was to provide drama-based lessons at all grade levels, along with professional development for Metz classroom teachers. A private grant funded the project for five years; I served as a Teaching Artist in the program from 1994 to 1997. In this essay, I reflect on what it means to move across literal and figurative borders as a Teaching Artist. I ask, "How can a Teaching Artist intentionally engage with a community that is not her own?"

Geneva Gay (2010), author of *Culturally Responsive Teaching: Theory, Research and Practice*, explains, "Stories are powerful means for people to establish bridges across other factors that separate them (such as race, culture, gender, and social class), penetrate barriers to understanding, and create feelings of kindredness" (3). And so, I begin with a story…

I have never felt heat like this before. The concrete emits as much warmth as the beating sun. I walk up the sweltering steps to my first teaching job. I am in Laredo, Texas. I am 21 years old. I moved here just days before with only a few bags and boxes. I have never been to Texas before; I know no one. As I turn back to the parking lot, I see flat land, cacti and two flags indicating each side of the Texas–Mexico border. Nothing is familiar; even the air feels and smells foreign.

I feel panic. Am I ready for this? Did my schooling in Boston really prepare me for this? As I walk into the empty school I feel the tremendous shock and respite of the cool air conditioning. I let out a sigh of relief. It is not only the heat that I have escaped, but the foreign geography; suddenly, I recognize everything. The hallways, the glass doors leading to what must be the office, the signs telling me where the bathrooms are. I could be in Massachusetts. This is not so different from what I know. I'll be okay.

The student body at the school was 98 percent Mexican American whose first language was Spanish. Many of the students recently immigrated to Texas from Mexico, which was a short distance from the school. I was the school's first ever theatre teacher, one of few white teachers in the school and I was not yet a Spanish speaker.

The first play I chose to produce at the high school was *Tartuffe*. I had read and seen the play in college, and I was eager to direct it. After all, none of these culturally depraved students had ever heard of Molière. My job was to teach these students the most important elements of theatre. To my mind, Molière was a great choice.

Louise Derman-Sparks (1995) argues that US classrooms expect assimilation and deny students' cultures, languages and experiences. She writes, "Under such a misguided approach, education is used to eliminate cultural difference by teaching children and parents new cultural habits and thereby curing their 'cultural deficits'" (18). Over the course of the next several weeks in Laredo, I came to realize that I had a lot to learn about my students, about my own biases and assumptions, about pedagogy—what I would someday learn to call culturally responsive teaching.

My second week in Laredo, Ms. Rogers, a seasoned history teacher, lectured me in the teacher's lounge, "Miss Schroeder, don't you let them speak Spanish in your classroom. They'll walk all over you." I took that comment to heart. I offered dramatic monologues, scenes and plays only in English and wondered why most of my students struggled to connect to the characters. A few weeks later, one of my students, Guillermo (pronounced gee-YAIR-moe), watched me work on a lighting system in the cafetorium. Recognizing his interest in what I was doing, I greeted him and invited him to help. Guillermo quickly jumped in, explained to me with hand gestures and fragmented English that his father was an electrician; he would love to help. Together, we had the light trees and eight par cans up and running in no time. Soon, Guillermo was teaching me how to run the new light board.

Days later the Principal asked for a student who could run the lights for an upcoming ballet folklorico performance in the cafetorium. I recommended Guillermo and the principal assured me that he would permit Guillermo's absence from classes. The next afternoon, Ms. Rogers caught me in the hallway, "Miss Schroeder, I understand that Guillermo (pronounced GWIL-er-moe) missed my class this morning because he was running the lights for you?" She informed me that he was failing her class. I wondered how hard I would work for a teacher who failed to correctly pronounce my name. Soon, Guillermo was in afterschool theatre, which required him to pass all of his classes and enabled me to monitor his grades, which immediately improved. He even passed Ms. Roger's class the next marking period.

I began to wonder how my actions with students represent my values, as well as reflect and impact my larger intentions to cross borders. Toward the end of my first semester, a student referred to a monologue she wrote for class, "Miss, can I just do this in Spanish?" "No, Claudia, I am sorry. These need to be in English. You need to practice your English. And, I won't understand you if you do it in Spanish." I was shocked by her response, "But, Miss, I already wrote it in English, so you have the translation right there. Are we learning English or Theatre?" I eventually agreed and Claudia performed the monologue in Spanish. I was moved as she connected to the language in deep and meaningful ways. And I didn't need the translation. The context and her inflection told me everything. I realized that most of my students saw English as an academic language, while Spanish was used at home where people were more likely to emote and share intimacy. The students were translating everything into English; no wonder they were having trouble 'dropping' into the material. Soon, I encouraged Spanish in my class: I found bilingual scenes and monologues; I created lessons where students wrote their own works with characters that resembled their family and community members; I took even more care to pronounce the students' names as they taught me to and to ask until I got it right. Eventually, I learned to speak Spanish—mostly from my students!

Socorro Herrera (2010) speaks about the need for schools to recognize and value the lived experiences that culturally and linguistically diverse (CLD) students bring to the classroom. She asserts, "More often than not […] CLD students' assets are left untapped because the classroom does not provide a place for them to become part of the curriculum" (Herrera 2010: 17). In graduate school, after three years of teaching in Laredo, I was introduced to Paulo Freire, Lev Vygotsky and other scholar educators who gave me the language to understand the necessity for developing a pedagogy that considers agency and cultural perspective, parts of the puzzle that my initial teacher education program failed to offer me.

Years later, I walked into the Open Hearts/Open Minds program in Austin, armed with my memory of Guillermo and my Laredo experience. I intentionally brought resources of, by and for Latinos, and a series of lesson plans, which I developed specifically for the Mexican American youth at

Metz. I walked in with the intention of being open to exploring, writing and speaking in Spanish.

Before entering the classroom, I met with Mrs. Acosta, an experienced Latina classroom teacher. I asked her questions about her classroom management techniques and curriculum goals for the unit. I studied the classroom demographics and asked about students with special needs. I practiced the students' names in advance. I started the first day, with an enthusiastic "¡Hola!" The students stared at me blankly. I began to notice that some of the students anglicized their names on their name tags—that 'Miguel' was 'Michael'; 'Margarita' was 'Margie'; 'Roberto' was 'Bobby.'

For the first day, I created an activity called "Donde estan las llaves" where students sing a song about lost keys while one participant looks for the keys. I was surprised to learn that I had to teach the Spanish words to the group. At the end of the class, I was perplexed. I asked Mrs. Acosta about the language skills of the students during our afterschool meeting. She explained the youth were reticent to speak Spanish at school. Most of them were second-generation Mexican Americans and their parents encouraged them to learn English as a method of getting ahead in society. I realized that what I learned in Laredo about Mexican American youth was not completely relevant in this other context. Despite my intentions, I had assumed all Mexican American youth were the same.

What was relevant though was that the Austin youth, like those in Laredo, had their own stories to tell. The classroom teacher expressed that the students struggled with issues of assimilation. They were developing skills at code switching, moving between their two identities and assessing which identity to forward in any given situation. However, as bilingual children in the midst of developing their own identities, they were further challenged with deciphering when they should speak Spanish or English. I shifted what I planned and developed a sequence of lessons, collectively called "Stories of My Life." Our goal was to create an opportunity for students to dramatize the multilingual stories from their own lives—to create a vocabulary around diversity and difference critical to fostering a pluralistic classroom.

We began "Stories of My Life" with a story drama based on the book *Elmer*, by David McKee. The book deals with a multicolored elephant who feels different and therefore inferior. The Elmer lesson spanned over three days, and the children eventually met Elmer (a puppet) and shared thoughts with him about difference. I wanted the youth to feel comfortable sharing their own stories, so we needed to establish language around identity and diversity. Mrs. Acosta and I hoped that exploring a character's challenges with self-identity would be much more meaningful to the youth than simply remembering to 'respect others' in the classroom. Furthermore, we focused on what Koppelman (2011) refers to as cultural pluralism, or a valuing of difference rather than a focus on how we are similar (9).

After several weeks of skill building around play, drama, storytelling and diversity, the children were ready to share a story. However, they struggled to write them. In front of a blank piece of paper, several froze; the same children who were verbalizing stories days before were suddenly overwhelmed. I considered how writing and speaking offered different challenges particularly for young people working in multiple languages.

Ultimately, the stories the Metz youth shared were compelling in a variety of ways. Every individual presented a story and every individual experienced 24 other stories, as they dramatized their lives and appreciated the lives of their peers. Mrs. Acosta offered her gratitude and surprise that children who rarely spoke in class were now enacting stories and talking about their personal experiences. I do not know of the long-term effects of this program for the children in the class, but I know my pedagogy was again reshaped by my experiences.

My revelations at Metz did not negate what I learned in Laredo, rather they added to my own story and evolving thoughts about culturally responsive teaching. Sharon Grady (2000) reminds us that, "from our own power positions as teachers, drama leaders, and directors, we need to develop the ability to look beyond our own ways of viewing the world" (xiii). The children at Metz, the teachers and students in Laredo, taught me that I don't know, that I will never know, and that not knowing is not only okay, but important. My intentional practice is now more about listening and recognizing when assumptions and bias shape my actions. Owning our 'not knowing' and honoring what we gain from other's knowledge is critical. Creating a safe space to honor cultural, personal identity is essential to my practice as a Teaching Artist—this intention, and perhaps only this intention, remains consistent for me in all contexts.

In working with pre-service theatre teachers, I now teach toward culturally responsive pedagogy, defined by Gloria Ladson-Billings (1994) as "a pedagogy that recognizes the importance of including students' cultural references in all aspects of learning" (7). But how does a teacher really come to know and embrace culturally responsive pedagogy? How did I really learn to (try to) live the practice of what I preach to my students?

Both theory and practice prove critical to my work as a culturally responsive theatre educator. My understanding develops through a back and forth between action and reflection, and my praxis is, of course, ever evolving. In working with Mexican American youth for most of my teaching career, I have come to understand the critical nature of listening to youth and recognizing them as experts of their own lived experience, and I still work at being intentional about this—every day.

Amanda Hashagen

DEVISED PERFORMANCE IN A GENDER-SPECIFIC JUVENILE PROBATION PROGRAM

Conformity plays an important role in the juvenile justice system. Many young offenders have entered the quicksand of the system because they have broken the laws that we, as a society, have established and (mostly) agreed upon. Sometimes the system strives to break down individuality to achieve conformity. However, there can be a threat of shutting down the entire child rather than just the unlawful actions they have committed. My personal artistic journey has led me to try to find ways to create a balance. How can we celebrate and redirect a young person's individuality, strengths and experience to help them achieve acceptance within the larger community? The belief that every human has the power to create better circumstances for themselves and their community through the discovery and sharing of their 'story' is at the core of my practice as a Teaching Artist.

I have worked with many facilities, parole officers, guards and teachers who completely understand the threat of shutting down the child's individuality and have done tremendous work to positively rehabilitate our young people. So, I must make it clear that the Teaching Artist helping young people tell stories is not the *savior* of the juvenile justice system. I see the work as a complementary tool in the rehabilitation of young offenders. A tool that strives to create a space of mental, physical and vocal freedom in the midst of locked cells and uniforms. In some cases, the structure and safety of the juvenile justice system actually affords young people the first opportunity they have to focus on themselves. My intention is to use this opportunity to help young people identify their goals and their obstacles to achieving those goals, to discover the strength and skills they already possess to overcome their obstacles, and to recognize the people and services in their community that can be their allies. I help young people tell their stories to one another and the wider community through CreativeWorks, a nonprofit that uses applied-theatre techniques to engage marginalized youth. I believe through this type of interaction we can become a stronger, more connected community.

It is vital to remember the power of the facilitator when helping young people tell their story. The young people we work with have numerous vivid, painful, disappointing, inspiring and powerful experiences. I began to wonder, "How can I most effectively use my position as a facilitator to help determine which of their stories should be told?"

In November of 2012, the Jackson County Family Court asked CreativeWorks to provide a 16-week theatre program for teen girls on probation that was to culminate in a presentation for peers, family and members of the juvenile justice community. The following case study examines the intentions, thought processes and guiding principles behind the planning and process phases of this project.

Planning

As we began to plan the project, it was necessary to consider the needs of the multiple partners involved and each of their intentions. I met with all parties who had an interest in the project, including the Director of Family Court programming, as well as the Probation Officer who was currently working with the group. I kept track of which intentions they had for the project that were not negotiable and which expectations might be in direct conflict with CreativeWorks' intentions. Thankfully, I found my objectives were very similar to the partnering organizations'. We determined that we would work with the young women to devise and perform their own script based on their experiences. I did not have specific expectations for the content of this project. My main goal was to design a semi-structured program that would create the space for the participants to work from their own priorities.

For years I set out to find the perfect method to facilitate devised theatre for young people. I thought, if I could just create a set curriculum that I use with every project, I could save a lot of time creating the content of each performance. Then I could devote more attention to developing the aesthetic value of the final product. Time and time again, however, I found that I could not reconcile creating such a curriculum with my intention for the programming.

My work is rooted in Paulo Friere's theories outlined in his book *Pedagogy of the Oppressed* (2006). The Brazilian educationalist's philosophy focuses on conscientization, or critical consciousness. The idea is that the facilitator is in dialogue with the students to name their own world so that they may see social and political obstacles that confront them. Once they have a more thorough understanding of these obstacles from their own perspective, they can then take action to overcome the barriers. I come to the work focused on helping young people see the strength and skills they already possess that can help them overcome barriers they must prioritize themselves. A completely structured curriculum cannot help me accomplish this. I must approach the work in an organic manner and be open to the possibilities and the direction that the students guide the project in. "Which stories should be told?" This is a question those who are telling the stories must answer for themselves. I had to create a structure made up of various exercises and mediums—for example, improv, poetry, drawing, writing in response to music—which would encourage the participants to discover and honor their own viewpoints as well as increase their capacity to join in dialogue with their peers.

The majority of my devising programs follow this basic structure:

- Team and trust-building
- Working around a generative theme
- Identifying and prioritizing issues the groups face in their daily lives
- Creation of performance material, for example, poetry, storytelling, dialogue, movement, music
- Clarifying message and method
- Editing

Friere suggests beginning with dialogue about a generative theme, a universal concept that the participant group can relate to. The idea is that the facilitator introduces a topic to work with, and through discussion, dialogue and improv, the priority issues that the group really wants to work on begin to surface. During my initial meetings with the parole officer, she told me she would be teaching from the Girls Circle curriculum right before each of my sessions. I had used this curriculum in the past, and knew that it focused on girls' relationships with their own bodies, their friends, parents and dating partner. I wanted to connect the generative theme to what they had already been discussing. So I decided on the following starting point: what expectations are placed on teenage girls by their families, friends and society?

Process

Team and trust-building

There are numerous games and activities to choose from when facilitating team and trust-building. The key for me in every project, including this one, is to scaffold these games from the most fun and least amount of physical and verbal commitment to activities that require entering the personal space of others and analyzing serious topics such as power dynamics. I often tell the participants that they will soon be acting, but not to stress out about it, because we will start slowly and ease into it.

Working around a generative theme

We began to explore the expectations placed on teenage girls by their families, friends and society through a few activities that helped us examine the influence of the media on young women's appearances and behaviors. The dialogue and storytelling around this topic led to several girls talking about pressure from their family and peers at school to be and look a certain way. They also discussed the repercussions if someone did not fit into this mold, which lead to conversations about bullying.

Identifying and prioritizing issues the groups face in their daily lives

After a couple of sessions focused around the generative theme, we began to brainstorm together what types of issues kept coming up. We kept a list of these issues on chart paper. Each girl could offer as many suggestions as she wanted; every suggestion was written down. After voting on the listed suggestions, bullying was chosen as our topic of focus for our performance.

Creation of performance material

The next project session used the topic of bullying as a starting point for personal storytelling. The participants were asked to share a true story about bullying. As we went around the circle telling stories, I noticed that many of the girls were having difficulty thinking of a one-minute story to share. While a couple of girls spoke of years of being subjected to bullying, others seemed disinterested, and some even said that bullying wasn't a problem at their school. I pushed the girls that didn't see it as an issue to think of something they had heard about happening, and the results were passionless hearsay.

Once our hour session was completed, I felt a little deflated. Clearly bullying was a relevant issue, and one that was rich in possibilities for performance. The girls had chosen this topic. If the intention of my program was to help the participants identify their own intentions, their own stories,

I should honor their decision. Right? To me, the tricky part of this work is knowing when the group as a whole has reached the point of identifying their intentions. Our program process asks participants to identify issues, tell stories, narrow down the issues, tell more stories and so on, until the cycle settles on stories that are so pertinent to the participants that they must share them. The girls' lack of urgency and connection to the topic of bullying led me to believe that this wasn't their priority issue. The storytelling/narrowing cycle was not complete.

I shared my thoughts with the girls. I told them we could do a performance about bullying, but that it felt like they weren't really into it. I told them this was their project, and I wanted them to have the opportunity to say what they wanted and needed to say. Most of them agreed that the topic wasn't really moving them. I asked again,

> What is something you have to deal with all the time that you don't always know the best way to handle? What do you want people to know? What do you want people to think about?

Discussion ensued, and one girl said, "I have to deal with my mom every day. I love her, but she makes me so mad. If she could just understand me maybe we could get along." Upon hearing that, several of the other girls confirmed they felt the same way. The girls spontaneously started talking to one another and shared stories about their relationships with their mothers. This was the urgency and passion necessary to follow through on the creation of a performance to tell their stories. We had finally discovered our topic!

Over the next few session we did activities, such as storytelling, improv and writing from prompts such as music and images, which helped the young women connect with how they felt about their current relationship with their mothers, how they wanted that relationship to be and how they might achieve that type of relationship.

Even though there was a definite surge in motivation for most of the young women, there were a couple more hurdles for me as a facilitator to confront. One of the young women informed me that her mother had abandoned her as a child and that she didn't have any kind of relationship with her. Another girl told me that her mother suffered from schizophrenia and dementia, and that even though her mother was there, she was not really 'there.' It was clear that even mentioning the word 'mother' was a trigger for these two. I had to commit to making sure I spent as much one-on-one time with them as we went through the process. We talked about how even that lack of a relationship was a type of relationship. The girl who had been abandoned easily transferred the topic to her relationship with her grandmother, as her grandmother had become her mother. The other girl's story was still about the relationship she wanted with her mother, but it was also an acknowledgment that it could never be her ideal relationship. She focused on what she had learned from her mother fighting disease, how it made her realize she wanted to work with people with disabilities. She also used her story as an opportunity to ask others to not take their relationship with their mothers for granted—by spending time with their moms, listening to what they have to say and by looking to them for guidance and protection.

Clarifying message and method

Once we had created several prose and poetic writings around the topic, we again discussed what we wanted our point to be. What did we want people to know? What did we want them to think about? What did we want their help with? I used this discussion as a guide for editing their work into a performance script.

Editing

When devising performances with young people I typically have them write their own script as a group to gain skills in script writing, communication and negotiation. This works well when there are at least four hours a week for several months to work. This project, however, lasted a total of 16 hours, which forced me to decide which elements to focus our time on during our sessions. I became the editor for this project. There is a great power in editing as it guides the direction of a story. How could I wield this power in a way that still honored the girls' own intentions? I decided to use the group discussion we had about clarifying the message to guide my edits. I used only the words they had written. The girls did a read through of the first draft. We then discussed what worked, what they wanted to change and what we needed to do to fill in some of the holes in the script. I then revised the script. We went through this process until they were satisfied. Some of the participants had changes they wanted to make. Although a majority of the girls wanted to share a story about the relationship they had with their mother, this was clearly not a prioritized issue for all the girls. Considering this, did my intention for the program fail? I'm not sure. Perhaps, to some degree it did fail. I do believe that within the thematic framework chosen by a majority of the participants, I was able to help those two girls discover a story that was important to them.

Conclusion

We all have numerous stories that dwell within us. Which stories should we tell? The answer to this question will be different if the teller is one-on-one with the listener. It will change again if one person is telling their story to multiple people. Again it changes when a group is trying to collectively share their stories with multiple people. I must continue to work toward creating a program structure that can connect the group's stories while allowing the space for every participant to share the story they need to tell.

One thing is clear: through the sharing of their individual stories, the girls were able to express why they had difficulty conforming to society's expectations. They identified that their recent behavior would prevent them from achieving the goals and relationships they strove for. Through their performance they were able to open up a dialogue with their own mothers to try and find new modes of communication to establish understanding and cooperation. In this sense, the program was successful in both maintaining individuality and addressing the conformity necessary to keep them out of the juvenile justice system in the future.

Lisa M. Barker

AUDITION NOTICE(D): TAKING STEPS TO ALIGN MISSION AND ADMISSION

I partially credit the movie *Braveheart* with the launching of my career in educational theatre. I did not work on the film; rather, I happened to see it the summer before an audition that went well. In the fall of my sophomore year at Northwestern University, I auditioned for Griffin's Tale, a student-run children's theatre company comprised of college-aged actors who adapt and perform stories written by local children. During the callback, my scene partners and I were tasked with improvising a family dinner in the genre of *Braveheart*. Luckily, I had enough schema—Scottish warriors, Mel Gibson, something about 'freedom'—to make choices that were compelling enough to keep me in the running. What I did not have was a set of strategies I could apply to the audition experience—what to write on the audition form, how to enter the audition space, how to interact in an upbeat and collaborative manner with fellow auditioners against whom I was essentially competing. I also did not have a clear idea of what Griffin's Tale was looking for in new members. I had seen the company perform for a college audience, so, although I had some sense of their aesthetic and final product, I knew little about their adaptation process (i.e. how a child's story gets transformed into a piece of theatre) and the particular capacities they were looking for to serve this process and product.

Despite lacking auditioning skills and a sense of Griffin's Tale's criteria, I must have done something right. And thank goodness. Through Griffin's Tale and its professional offshoots, I spent the next decades with access to social networks and a set of interactive and aesthetic modes that shaped my personal and professional life. The ensemble-based model meant that I had a consistent community in which to develop my identity as a performer for young audiences. Weekly rehearsals served as an apprenticeship into the adaptation process, and I could look to veteran Griffin's Tale members for mentorship. The experience of being a company member was transformational, and only available to folks who knew about, signed up for and nailed their auditions.

Over the years, I have wondered:

What was it about my audition that wooed the casting directors? Did my allusions to *Braveheart* have any influence on the outcome of the audition and, accordingly, on the trajectory of my career? What else among my choices and interactions pleased the company?

As a teaching artist, director and teacher educator, I continue to wonder:

What does the design of admission processes—the format, tasks and interactions that characterize an 'audition,' for example—say about our intentions in terms of attracting, assessing, securing and sustaining members who are a good fit for our mission? What steps can we take to align admission and mission? That is, how can we ensure that our audition-like processes assess the kinds of capacities that are authentic to the nature of our work?

In this essay I consider these questions as I reflect upon my experiences as an actor in Griffin's Tale and, later, as founder and co-director of Flying Treehouse, a children's theatre company at Stanford University. I discuss each company's *mission* (i.e. official, stated purpose), *admission* (i.e. the process by which students gain access to company membership) and inferred *intention* (i.e. what the admission process suggests about the company's underlying motivations and values). I also juxtapose my experiences in these companies, not to suggest that one model of admission is better than another but rather to reflect on the relationship between admission processes, like auditions, and our intentions as arts organizations.

Founded in 1990 by Melissa Chesman, Griffin's Tale is a children's repertory theatre company consisting of undergraduate student actors who collect stories written by local elementary-school children, adapt the stories into songs and sketches, and perform these pieces at the young authors' schools and on the university campus. The mission of this adaptation and performance process, as stated on the company's website, is to "[encourage] imagination and creativity." While this encouragement is aimed at the children who author the stories and attend the shows, I would argue that this mission extends to the college-aged actors who adapt and perform. My three-year experience as an ensemble member of Griffin's Tale served as a delightful apprenticeship into how to adapt text into playable action, improvise throughout this adaptation process, and perform audibly and flexibly for young audiences in a range of in-school performance spaces (e.g. libraries, gyms, cafetoriums). Griffin's Tale was indeed my primary source of imagination and creativity as a young adult.

When I auditioned for Griffin's Tale, the process consisted of two parts. First, interested undergraduates individually prepared and performed two minutes of any material they wished, such as a monologue, song or, in my case, the reading aloud of a children's book. Second, a subset of these auditioners was invited to a callback. During this callback, company members observed and encouraged auditioners, who engaged in collaborative improvisational exercises and individually sang popular songs in the style of specific characters (e.g. "Happy Birthday" as a pirate, "With a Little Help from My Friends" as an escaping prisoner).

The performance tasks in the callback suggest that the company's intention was to secure new members with a capacity to improvise—to be upbeat and supportive in collaborative settings—and a willingness to make bold musical and character-driven theatrical choices. These admission criteria align with the work of the company. Griffin's Tale's adaptation process consisted of using improvisation to turn children's stories into theatrical sketches and songs, and the product—a touring show—consisted of a sequence of ten to 15 of these stories, requiring us to distinguish (and transition nimbly) between a range of roles (e.g. gym teacher, lion, girl scout). While the skill set assessed by the callback aligned with the aesthetic, I wonder to what extent it matched the stated mission. What does the capacity to "[encourage] imagination and creativity" look like? To what extent is the ability to improvise a solid proxy for this capacity? How do we inspire and assess this capacity through the audition process? How do we nurture it once we have cast a group of bold, upbeat folks in the company?

I grappled with these kinds of questions over the next 15 years as an actor in Griffin's Tale and its professional descendants, Barrel of Monkeys in Chicago and the Story Pirates in New York; as a high-school theatre teacher and director; and, in 2011, as founder of Flying Treehouse, a children's theatre company that I co-directed with Dan Klein at Stanford University. Flying Treehouse's mission was to cultivate and celebrate young people's imaginations and language arts through creative-writing workshops in local elementary schools, in-school performances of the young authors' stories and an annual on-campus public performance of this work. In this mission, the adaptation process was preceded by a four-week teaching residency, during which time we partnered with local second-grade classrooms to team-teach creative-writing lessons, which would yield the stories that would populate our productions. This curriculum was heavily influenced by the six-week residency model of Barrel of Monkeys. In this way, I founded Flying Treehouse with the intention of importing into a university context the community-based value system and partnership model of Barrel of Monkeys.

Although both Griffin's Tale and Flying Treehouse are situated on college campuses, the contexts and the companies' missions differ. Therefore, as we decided on how to garner participants, Dan and I asked ourselves, "How should our context and mission shape our admission process?" Northwestern University has one of the top theatre departments in the United States, and the turnout for Griffin's Tale auditions, especially given the company's long history, was often overwhelming. A system for selection based on a set of criteria (i.e. an audition) was arguably necessary. By contrast, at the time of Flying Treehouse's founding, Stanford's vibrant arts community included students who, for the most part, participated in performance as a fulfilling endeavor rather than a program of study. We would therefore have to look beyond Stanford's arts departments during recruitment. Flying Treehouse's newness as an organization meant that we also had to work to establish an identity that would lay the foundation for the company's future. Moreover, because teaching was central to our mission and we wanted our admission process to assess both performance-related and teaching-related skills, we prioritized a set of dispositions and capacities—kindness, intellectual agility, seeing children as whole and complex human beings—that are difficult to assess through a conventional audition process. In sum, at least during Flying Treehouse's inaugural year, we felt that we would have lost more than we would have gained by requiring interested students to audition.

Dan and I decided that Flying Treehouse's founding members would be any student who would commit to the company. No audition necessary. Interested students would enroll in "Creating Theatre for Children," a course I designed and co-taught with Dan. The intention behind our decision to forego an auditioning process and instead host a course was twofold: (1) to increase access to the company and to hopefully therefore diversify the skill set and the linguistic and cultural gifts of its constituents; and (2) to train students in the components of our practice—how to collaboratively facilitate drama-based writing workshops, adapt children's written text into sketches and songs, and perform these pieces effectively for child and adult audiences. As a doctoral candidate in teacher education at the time, I based this course and its pedagogy on my philosophy that the features of good teaching, adaptation and performance are discernible and teachable.

As with most decisions that matter, any admission process comes with some gains and losses. What can be gained through an audition process is assembling a group of folks with a baseline level of confidence and experience in auditioning, which can correlate with effective performance skills. Moreover, in the case of interactive, improvisation-based callback formats like I experienced in Griffin's Tale, successful auditioners may be adept at the kinds of collaborative skills that serve an ensemble-based adaptation and performance process. These assets proved true for my Griffin's Tale colleagues, who are some of the most talented, generous performers I have encountered.

What can be lost through audition processes is the extent to which a diversity of skill sets and perspectives are represented among company members. This was also true for my experience in Griffin's Tale; all company members were white (including me) and almost all majored in a performing art (not me). This composition may have merely been a random sample from Northwestern's mostly monochromatic Department of Theatre. Or, it is worth reflecting, a college student who would ace an audition may be characteristically different—economically, culturally, linguistically— than students who would have interest in the company's mission but lack auditioning experience or familiarity with the genre. Perhaps the successful auditioner, for example, had a theatre program in their high school or a working understanding of children's theatre or ensemble-based performance because they had seen or participated in similar projects in their home communities. If we believe that diversity—of theatrical forms, physical appearances, artistic capacities and linguistic gifts—makes for better storytelling, then we must be intentional about aligning our audition-like processes with our organizational missions, lest risk constructing access points that function more like barriers than as gateways into our artistic communities. Moreover, the clearer we can communicate our audition criteria to community members, the more likely we may be to assemble ensembles that serve our missions.

Like Griffin's Tale's audition-based model, our decision to require course enrollment for admission into Flying Treehouse came with losses and gains. The course met in two-hour sessions three times a week for ten weeks, yielding over 50 hours of scheduled time together. Insisting that students attend class for six hours per week (plus additional hours on assignments and production-related tasks) likely excluded students who didn't have flexible schedules. For example, students in majors with strict course sequences— and therefore minimal wiggle room in terms of electives—may not have been able to participate in our program. Such students might have had access, however, had we launched a model like Griffin's Tale—a student-run extracurricular organization with more flexible scheduling. Another byproduct of our no-audition approach was less control over ensemble size: 22 students enrolled in the course. While this is not a large class size, it made for a big cast. Shows performed by Griffin's Tale typically featured eight to 14 cast members, and 22 felt unwieldy given my past experiences and the size of available performance spaces. Among the 22 Flying Treehouse cast members, only three students had majors in Stanford's Department of Theatre and Performance Studies. Although several students had majors like Child

Development, Comparative Literature and Education—realms relevant to the company's mission—most cast members represented fields like Engineering, Economics and Earth Systems. While the company included several improvisers and actors, the majority of students had far less performance experience than students who typically sought out and succeeded at audition-based productions and ensembles.

Though the company's size and variable performance experience was a new challenge for me, our ensemble's composition suited our mission. Approximately half of the young authors with whom we partnered were children of color, several of whom spoke languages other than English at home. Around one-third of Flying Treehouse members were students of color and, in addition to English, cast members spoke French, Italian, Mandarin, Russian and Spanish. While our racial/ethnic composition was still disproportionate to our community partners and the larger population of degree-seeking Stanford undergraduates, approximately 58 percent of whom identified as nonwhite in the 2010–2011 academic year, it was a notable leap from the proportion of students of color in many other campus arts organizations. In addition, cast members had a wide range of skill sets that served our mission. Their experiences in creative writing, music (e.g. piano, guitar, violin, voice) and movement (e.g. dance choreography, stage combat, varsity wrestling) enriched our teaching residency and adaptation process. Their skills in sewing, film, photography and graphic design supported production-related tasks and promotional materials.

Since its founding, Flying Treehouse has become, like Griffin's Tale, a student-run company that embraces an audition-based admission process. Still on the company's listserv, I learned that Flying Treehouse's audition notice in September 2012 was as follows:

> Bring [...] something to teach us in three minutes or less (your favorite hobby, something you're good at that nobody else knows how to do, or just a better way to do something we already do know how to do) and a big smile. We'll chat, we'll play with the kids' stories, and we'll have fun.
>
> (Personal communication)

These audition tasks—teaching, and adapting stories written by children—are authentic to the interactive practices in which the company engages and open up the possibility of assessing prospective members' capacities to collaborate and communicate effectively. These tasks also provide prospective members with a sense of the company's adaptation process and aesthetic and, therefore, support auditioners in determining whether company membership would be a worthwhile way to spend their time.

As Flying Treehouse evolves, I hope its gatekeepers will continue to seek intentionality in the admission process. I envision this intentionality situated across the following four sets of questions:

- *Understanding our mission and context*
  What is our mission? On what core values is our mission based? Who are our community partners, and what are their values?
- *Articulating criteria and assessing our needs*
  What skills and dispositions are fundamental to our process and product? Among these skills and dispositions, which are prerequisite for admission to our organization, and which can be taught once members are aboard? What are the assets and areas of need within our current membership?
- *Designing admission tasks and procedures*
  What kinds of performance tasks (e.g. the reading aloud of a children's story, an improvised family dinner, a three-minute teaching demo) are authentic to the nature of our work and can assess the capacities that serve this work?
- *Recruitment and communication*
  How can we inform current and prospective members about our admission process in ways that are clear, inclusive and compelling? To what extent can we make our admission criteria transparent to all who would desire access?

As I continue to teach, direct and perform, I plan to return to these questions in the hopes that I can more purposefully align mission and admission, and therefore lessen the risk of relying on brave-hearted coincidence.

Notes

Barrel of Monkeys and the Story Pirates were both founded by Griffin's Tale alumni. Erica Rosenfeld Halverson and Halena Kays founded Barrel of Monkeys in Chicago in 1997. Lee Overtree, Drew Callander and Jamie Salka founded the Story Pirates in New York in 2003, with an extension in Los Angeles as of 2009.

Acknowledgments

Many thanks to Sophie Carter-Kahn, Dan Klein, Lee Overtree and Erica Rosenfeld Halverson for their feedback and friendship.

Michelle Dahlenburg

REMAKING HOW A SITE IS PERCEIVED
AND EXPERIENCED: THE GHOSTS OF
WALLER CREEK PROJECT

Most of us have countless ghosts, or site-specific memories, haunting infinite number of places. Even new places can remind us of old ghosts—for example, why do all elementary schools smell the same? Memories emotionally connect us to the places and spaces in our lives. But if we don't see ghosts at a certain site, can we still care about it? If we want others to care about a place, can we conjure site-specific memories through collaboration? As a Teaching Artist, I am interested in how theatre and storytelling can engage people in community, civic and social-change issues by creating new memories in unfamiliar places.

Waller Creek is not a place that most Austin, Texas residents associate with positive memories. Running through downtown Austin, Waller Creek is a site of urban decay, flooding, homeless encampments and neglect and is currently undergoing massive redevelopment. In 2010, for my practical thesis research at The University of Texas at Austin (UT), I created and facilitated a pilot program called "The Ghosts of Waller Creek" with urban designer and doctoral candidate Lynn Osgood. Lynn acted as co-facilitator, Waller Creek historian and member of the City of Austin Waller Creek Citizen's Advisory committee. Our intention was to use site-specific performance workshops to help Austinites connect with the creek and remake their perceptions of it by exploring its ghosts—its past, present and future civic issues.

Establishing the project goals was a fluid, ever-evolving process, influenced by my own interests, my project partner, the participants and the physical workshop site. In this essay, I examine the internal and external influences that shaped the project, including the workshop focus and content, participant selection and physical location. I conclude by situating my project within a larger systemic change movement geared toward integrating teaching artist work within government institutions.

Why Waller Creek?

In spring 2010, Lynn approached me about piloting an arts-based project related to Waller Creek. Her doctoral studies focused on the role of joy in public space, and she wanted to use the arts to inspire Austinites to see Waller Creek as an enchanted place, one worthy of their interest in light of the proposed redevelopment. I wanted to find a thesis project focused on community, civic and social change. I hoped to escape the ivory tower of the university, get involved with my city and form lasting relationships with other Austinites. I also wanted the project to intersect with theories and practices from applied drama and theatre, critical pedagogy and arts-based civic dialogue.

Lynn's idea seemed like a perfect opportunity to achieve many of our desired goals. Though I knew little about the creek, I was interested in working at an outdoor site with rich historical and political resonances, with opportunities to experiment with theatre for civic dialogue. Though we weren't sure what the project would look like, Lynn and I enthusiastically began our collaboration.

Why are we doing this?

In the weeks following, my excitement waned, as I began to feel unsure about the project's purpose. In my previous experience as a Teaching Artist, I had always worked closely with a partnering organization with specific goals. Though Lynn was a member of the Citizen's Advisory Committee, we did not have an organized partnership with the city. We saw the project as a potential pilot for future work, but without a partner organization directing our goals and priorities, we had to establish our own.

In one of our weekly meetings, Lynn talked about the typical ways city planners engage with the public, such as hearings, surveys and meetings, and that they often only reach the most vocal and interested stakeholders. These methods can discourage busy people who feel their voice won't make a difference. I asked her, "Is the goal for people to help make some sort of decision about what happens with the area?" "No," she said, "That probably won't happen. My goal is for people to love Waller Creek." Lynn explained that the city's initial tunnel development project would convert 20 city blocks of floodplains into usable land. But funding was not available for the redevelopment of the area, which has potential for green spaces, public art, businesses and recreation. She said that the city needed business owners and other people with money to be involved. I worried that the project had the potential to become mere propaganda. I wanted the project to raise questions and invite participants to investigate the creek area for themselves, not simply present a one-sided narrative about the space. "Why should people care about this?" I wondered. "So they'll vote for a bond issue that funds the redevelopment?"

Who needs this project, anyway?

When I begin a project, I spend the bulk of my time asking questions and listening, in search of the needs of the participants and partners. I also look for the dramatic tension or heat in the situation, the place where the most interesting part of the story or issue resides. These places are often the most powerful catalysts for change among the participants and/or audience. As I learned about the situation at the creek, I found that heat in the tension from the current stakeholders of Waller Creek and their reactions to the redevelopment plans. People and businesses in the area wanted to have a voice in how change would manifest: as property values rose, music venues, small businesses and homeowners could be priced out of the neighborhood. In addition, homeless advocates were concerned that the homeless in the area would be displaced. I imagined interviewing music venue owners, homeless advocates and city planners, and, with their permission, creating a piece of theatre that explored their feelings about the redevelopment. A post-show dialogue would follow, in which different stakeholders could connect with each other and city officials in a nonthreatening way. I hoped this could break through barriers created by traditional participation processes—lack of inclusion, collaboration and dialogue—while creating a new narrative about what was possible at the creek.

When I mentioned these ideas to Lynn, she liked the idea of a theatre piece, but was wary of exacerbating existing tensions between the stakeholders and the city. The city was working with these groups, she said, and felt their concerns were already being heard. She worried the piece would be too political and undo work already done. I asked myself, "Isn't theatre's job to provoke and challenge? What's the point of a project that doesn't work toward change?"

Through my conversations with Lynn and others, I realized that my desire to create a theatre piece was driven more by my own interests and perceived needs of the stakeholders, rather than their actual goals and needs. As a newcomer to the situation, I deferred to Lynn's expertise. Instead of a theatre piece, we decided to use five outdoor site-specific performance workshops to raise awareness about the redevelopment with everyday Austinites and students who knew little about Waller Creek.

This new direction felt daunting. Why would people care about this creek and its redevelopment? I realized that, like potential participants, I also had little prior knowledge of the creek. Before I could figure out why others should care, I had to discover that for myself.

Meeting Waller Creek

On a hot July afternoon, Lynn suggested we walk along Waller Creek downtown. As she shared the area's history, I was astonished by the raw beauty of the space, but appalled by its abandonment: cracked sidewalks, soda bottles floating in murky water, crumbling walls, graffiti under bridges and overgrown weeds. Lynn explained that the once well-to-do area had flooded in 1913, destroying Victorian homes and lowering property values. Later, lower income citizens of color lived in small houses by the creek. In 1976, the city redeveloped Waterloo Park, which is located along the creek. Through this historical overlay, I intuited the ghosts of Waller Creek. I could see the remnants of that redevelopment effort, and imagined possibilities: walks, bike rides, picnics and concerts. The area wasn't currently conducive to these kinds of activities. Yet I realized that as a Teaching Artist, I could use the arts to help everyday Austin citizens understand and care about the creek's history and imagine its future.

Location, location, location

Lynn and I developed a plan for two three-hour workshops with an undergraduate design class at UT, taught by a colleague interested in the relationship between performance and design. At first, I didn't believe that the location of the workshop along the creek would affect participants' sense of connection to it. With temperatures over 100 degrees, we spent most of the first workshop inside an air-conditioned classroom. We planned to conduct the outdoor portion of these workshops at a section of Waller Creek that runs between the art and theatre buildings at UT. This section of the creek is not part of the proposed downtown redevelopment, but it was more convenient given the extreme weather and lack of transportation.

The second workshop illuminated the importance of being at the specific site of the downtown redevelopment. In preparation for an image theatre exercise, I asked the group to brainstorm words and phrases associated with Waller Creek's issues and history. The group struggled, and in time grew frustrated. I felt like I was failing the group, and doubted the project. Finally,

I asked, "Why is this hard?" There was a pause, and then one student said, "Because we don't care enough about Waller Creek." "Why don't we care?" I asked. "Because it's just some creek. Why would we?" I asked, "Well, are there any bodies of water in Austin that we do care about?" They thought for a moment. "Yes—Barton Springs!" "Why do we care about Barton Springs?" "Because we swim there, and there are fun things to do." "Great, let's go outside." Once at the UT section of the creek, I facilitated the rest of the workshop, ending with an exercise that asked the students to create devised performances based on a set of creek-specific criteria. Though they were skeptical at first, the performance exercises gave them permission to step off the path and experience the creek in a new way. By the end of the workshop, the students had transformed into energetic, playful performers, splashing around the water as they danced, played tambourines and chanted, "This is our creek!"

Though surveys indicated that the workshops had an effect on the participants' relationship to the space, it bothered me that we hadn't taken the students to the redevelopment site. Originally, I had assumed that participants who were interested in the creek's university section would be able to transfer that connection to its downtown area. According to survey responses, this was not the case. Many participants' comments contained the word 'campus,' referencing UT-specific performance experiences. The downtown area of the creek was very different, and I could not assume students who felt attached to its university section would feel the same about areas they had not visited.

Revisiting intentions

At this point in the process, I realized that if we wanted to help people in Austin understand the issues at Waller Creek and form memories in that space, we needed to take them to the proposed redevelopment site. I had not felt as invested in its future until I visited the downtown portion, and I suspected others would feel the same. Lynn and I held three more workshops with UT students, Austinites and city planning professionals downtown. From my field notes and videos from the workshops, it is clear that participants experienced changes in their relationship to the creek because of the program. For many participants, the performance work shifted the creek from being an unfamiliar *space* to a more familiar *place*, one full of possibilities for future activities. While our original intention was to provide a space for participants to form connections with Waller Creek and remake their perceptions, the last three workshops revealed additional discoveries: the workshops could explore design interventions with landscape, lighting and signage; relationship-building was key to engaging people in civic issues; and the workshops' playful nature leveled the playing field between city planners and Austinites, creating a safer space for dialogue.

In a recent *HowlRound* essay, Michael Rohd (2012) invites theatre artists to engage in civic practice, "employing the assets of his/her craft in response to the needs of nonarts partners as determined through ongoing, relationship-based dialogue." He argues that Teaching Artists have the listening, facilitation and problem-solving skills required to catalyze community, civic and social-change projects reflecting community partners' ever-changing needs.

As we moved through the project, I realized my desire to create change within individual participants revealed a personal goal to affect systemic social change—to use the arts to interrupt and shift the power dynamics within traditional methods of civic engagement. Just as Teaching Artists shift power dynamics in classrooms and theaters toward a more equal footing, we can also use similar arts-based processes to shift hierarchies between citizens, planners and various citizen stakeholders. I realized my intention was not only to bring about change within individuals visiting Waller Creek—my goals also included integrating teaching-artist practice into city government, and transforming traditional methods of civic participation by situating them in more collaborative, inclusive and creative spaces.

The ghosts of our project: "Are you 'Flocking Michelle?'"

At a recent party, a friend I'd met through the project introduced me to his wife. "Wait, are you 'Flocking Michelle?'" she asked. I laughed. Flocking is a movement exercise I led at each workshop, a metaphor for positive collaboration that shifts roles between leader and follower, based on the group's needs. Several partygoers had been in attendance at the workshops two years prior, prompting a lively discussion of Waller Creek memories and the new Waller Creek Conservancy, which has taken over the stewardship of the creek. "Have you seen the proposed designs? Which ones do you like best?" I realized this conversation happened because Lynn and I intentionally worked with everyday Austinites, who now experienced a deeper relationship with the creek and people they met.

As of this writing, the Conservancy has just announced the winner of an international design competition to redesign the creek area. Years from now, when we walk along the newly developed Waller Creek, I imagine we will still see its ghosts: the floods of 1913, the homeless encampments, students splashing in the water and our flocking exercise in Waterloo Park. Waller Creek will never look the same to any of the participants. This project reminded me of the power of storytelling and performance to connect people to one another and place. My hope is that by creating these ghosts, we each felt welcome at the creek and personally engaged in its future. In the words of one participant, "Now we have Waller Creek friends."

Chapter 4

Quality

Quality: 1. An inherent feature; a characteristic. 2. A judgment of excellence; a feature of value.

(Seidel et al. 2009: 5)

As artists and educators we, the co-authors, embrace quality's multifaceted meaning. As reflective Teaching Artists, quality's chameleon-like aspect challenges us to consider carefully what characteristics, or *qualities*, contribute to the *quality* of a specific experience in order to make an informed decision—or when applied to facilitation—to construct common understanding among all participants. Quality can be subjective; it is often based on personal experience or opinion. The Harvard study *Qualities of Quality* (Seidel et al. 2009) sought to codify quality, but also noted that material conditions and elements such as place, history, geography and identity influence can contribute to our definition, understanding and recognition of quality. Quality, then, is circuitous—it exists through and is codified by ongoing conversation and reflection.

In this section we build on a premise introduced during our discussion of Intentionality. We argue that quality drama-based experiences are contextually situated; their value is based on a specific set of factors determined by the relationship between the Teaching Artist, the participants and their environment. We believe that quality, drama learning experiences benefit from a shared, transparent understanding of intention and pursuit of quality, which is co-constructed and refined throughout the entire process. The reflective Teaching Artist can involve participants in discussions about the essential purposes of an experience, co-create criteria that define achievement within the journey and co-determine and delineate end results. Each of these efforts will support quality within the reflective experience.

This section closely considers three specific ways the reflective Teaching Artist can engage with participants in an exploration of quality. We consider how to

- Pose a compelling or essential question
- Set common goals
- Define criteria for achievement

Posing questions, defining criteria and setting goals can contribute to a purposeful, insightful, *quality* drama learning experience. "Teacher/artists, parents and mentors need to take time to examine decisions that students make and help them consider their choices and the impact of those choices on the quality of their learning experiences" (Seidel et al. 2009: 85). Clear intention creates pathways of discovery and learning where participants, individually and collectively, identify and characterize quality practice. When students consider what achievement looks like and construct goals as a part of the learning experience, the multilayered process encourages further growth and ideally leads to deeper personal understanding and commitment to the process itself.

As Teaching Artists and their collaborators co-construct a definition of quality practice, they should also anticipate the unexpected. Bogart and Landau (2005: 18) note that

> a project needs structure, and a sense of direction, but can the leader aim for discovery rather than staging a replica of what s/he has decided beforehand? Can we resist proclaiming "what it is" long enough to authentically ask "what is it?"

Questions, criteria and goals should excite the collaborators and stimulate a desire to explore; in this section we consider how to put each into action.

COMPELLING QUESTION: HOW DOES A QUESTION PIQUE STUDENTS' INTEREST ABOUT A TOPIC OF EXPLORATION?

Framing an experience with a single compelling question is difficult. What question will excite your students? What question is engaging to you? What question will prompt other questions? How does the question build from and/or connect to participants' lived experiences? What question will guide each step in the drama learning experience? Constructing a successful compelling question requires a thorough understanding of how and why a particular process is being undertaken. It needs to synthesize these ideas into a tangible, engaging and relevant call toward exploration. A compelling question is simple in design, but grand in scope. It promotes answers that are personal, relevant and offer the possibility for varied and deep exploration. For example, a Teaching Artist facilitating an afterschool theatre program with teens might implore the ensemble to consider this: "What are an actor's tools?" The question is clear and simple, but the focus is on knowledge acquisition or a test of memory. Instead, this same Teaching Artist might ask: "How does drama help you understand other people's perspectives?" This question encourages an exploration influenced by many factors, hopefully promoting a thorough examination of the drama/theatre form that can grow more dimensional over time. A compelling question helps the learner peel back the layers to discover foundational as well as new knowledge driven by answers that spur new questions.

Kieran Egan (2005) writes that an engaging learning experience will contain mystery that grabs and holds our imagination, making us desire to learn more. A compelling question provides the invitation to the opportunity. Woven into the design of a program, the question elicits other questions and possibilities for exploration. The process compels students to seek more information, explore other perspectives and gain a more thorough understanding to help them construct informed answers to the query. It makes the learning journey relevant and responsive to the participant's experience, interests and life.

The development of a compelling question is essential to backwards instructional design (Wiggins and McTighe 2006). It provides a specific and focused purpose to a drama learning experience that will substantially include students in the big picture pursuit of the experience. As a Teaching Artist designs the instruction, the question will determine what strategies and activities will feed into the investigation of the question. Reflective moments will help learners gain greater understanding of the question and consider multiple possible answers. Each question encourages students to formulate their own, independent conclusion. Possibly the greatest advantage is the depth with which students become involved in the process in backwards design. What they do takes on greater purpose as they are invited to articulate why they are involved and how they may benefit from the experience.

Take a moment to play
Think of a recent residency or lesson you facilitated. Play for a moment with constructing a single, pithy question that both introduces a couple of core concept vocabulary words as well as invites multiple answers for consideration.

CRITERIA: HOW DO WE KNOW ACHIEVEMENT WHEN WE REACH IT?

The question embedded within this question is: "Do participants attain greater achievement if they strive for predetermined, standard criteria or do they attain more success when invited to help define what the achievement should or might look like?" As is evident from this particular section, we believe that participants should be as much a part of defining achievement as striving for it. While it is understood that a participant may be a novice in the art form, lacking the expertise of the necessary artistic skill, aesthetic vocabulary or past experience, they can still contribute to the conversation about what quality achievement may look or feel like. The Teaching Artist has to consider, then, how to create that foundation of understanding necessary to engage in discussion about criteria for success. Sometimes this is about providing an opportunity to experience theatre, as is discussed in our chapter on Artistic Perspective, so a participant can develop an aesthetic vocabulary. Ongoing discussions about theatre from audience and performer perspectives help students construct a greater understanding of what defines quality achievement. Other times the prior knowledge supporting our determination of quality is based primarily on our understanding of who we are and what we believe. Drama/theatre practice at its core is about how humans make sense of who they are with each other and within the world. All participants are experts in their lived experience and, at a basic level, can facilitate a conversation of what they see and how it makes them feel, an essential step in determining a larger common goal or marker of achievement.

This connection between what we see, feel and believe is at the heart of every drama learning experience. The more exposure and experience, the more we practice articulating these connections through questioning and discussions, the richer each drama learning opportunity. Embedded within this process, ideally, are frequent chances for reflection on what has been achieved and how to further improve. For example, a fifth grade class working in small groups to create silent movies based on major scientific discoveries in the twentieth century might be asked to share their staged progress for the last portion of their working session. The Teaching Artist asks students to describe what they see, hear and feel as they watch each work in progress. They identify images that stick in their mind (e.g. the characters of Thomas Edison and Lewis Howard Latimer slamming their hands down on the table in frustration as they try to perfect the filament for the light bulb prototype) and how specific aesthetic choices made the moment memorable (e.g. the actors' faces and bodies really communicating how tired and frustrated their characters felt). As students are guided to describe what is memorable or impactful about their peers' work, they begin to define and develop criteria for achievement (e.g. making large choices with your face and body is necessary to communicate your character's opinion in a silent film) through specific, tangible ideas for shaping and clarifying their artistic choices. The reflection, guided and shaped by the Teaching Artist's questions and prompts, also helps create a common working vocabulary between participants and the Teaching Artist.

As work progresses, and observation skills and knowledge deepen, the shared criteria often become more rigorous and detailed. Students become

Consider for a moment
What skills do you regularly develop in your participants? What questions might help participants recognize the hallmarks of each skill as they explore them?

more astute critical aesthetic purveyors of their own work and the work of others. As they design and develop their own process for identifying quality practice, they build a rigorous understanding and commitment to quality that will (hopefully) be evident in future pursuits. Extrinsic requirement permeates too many learning experiences (i.e. *If I do what you tell me to do, I will be good!*). Engaging participants in creating criteria for success encourages intrinsic motivation (i.e. *I determined that this is good, so I want to achieve what I THINK is good when I participate, practice or perform!*).

GOALS AND OUTCOMES: WHAT IS THE BENEFIT OF CO-CONSTRUCTING OUR PATH AND END POINT?

Goals are used in a drama learning experience to state how we hope participants will benefit from the exploration. Outcomes are the measure, the proof of the articulated achievement. Together, goals and outcomes can set a definable path for an experience, with purposeful checkpoints along the way. Goals give us a reason for the journey; the compelling question engages us in the endeavor; the criteria define the steps that drive us to greater achievement; and the outcomes are our agreement of what the ending will look like when we have arrived. A range of sources may influence goals and outcomes: from school or national standards, to competition guidelines, to individual or group interest, to personal enrichment and so on. They should be challenging to, yet attainable by, the specific participants of the program. Goals and outcomes should stimulate growth in students. They should be present: put the goals up on the wall and let them stare you in the face. Quality goals and outcomes help build common vocabulary, relationships, an approach to working and a common purpose. Before exploring, you need to know what it is you are hoping to accomplish. Twyla Tharp writes about the boxes in which she keeps collected materials for ongoing projects as her 'goals':

> It's what I can always go back to when I need to regroup and keep my bearings. Knowing that the box is always there gives me the freedom to venture out, be bold, and dare to fall flat on my face. Before you can think out of the box, you have to start with a box.

> (2003: 88)

To understand whether or not an individual or group has met a goal and achieved the hoped for outcome, participants should fully agree on the expectation of each goal and how to improve the outcome if the goal is not initially achieved. The challenge is that the Teaching Artist and/or supporting organization often set goals without participant input and can, at times, not even share the goals with the participants at all. Without an awareness of the goals, how can there be an understanding of what, why and how work is to be done? Students should know the project goals at minimum, or, ideally, they should contribute to constructing and revising goals and outcomes as a daily effort as the experience proceeds. It is not about simply achieving the goals, so much as understanding the why or why not and considering what will be the next course of events in relation to the outcome.

> **Create the space**
> At what point in the drama learning experience do participants have enough context to help construct challenging, purposeful and achievable goals?

AND CONSIDER …

Somewhere in here is the argument, "What if we desire to simply explore and see where the journey takes us?" Michael Rohd (1998: 3) describes his "Hope is Vital" process as

> a journey. Like any journey, it has a beginning, a route, and a schedule, but it does not have a predetermined destination. It just gives directions to start. [It is] a general map, which will change with every journey you take.

Goals and outcomes define and inspire the journey; they don't set a regimen for daily activities or provide a script for what participants have to do. These elements simply ask that you be clear about your purpose. Is this about … Skill development? Creating a product? Investigating an issue? Exploring a story? How do each of these factors contribute to building a quality practice and product?

TEACHING ARTIST INVESTIGATION OF QUALITY

Our contributing writers consider the idea of quality and its impact on their varied work and programs in the following case studies. Tamara Goldbogen considers how to translate the quality of European youth theatre performance to American stages. Nicole Gurgel negotiates moments of political and personal tension in a devising program facilitated in Texas schools. Gary Minyard questions how to find relevance for young performers and their community audiences during the staging of a classic play in a professional youth theatre. Michelle Hayford contemplates how prior experience impacts and enriches a devising program with youth in foster care. The final essay, by Kati Koerner, discusses her journey to determine criteria for success in a drama residency program with English Language Learners.

Quality
Case Studies

Tamara Goldbogen

WHAT DOES QUALITY THEATRE FOR YOUNG AUDIENCES LOOK LIKE?

In my position as a Theatre Arts Lecturer at the University of Pittsburgh I spend a lot of time thinking about quality of work. In my case this refers to theatrical productions that I send into schools, foundational pieces that I include in my courses and, of course, work that I create on stage for young audiences. Every year I get to revisit the big question, "what does quality Theatre for Young Audiences (TYA) look like?" when I teach my introductory course, Theatre for Children. Day one always begins the same way: oversized paper goes up on the walls and I write questions like, "What is children's theatre?" or, "What is the first children's theatre experience you remember?" Students grab markers and begin to write. With this simple exercise, the door is opened and our collective effort to define and assess quality TYA has begun.

Early on in my own development as a TYA practitioner, I became acutely aware of audience engagement and how significantly that element of the theatrical experience defined the way in which I identified quality work. My formal TYA training began at the University of Texas at Austin where I watched Suzan Zeder navigate the ambiguous new-play development process to create quality work. Suzan practices audience engagement on many levels with students, artists, playwrights and young people. Her abilities as a dramaturg and teacher are ones that I try to emulate on a daily basis in my life—both personally and professionally. My next stop was the Children's Theatre Company (in Minneapolis) where I was challenged and inspired by artistic director Peter Brosius. He easily fits my definition of a visionary thinker. In one of our weekly meetings, Peter asked me to think about who was doing the best TYA work, not just nationally, but internationally as well.

"Who do we want to work with?" he dared. This was a defining moment for me—Peter opened up my worldview of TYA. No longer limited to US-based work, I began to attend the International Association of Theatre for Children and Young People (ASSITEJ) festivals around the world in search of new exemplary models of quality TYA.

My exposure to international TYA led to my interest in the beginnings and endings of the TYA experience and the way artists and practitioners invite young people to experience the world of the play. I wanted to know how audience engagement shaped the way in which young people processed the stories that were being told on stage.

When does the story begin for young people attending a theatrical performance? Imagine that audience members arrive at the theatre, are presented with a piece of string and asked to see where the string goes. When a young person recounts his or her version of the events will it begin with the discovery of the string? Will it begin with the characters' storylines? How expansive will their recollection be? This avenue of thinking challenged me to reconsider my own notions of audience engagement and how I approach my own work.

My exploration centers on two productions presented at the ASSITEJ World Congress in Australia (May 2008): *Cat* by Windmill Performing Arts of South Australia, and *Goodbye Mr. Muffin* by Teater Refleksion and Teatret De Rode Heste of Denmark. These international productions provided a wealth of material for subsequent application in my own work directing *Tomato Plant Girl* at the University of Pittsburgh (2009–2010). My intention was to draw from the international audience engagement techniques that I encountered and to put them into practice with US audiences.

International inspiration

The production of *Cat* by Windmill Performing Arts of South Australia provided an excellent example of what I consider to be a liminal beginning to a TYA production—one that is ambiguous, open and blurred. This was my experience:

> I'm ushered into a small area lined with comfortable cushions where young people and their parents are waiting. It isn't long before music fills the room and butterflies appear. Beautiful butterfly finger puppets—controlled by actors—flutter among the families here to see the play. Children hold out their fingers to provide a resting place for the butterflies.
>
> (May 14, 2008)

The butterfly puppets serve as guides, leading the audience to the playing space, showing people where they can sit, and indicating where the action is going to take place. The butterfly puppets stay with the audience for the entire theatrical event—weaving in and out of the story that follows.

Windmill's production of *Cat* is what the company calls an installation theatre piece, that is, a play in a flexible space rather than a formal theater setting. This approach allowed the production to transform a playing space into a place. In their book, *Spaces of Creation* (2005), authors Suzan Zeder and Jim Hancock explain the fundamental difference between a space and a place: "place is bounded space [... P]lace is given meaning and significance by the attachment and memories we associate with a specific location, object, artifact, or event [... W]e remember this place with all of our senses." Only by engaging the senses of our TYA audience members can we truly begin the work of transforming the performance space into a place of storytelling and discovery.

While the content of Windmill's production of *Cat* itself does not stray far from conventional participation theatre, what happened at the conclusion of the 'performance' was, in my view, unique and unlike anything I had experienced in TYA productions in the United States. The actors stepped out of character and presented the young audience members with three options for post-performance activities. Option one was listening to and re-enacting the story as one of the actors read the children's book on which the play was based. Option two was learning a song together from the play and trying out some of the instruments that were used by the musician such as terracotta flower pots, wind chimes, a glockenspiel and a recorder. Option three was a guided exploration of the shows props and puppets with one of the actors.

All of these activities took place simultaneously, immediately following the performance, and were located in the playing space. It was the child's decision which activity to choose. I was amazed at the confidence and ease with which the young people navigated the options that had been presented to them. I watched closely as the children gravitated toward their areas of interest and were immediately engaged in an extended learning activity. As an observer, it seemed to me that these activities opened up further explorations into the world of the play for the young audience members.

Another production at the ASSITEJ festival that captured my attention was a show from Denmark, *Goodbye Mr. Muffin* by Teater Refleksion and Teatret De Rode Heste. The main character, Mr. Muffin, a 7-year-old guinea pig, is nearing the end of his life. His is a tale about life and death told with great warmth, wistfulness and dignity, helping the audience understand grief and sorrow. This was my experience:

I enter a converted black box space with a small seating area facing a shoebox on a table at the front of the room. Adults and children sit side by side on child-sized benches. Two actors appear and stand on either side of the shoebox—a woman holds an upright bass and a man sits on a stool and addresses the audience. A few plucked notes come from the bass and the male actor begins writing a small note that opens with, "Dear Mr. Muffin, I am so sad…." The male actor delivers the narration for the piece, manipulates the shoebox (which transforms into Mr. Muffin's home), and is the puppeteer. The female actress provides the musical narration for the story with her instrument. From the instant when a tiny door on the shoebox opens and an equally tiny guinea pig puppet pops his head out, to the moment Mr. Muffin is buried in the ground, the audience is transfixed.

(May 16, 2008)

Goodbye Mr. Muffin is a simple and straightforward puppet theatre piece. There were two main conventions employed in this play that sought to engage the audience. To achieve an intimate setting, the company requires a limited audience, minimal lighting focused on the simple set (the shoebox) and the absence of a raised stage. All of these elements help to tell this story in a heartfelt way.

Another engagement convention used was almonds. The narrator carried a bag of almonds, Mr. Muffin's favorite food, around in his pocket. When Mr. Muffin was unhappy the narrator would offer him almonds and that always seemed to help. When Mr. Muffin dies there is a pervasive feeling of sadness and the audience is allowed to grieve the loss along with the narrator. When Mr. Muffin is buried, the narrator includes a small tribute of a few almonds. The almonds continue to weave through the narrative providing the audience with something familiar and unassuming to follow throughout the story. At the conclusion of the piece, the narrator invites the audience members to come forward to visit Mr. Muffin's grave. As the families respectfully approached the burial site, the narrator remains in character and produces the bag of almonds to share with audience members. The post-performance conversations between the narrator and the audience members were hushed and brief. The children munched on almonds and stared at the little grave. Here is an excellent instance where sensory engagement successfully transforms a playing space to a place.

Putting inspiration into practice

I returned from the ASSITEJ conference in Australia determined to bring some of these new audience engagement techniques to my own work, and excited to offer new theatre-going experiences for young people in my community.

My first opportunity to try out these new approaches was on a touring production of *Tomato Plant Girl* at the University of Pittsburgh. Having worked on the inaugural production of *Tomato Plant Girl* at the University of Texas at Austin, I had useful insight into the play's potential to connect with a wide range of young people and families. The University of Pittsburgh's production of *Tomato Plant Girl* was created in a TYA course that I taught in Spring 2009. The class comprised 20 graduate and undergraduate students from a variety of majors. Students learned about the history, literature and current practices of TYA, and took on vital roles in the theatre process—acting, production, outreach and marketing. As a class we were able to address the question, "what does quality TYA look like?" because we actively engaged in the process.

It was my creative partners, production designer Lisa Leibering and musician Buddy Nutt, who helped me to create the world of the play and to begin to think about sensory audience engagement in new ways.

As production designer, Lisa shared my desire to create a world for the play that would engage audiences on several levels. My concept was to create a highly stylized world for the characters to inhabit—a place where a tomato plant girl growing out of the ground could be possible. Lisa accomplished this task by designing a set made almost entirely out of fleece material.

This project also served as a case study for Lisa's research, which looks at the unique challenges of designing for young audiences and the connections to cognitive functions. New brain-based studies have shown that today's children are capable of processing much more visual stimuli than previously thought, and that this visual processing has demonstrable cognitive benefits. We worked to incorporate these new developmental theories into theatrical designs for the production so that the audience members would be stimulated deeper cognitive level.

This research led us to create a Fabric Touch Board that audiences encountered as they entered the playing space. It was made from a board covered with swatches of material used on the set and in the costumes. Text in the center of the board read, "Come feel these fabrics used in our production!" I watched as young people would touch the fabric samples and then easily identify where the fabrics were located on the set. It was clear to me that the board helped young people *get acclimatized to the place and jump-started* their imagining of what was going to happen in this new world.

In an effort to provide Leibering with substantive feedback, we included a section in the *Tomato Plant Girl* study guide that centered on post-performance feedback. We asked students to draw the world of the play after they returned to their schools or homes. We asked them to remember as many things as they could and to include colors in their drawings. It was evident from the pictures we received that the textures (clouds, costumes), colors (green grass, pink dress), characters (they are in every drawing) and puppets (tomato plants, giant mother hands) all had a significant impact on the theatrical experience of these young audience members. The Fabric Touch Board and study-guide feedback all provided fodder for Lisa's research and my own greater understanding of how effective sensory engagement techniques can be.

I also collaborated with local musician Buddy Nutt, a one-man band of unique instruments including the didgeridoo and the musical saw. In our first meeting, Buddy was able to articulate his ideas for a soundscape that elevated my understanding of the story. The world of *Tomato Plant Girl* was fully realized by pairing Lisa's visceral designs and Buddy's odd-ball musical style.

We ended each performance with an invitation for young people and families to come into the garden to talk to the characters, ask questions, touch the set, smell the fake dirt, and look behind and inside things on stage to figure out how things work. I observed this interaction working on many levels. Even the shyest audience member could not resist the opportunity to step onto the plush, fleece ground covering and touch the soft stuffed flowers. There was always a parent or two who went straight backstage to figure out how the set folded down to fit into a van for touring. The most meaningful feedback about the production came from the audience members who chose to come up on stage and engage in the world of the play.

I believe TYA in the United States can benefit from continued research of audience engagement techniques utilized in international productions. My search for quality TYA has led me to understand the importance of sensory audience engagement. As TYA artists and practitioners, we must continue to find new ways for our young audience members to connect with and navigate the theatrical experience. I look forward to asking the question, "what does quality TYA look like?" every semester with a new group of students who will help to shape the future of this field.

Michelle Hayford

SUIT MY HEART: STAGING FOSTER YOUTH NARRATIVES THAT HIT HOME

I was introduced to the mentoring nonprofit Footsteps to the Future (Footsteps) when I cast an aspiring young actor in her first-ever role for a local production of Eve Ensler's *Vagina Monologues*. Artkeda, a Footsteps mentee, owned the stage after weeks of learning her lines by listening to a recording of the monologue. She overcame her literacy challenges in order to pursue her dream to act.

I had also cast Judi, the Founder and Executive Director of Footsteps, whose rehearsals were largely (and happily) taken over by *un*scripted monologues about 'the girls' she serves with the nonprofit. ('The girls' is a loving term of endearment Footsteps mentors use for the young women in the mentoring program: "It's all about the girls!") Judi founded Footsteps after being asked to donate suitcases to foster youth, whose frequent moves to and from foster homes and youth homes are often accomplished with trash bags. She discovered that many foster youth are underserved by the agencies meant to protect them and often vulnerable to abuse and deprived of education. The Footsteps mission is to empower young women in, and aging out of, foster care (approaching the age of 18) to safely transition to living independently.

Judi accepted my proposal to partner my theatre students with Footsteps to create an ensemble play at Florida Gulf Coast University (FGCU) based on interview narratives with Footsteps mentors and mentees. Our collective endeavor with the production was to represent and empower the foster youth; *Suit My Heart* (title from mentee Brittany's poem 'My Heart is a Mime') allowed the audience a window into the disenfranchised lives of those entangled in the foster care system.

While devising *Suit My Heart*, I relied upon my training in the 'three A's' of performance studies conceived by my late mentor Dwight Conquergood as "artistry, analysis and activism" (2002: 152). With these 'three A's' in mind, I set out to facilitate a devising process and create an artistic product that would positively serve all communities involved. The quality of the project would be determined not only by the efficacy of the play that we produced in the end, but by the personal growth of my students and the empowerment of our community partners throughout the process. Discovering the reach of my authority and breaking open my own painful family history in order to grow as a Teaching Artist were not original goals for this project, but turned out to be necessary developments.

'Artistry' meets 'Activism': Getting acquainted and accepted

Judi invited me and my family to the annual Footsteps retreat on Captiva Island as the first step in our collaborative journey. I relished the opportunity to reconnect with Artkeda and be introduced to more of the 'girls' and their mentors through a Storytelling Workshop and unplanned "deep hanging out," the informal "participant observation" mode most conducive to building community (Geertz 2000: 107). If I proved myself trustworthy and delivered a meaningful storytelling workshop, I knew I'd be able to secure interviews. The "deep hanging out" went well, the only exception being the initial odd presence of my husband. He was the only man invited that weekend and upon our arrival his presence was met with palpable discomfort. I was immediately sensitized to the 'girls' deep mistrust of men. I sensed then that men were associated with abandonment and abuse due to the girls' tragic life experiences and chastised myself for bringing my family with me. But his hands-on caring for our two small children had him quickly welcomed and freed me up to bond with my new community. I was aware that I may have made an unwelcome first impression: an intact heteronormative family with a doting husband, two kids and two dogs (yes, we even brought our dogs!) in the midst of a retreat for young women in, and aging out of, foster care who had been failed by their families, and many of whom were struggling to be self-sufficient single parents. I was cautious about being perceived as the "slumming" academic whose project would result in a "custodian's rip-off" (Conquergood 1985: 5–6).

The Storytelling Workshop began awkwardly due to the cramming of all the participants into the small living room of one of the hotel suites. But after moving furniture and breaking the ice with light-hearted theatre games, randomly selected pairs went off on their own to share one story of "personal triumph" (Rohd 2008). After the allotted time for sharing stories was up, I asked everyone to remember one notable sentence from their partner's story. They then were directed to create a five-count sequence of movements that represented their partner's story, and put the two elements together as a short representation of their partner's story through text and movement. This activity resulted in deep communion between the paired storytellers and resonated with a tearful audience as each pair in turn overcame any performance jitters to show their partner that they were *heard*.

This storytelling workshop demonstrated the power in seeing one's personal story transformed by another and crystallized into a simple yet loaded performance. The take-away was a reaffirmation of the resilience of those present by bearing witness to each other's life stories and collectively celebrating those moments of triumph each saw reflected back to them. The list of names and contact information I received after the workshop filled the front and back of a piece of legal-sized yellow notepad paper. I was relieved that the girls and mentors had perceived me as an artist with purpose who had effectively collapsed 'artistry' and 'activism', and proven that their lives were worthy subjects of the art we would make together. What I couldn't have anticipated was that I also would be validated by seeing my own story mirrored back to me in our final production.

'Analysis' meets 'Activism': Inspiring action

My next task was to inform the ensemble of FGCU theatre students about our project for the next ten months, and ensure that they continued to build trust with our Footsteps partners. I emphatically told my students that this was not a project to take lightly—many of these young women had been repeatedly let down by people they had trusted, and my students were not to be added to that list under my watch. Fortunately, my insistence on their dedication was unnecessary because my students were an empathetic group that quickly felt the weight of their ethical responsibility to do right by the young women they befriended despite their differences. The student ensemble was multiethnic, co-ed and from diverse socioeconomic backgrounds, yet aware of their status as privileged college students. With our attention to the dynamics of race and class (I myself am mixed race and first in my family with a terminal degree), we were attuned to the need to value diversity as the source of productive dialogue.

We were exploring universal themes while generating performance material—family, home, survival, transcendence, forgiveness and love. Many elements from the students' personal narratives worked their way into the final script. Everyone has a story of family and home, even in the sad case of its absence or destruction. And many of my relatively privileged students could relate to their interviewees' stories of family dysfunction—home and family is an often fraught aspect of our lives regardless of class, race or education. Personal growth, then, was measured by the willingness of my students to share their own struggles at home, be vulnerable with their peers and open their hearts to one another. It was a natural extension to bring this same generosity to the Story Circle events I facilitated at the monthly Monday night Footsteps meetings, borrowing Roadside Theater's Story Circle methodology.

The Story Circles solidified the strong sense of community and reciprocity among the mentors and mentees and my students, who participated fully in answering the prompts. My students' openness allowed the mentors and mentees to feel safe in answering the same questions with equal honesty. Notably, the fact that Artkeda and Florinda, two well-trusted Footsteps girls, were invested in the project as full participants in the cast also lent us credibility. Many of the mentees saw participating in the project as a chance to share a story their way. Some had felt misrepresented by journalists, newspaper articles and television, and saw an opportunity to have their words valued rather than manipulated. Sharing a story for *Suit My Heart* guaranteed a measure of ownership previously denied to them. In fact, the title *Suit My Heart* comes from a line of poetry shared by mentee Brittany, who acknowledges in the poem that love would "suit my heart" better than hate.

I also participated in the Story Circles I facilitated, but when the time came to transcribe, I skipped over my own narratives and deemed it solipsistic to listen to my own voice on the recorder, let alone consider my narratives for inclusion in our script. But I came to understand that my vulnerability as a Teaching Artist should not be mistaken for narcissism. After all, my own family history informs my activism and interest in working with foster youth in the first place. If, as Jan Cohen-Cruz argues, "[a]rtists must be as sensitive to their differences from community participants as to the common ground they share," (2005: 95), what is lost when Teaching Artists refuse to include their "common ground" as fodder for the project? My epiphany that I was valuing difference and acknowledging privilege to the exclusion of personal investment and risk had me rethink the editing out of my narratives and recognize that their inclusion came from a desire for reciprocity, not self-indulgence. Stepping away from the role of Teaching Artist as merely a privileged interpreter and instead democratizing disclosure greatly enhanced the quality of our process.

'Artistry, Activism and Analysis': Appreciating ethics

My worst failure as a Teaching Artist occurred when I didn't listen to my gut and allowed a local reporter to interview Artkeda alone in my office while I conducted rehearsal. I repressed my mistrust of him, and afterwards Artkeda admitted that she felt cornered into answering questions about her family's past and only spoke out of loyalty to me. I felt the painful privilege of authority as I recognized that I had failed to protect her from this journalist's predatory interview. I confronted the reporter, interrupting his interview with another cast member. I appealed to his conscious and asked that he not print Artkeda's family history, to which he said his only concern was "to get the story." I told him his methods were unethical and he cut me off, saying, "I don't need a lecture from a college professor about how to do my job," and left. I got the editor on the phone to complain about his behavior and to ensure the publication did not print Artkeda's interview. But the damage was done; I had exploited Artkeda's trust after so painstakingly building it, and while she accepted my teary apology, I kicked myself for not listening to my intuition. I discovered the necessity of playing gatekeeper to vulnerable community partners who grant me more authority than I recognized. I learned my authority as a Teaching Artist is a privilege and a gift, but can quickly become a curse if it is underestimated. The irony of having trained an entire cast in the ethics of interviewing, only to be undermined in my own office by an insensitive reporter was not lost on the ensemble. We felt the sanctity of our safe space had been, at once, soiled and strengthened. The ensemble's generous forgiveness for my mistake allowed us to move forward in solidarity and with a greater appreciation for our shared ethics of loyalty and trust.

When I delivered the final script, the ensemble found that I had taken their cue and had contributed my own personal narratives with the inclusion of scenes that dramatized conversations between me and my brother as we came to terms with our separation during childhood and the traumas that prompted it. This modeling of vulnerability gave my students the opportunity to bear witness to my story as I had borne witness to theirs, further cementing the family our ensemble had become. I had realized the hypocrisy in asking my students and our Footsteps collaborators to crack open their home lives without doing the same. Although we had ensured anonymity by removing identifying information and creating composite narratives, the act of sharing demanded courage. To feel the unease shared by my cast and Footsteps collaborators inherent in making family secrets public was an incredible learning opportunity for me. To agonize firsthand with the fraught ethics of navigating the individual's right to share family history by way of reclaiming, reframing and healing the past was instructive of what a reciprocal applied theatre project *should* feel like. Rather than rest in the comfort of writing off self-reflexivity as undermining of my authority and merely egotistic, I risked the same discomforts of feeling exposed, disloyal and conflicted, with the result that my cast and Footsteps collaborators recognized the emotional resonance of their stories and entrusted me as the 'head' of our newly configured family.

Suit My Heart inspired us to share that which is not politely discussed— the shortcomings and intimacies in our homes, the awe we have for one another's strength to transcend and thrive, and the love we find with the families we choose. Perhaps the synchronicity of Conquergood's 'three A's' is best epitomized, fittingly, by another story of personal triumph. After the successful run of *Suit My Heart* at FGCU, Artkeda was thrilled to tour as part of the cast to the Community-University Expo in Canada to perform *Suit My Heart* as an example of best practices in applied theatre. She boarded her first flight, left the country for the first time, and upon descending the escalator in the airport in Canada, Artkeda declared, "I am proud of myself." This moment reminded me that Artkeda's accomplishment was shared by the entire ensemble for whom 'artistry, analysis and activism' had hit home.

Gary Minyard

HOW DO WE FIND RELEVANCE?

In my work, I constantly challenge myself to find the relevant connections between theatre, history and community—then intersect those connections with the lives of the young people who work with me. By creating a rich path of discovery for a cross-section of our community as performers and audience members, I hope to create a high quality theatre experience for all involved.

One of those experiences challenged me to push my own limits as an artist. In the spring of 2009, while Artistic Director at Pennsylvania Youth Theatre (PYT), I added a rare gem into the season: Yasha Frank's *Pinocchio*. Written in 1937 for the Federal Theatre Project (FTP), Frank's extravagant musical was the most popular show during the brief history of the FTP. Despite the political firestorm in Washington about a socialist agenda infiltrating many of the plays created for America's youth, tens of thousands were able to share in Yasha Frank's clever adaptation of Carlo Collodi's book. I had always been attracted to the show, but my biggest question became, "How do I make Yasha Frank's inspiring story relevant to our young people today?"

Bethlehem, Pennsylvania was hard-struck by the Depression. Bethlehem Steel was one of a handful of powerful steel mills producing the world's steel, and when the economy turned in the early 1930s, so did many family's fortunes. The Steel, as it is known in the Lehigh Valley, permanently closed its plant on the banks of the Lehigh River in the early 1980s. It left behind a trail of confused and angry workers. The Steel's absence still affects the area today, more than 30 years later.

Seeing those steel stacks for the first time sitting quiet along the banks of the river was (and still is) a startling image to me. I was on a bus during a cold November day visiting the area for the first time. The Steel was silent, but for some reason I could feel the ghosts of the steel works – the men and women who worked day and night to create the skeletons of our bridges, our war ships, our famous buildings, our backbone – asking me to connect their stories to something from America's past.

It was the similarities between the Great Depression and the Great Recession that inspired me to produce this show. America's economic condition since 2007 has left many people out of work, families in crisis, nonprofits scrambling for support, schools unable to provide important programming and more people wondering when or if the tide will turn. The impact of the more recent Great Recession serves as a powerful backdrop for exploring the concepts of deceit and greed as they relate to young people in today's world. My challenge, though, was finding a way to make the history of The Steel and the current economic conditions in Bethlehem, Pennsylvania a relevant point of connection and focus for the young performers.

My first task was to determine how to meld the history of the play with a community today. I knew I had to create a rehearsal process to accomplish several things: (1) train the young actors to become accomplished performers in a variety of styles while keeping the high-quality production values audiences expect; (2) add modern relevance to the 80-year-old messages of greed and deceit in the script; and (3) infuse national and local history into the rehearsal process to build relevance and interest in the play themes for the young participants. Running parallel to these goals, I also needed to construct a way for the community to have dialogue about the issues presented in the play.

My vision for this production was a fast-paced, uniquely physical style that was unfamiliar to most of the actors. I had to train the young performers in various styles of physical theatre in order to create an updated show for a modern audience. At the same time, I needed to be hyperaware of the pitfalls of such a quest. Did I have the time to train them and ensure the quality I needed for the show? Could I safely teach a young person something physically demanding? Utilizing a series of physical theatre exercises over the rehearsal process, I successfully trained 55 performers in a variety of styles including circus arts, stylized movement sequences and a modern presentational style. Throughout I attempted to stay close to the story: how does The Steel serve as powerful metaphor in our performance?

I begin every rehearsal with a ritual simply called a 'check-in.' This allows all cast members to share with the group where they are physically, spiritually and emotionally before work in the rehearsal room begins. Without this formalized time, I find that young actors will wind up spending precious energy sharing this information during rehearsal, which distracts from the work at hand. In order to build an ensemble, I pair this ritual with warming up as a group through a powerful exercise called: 'Milling and Seething.' I use it to teach young performers spatial awareness, physical control, balance, rhythm, teamwork, focus, eye contact and a variety of other performance techniques.

The bedrock of this kind of rehearsal process is training in a particular style—but there were immense challenges. Inspiring young people is easy compared to training them to perform something stylized and specific. Particularly, the Circus Arts are not easy to train for in a short amount of time with young people who have limitations of time and skills. However, tapping into a young person's natural skill set—either gymnastics, juggling, singing, playing an instrument or any other skill—proved to be the perfect entry point for the circus portions of the show. I particularly used humor and comedic 'bits' to highlight what skills they had. I also had a group of actors learn how to perform with wooden marionettes as part of our performance vocabulary. I also had to convince these young actors that the circus arts, stylized movements and marionettes are not 'old,' but cool, modern and relevant.

Many of those young actors, finally focused on the 'fun' circus training aspect of our rehearsal process, began to lose focus on the context of the scenes they were in, the characters they were to portray and relationships they might have to The Steel. As a portion of my intent with this production was to add modern relevance to the messages of greed and deceit inherent within the play, I realized I needed to help the company of young actors understand the correlations between the themes of the play with the realities of how those themes affected The Steel, the city of Bethlehem and families in the community. It is easy to say that greed and deceit led to the downfall of The Steel, but the truth is much more complicated. My goal was for each of our cast members to have a personal connection to that history, to build a personal stake in their city's past.

To deepen the personal investment in the play's themes for our actors, I supplied them with research on the FTP, The Steel and the city of Bethlehem. I asked them to consider connections between the city's past and current circumstances. The young actor who played Pinocchio shared a story of the father of one of his good friends who had recently lost his job. He described how the family had very little money—his friend could not go on vacation, buy new clothes, go to the movies or even go out to eat. Just like Pinocchio's father Gepetto, money was a struggle and sacrifice became normal. This conversation during rehearsal led others to make connections to this kind of difficulty in their own lives—their own friends, family members and even news stories—all of their observations became a relevant part of the conversation. In the end, each of the young actors found something impactful to connect them to the historical context, bringing a modern sensitivity to the predicaments around them. Each actor in their own right brought those perspectives to the stage.

Yasha Frank was the head of the FTP's children's theatre division in Los Angeles where *Pinocchio* premiered. It then opened in several other cities across the country because of its popularity. In fact, *Pinocchio* was so popular that there is no way to calculate how many people actually saw it. One of the reasons his fantastical adaptation was such a hit with audiences was *The Lesson of the Penny*. It is certainly the prevailing message that resonates throughout the play. Frank wrote the Blue Haired Fairy Queen's lines in order to include the adults and the children in the crowd:

BLUE HAIRED FAIRY QUEEN: Pinocchio! By word and deed!
You've triumphed over human greed!
And very soon you'll know the joy
Of being a living, breathing boy.
You've learned the lesson of the penny,
Some have too few, some have too many
But share with those who haven't any!
So let the bells proclaim our joy
While you become a human boy!
(Frank 1939: 43)

In 2010, as in 1937, that message of money and greed echoed in the rehearsal studio. All of a sudden, the Blue Haired Fairy Queen's words provided the cast with a tangible discussion point to which each of them, whether they were six or eighteen, could relate. Money permeates their lives, but the idea of helping someone in need trumped all of their wishes of being rich. I can only imagine that Yasha Frank had a similar sensation rehearsing his play when he realized that his cast and crew were practicing this play not for wealth but to help people.

I was fortunate to host Yasha Frank's son, Boris Frank, for opening night. He was a young boy when the show opened at the Beaux Arts Theatre in Los Angeles. Boris's personal recollections in the talkback provided an authentic voice to the audience and our casts, illuminating a time in our country's history that mere research could not do. He shared with our two casts the information that not only did his father write the show to help teach young people *The Lesson of the Penny*, but also to make sure that they understood a deeper lesson: that 'Everyone Participates.'

By hiring hundreds of unemployed professional performers and vaudeville acts, designers, musicians, costumers, stagehands and technicians, Yasha Frank not only provided those artists with meaningful work but also stayed true to his message of participation. Everyone has a stake, even young people, when the nation finds itself in crisis, and it was this brave artist who transformed a simple story of a wooden puppet becoming a real boy into so much more. It was entirely appropriate that so many young people were able to participate in PYT's production because that in and of itself embodied Yasha Frank's message.

Empowering young performers with the belief that they are each a brave artist, through the men and women who treaded the boards before them, became central to my efforts to make *Pinocchio* relevant to the cast. Each of my actors was challenged to step beyond their comfort zone and endure difficult training in order to perform this play. No one gave up. This process challenged their ideas of what an artist is, what performers do and how audiences are affected by meaningful messages. Boris Frank—through the connections he made between the actors living during the Great Depression and the young people in Bethlehem, Pennsylvania 80 years later—solidified this perspective in me.

I began to wonder how I could facilitate a similar experience for community members, who were not a part of the rehearsal process, so they could also dialogue about the important issues in the play. I decided to create an outreach program called "On The Nose: Pinocchio's Life Lessons" as an extension to the production. This interactive program provided an opportunity for young people who were not in the play to consider the ethical questions of greed and deceit directly, to express their opinions and to hear their peers' points of view. The production outreach workshops were held at the Bethlehem Area Public Library branches, and offered families a chance to explore and reflect upon questions of class and wealth through the community's local and national economic history. The quality of this program surpassed anything PYT had done in its past. Using an adapted play script and creative drama techniques, high-quality production values and a progressive educational approach, the young members of our audience were able to explore difficult questions with their families in a space of safety and support.

For example, during the first performance of this program two brothers sat up front and were deeply engaged with the actors and the action. During a question and answer section, the oldest brother revealed that his own father was unemployed and that they did not have a lot of money. His family, also in attendance, later shared how thankful they were for the opportunity to talk about their difficult circumstances in a safe environment.

In our work, we are challenged to find relevant connections between theatre, history, the communities we serve and the young people who work with us. By creating a rich path of discovery in a rehearsal process and an open forum to discuss these issues, I also learned an important life lesson: that the 'Everyone' in Yasha Frank's lesson of 'Everyone Participates' also includes me and the organizations and communities that I serve.

Nicole Gurgel

ON BOTH SHORES: TEACHING ACROSS PERSONAL/POLITICAL DISTANCE

> It is not enough to stand on the opposite river bank, shouting questions, challenging patriarchal, white, conventions. A counter stance locks one into a duel of oppressor and oppressed [...] At some point, on our way to a new consciousness, we will have to leave the opposite bank, the split between the two mortal combatants somehow healed so that we are on both shores, at once.
>
> (Anzaldúa 2007: 100–101)

Introduction

In January 2012, I and two other graduate students from the University of Texas at Austin traveled 315 miles south to facilitate the "Living Newspaper Project" in the border city of McAllen, Texas. Working with five classroom teachers, 75 fourth and fifth graders and one enthusiastic district administrator, our trio facilitated a six-week professional development/ artist-in-residency hybrid. Coupling Friday residency days with Saturday teacher trainings, each biweekly visit moved participants through the research, scripting and staging phases of the program. Throughout this process, our goal was to equip students and teachers with the tools necessary to create their own Living Newspaper performances about local social issues.

What excites me about facilitating the Living Newspaper Project is that it integrates critical, creative and civic engagement. This potent combination can inspire participants to investigate complex issues in new ways. The Living Newspaper Project's process is one that empowers students to consider art as activism and themselves as agents of social change, when it is done well.

When it is done well. There's that pesky word: *well.* A *good* residency. A *quality* project. These descriptors sneak into the language I use to discuss my work so easily, and remain undefined so frequently. What does it mean to facilitate the Living Newspaper Project—or any project—well? How do I as a Teaching Artist, working with an ever-changing community of collaborators, define a quality experience?

Through my work in McAllen, I arrived at a new understanding of quality, community-engaged arts work. This realization did not arise out of a moment where quality was undoubtedly present, but from a series of related moments where I felt it was lacking. In this essay I reflect on these moments, grounding my reflection in three questions: how do we define quality when working across personal and political distance? How do I as a Teaching Artist—and an outsider in numerous ways—maintain quality when on complicated personal and political terrain? Finally, how do we use our unique position as Teaching Artists—as those with one foot in schools and one foot outside of them—to impact the quality of student experience?

Background

The Living Newspaper Project interrogates and animates social justice issues through drama-based instruction and performance. Reviving the Depression-era Living Newspapers of the Federal Theatre, the program partners graduate student Teaching Artists with fifth through twelfth grade classrooms. It is housed in UT Austin's Department of Theatre and Dance and is affiliated with Drama for Schools, the department's professional development program in drama-based instruction. During the three years I worked with the Living Newspaper Project it expanded in scope, moving from a Teaching Artist-led program geared for high-school classrooms in Austin to a teacher-training model that accommodates fifth through twelfth grade curriculums both locally and regionally. McAllen was the pilot site for this threefold experiment: professional development training with elementary school teachers over a 300 mile distance.

As a Teaching Artist, this was my first time working across geographic distance. As a newly out queer woman, I was unprepared for the ways this distance would impact me. Far from my queer community in Austin, and in a professional environment where my queerness may or may not be well received, I engaged in the strategically undetectable dance particular to folks who pass (as straight) and find themselves in new and potentially unwelcoming territory.

It wasn't that I thought anyone would respond with overt homophobia. Outside of the experience I am about to unpack, no one from McAllen ever said or did anything that made me think it would be unsafe—physically, emotionally or otherwise—to come out. Coming out just seemed like a lot of extra emotional work for three already jam-packed weekends. So I remained quietly closeted.

In researching the lesbian, gay, bisexual, transgender, questioning, intersex and asexual (LGBTQIA) community in McAllen, my silence was echoed by the organizers of the area's first-ever Right to Prom. The event was designed to "create a safe environment" for local LGBTQIA students "'to enjoy their teenage life' by celebrating prom in an accepting space" (Chapa 2011). According to an article published only after the event, Right to Prom was promoted through primarily LGBTQIA channels "for security reasons and to prevent protests." Choosing to fly under the radar—by not publicizing an event, by coming out selectively—is not a new experience for queer folks. Depending on the context, silence can be necessary in order to protect our physical, psychological and emotional well-being. But, as I experienced in McAllen, it's a strategy that comes with baggage. This essay explores the way my queer silence, while strategic, locked me into what Gloria Anzaldúa calls a "counter stance" (2007) and ultimately compromised the quality of my work. Through reflecting on my experience in McAllen, I seek to become a more nimble Teaching Artist, one who is better able to embody Anzaldúa's call to occupy "both shores, at once."

Teaching across distance: A reflection in three parts

Scene one

It is my second residency day in McAllen. I ask each group of students to create three tableaus that tell a story based on the research they have collected. Near the end of the hour, each group presents from the cramped space we've cleared at the front of the classroom. As the final group takes the stage, the rest of us count them in with a "three, two, one, ACTION!" and they strike the first of their frozen images. *One*: three girls point toward a lone, lonely-looking boy, their faces contorted into sneers. *Two*: the lone student sits at his computer while the other three crowd around, as if inside his head or on his screen, still pointing and mocking. *Three*: the bullied student stands on a chair, head tilted to one side. He looks like he is about to hang himself.

I lead the class in applause, as I have done for the previous groups. As the applause fades, I feel panicked. Without using any words, this group of fifth graders has waded very close—if not directly into—a tragic epidemic that, in our polarized political climate, has added fuel to the culture war. It is just over a year from a string of highly publicized adolescent suicides, when children as young as 11 were taking their lives after being bullied because they were (presumed to be) gay. The outbreak inspired Dan Savage's It Gets Better video phenomenon as well as accusations from conservatives, like Tony Perkins (2010), that LGBTQ activist groups were "exploiting these tragedies [in order] to push their agenda." It is an issue that makes me unpredictable—cool and articulate one moment, angry and articulate another, and crying in front of the news the next. If I lead us into this, I don't know if I can trust myself to maintain my composure; if I don't maintain my composure, my response may also be my coming out.

This all flashes through my mind in the half-second before I guide the class through a boiler plate Describe–Analyze–Reflect. We never move beyond generic bullying language. I say something measured about how it takes courage to work on difficult issues like this, and then hurry everyone to move the desks to their original, orderly configuration before the bell rings.

Scene two

The next day, our group of teachers and Teaching Artists sit in a circle, in child-sized chairs in what once was an operating school. At our check-in activity, we create a reflection web, weaving a tangle of neon yarn while answering a series of questions. Everyone has shared one success they experienced during the past two weeks when I pose a second question: "What challenges are you facing?" The teacher whose students performed the tableaus ending in suicide says she is concerned about the group's topic. She doesn't want them to 'get any ideas,' and is worried about what their parents will think.

I look down at the string connecting me to her and think about how similar and dissimilar our responses to this moment are. Like her, the tableaus threw me initially. Once I had time to reflect on them, however, I realized how excited I was that a group of fifth graders would voluntarily address this issue, even if indirectly, even if they never uttered the words 'gay bullying.' I don't share these thoughts, however. I am still getting to know this teacher, and I am not sure that our views on this topic align. And as a queer woman five hours from home, I don't know what would happen if they don't. Would I get mad? Cry? Become too frustrated to lead this training?

While I keep my mouth shut, another teacher speaks up. Many of her students are investigating similarly serious topics. She talks about encouraging their choices. If students are already thinking about these issues, she reasons, this project creates space to work through them in the safety of their classroom, with the support of their classmates and teacher. To offset parents' concerns, she sent letters home asking them to familiarize themselves with their children's research topics. She offers to share the letter with our group. Grateful for her response, I briefly consider using it to unpack the situation further. Not wanting to alienate the first teacher, I thank them both and move on with the exercise.

Scene three

When I return for our final residency day, two weeks later, the group researching bullying is back to square one. Where their work two weeks ago had been clear, complex and moving, they now seemed confused, frustrated and stuck. I try to guide them through a storyboarding exercise, but they can't agree on a narrative. As the end of the hour nears, I leave them to work it out themselves. This is when the lone boy leaves the group for another. Feeling defeated, I gather the class for our closing exercise.

On both shores: Teaching inside/outside the system

In light of this trio of moments, how do we define quality when working across personal and political distance? For me, quality work is created when we as Teaching Artists critically, creatively and fully engage with the ideas and experiences that participants bring into the room. When issues arise that have direct and serious consequences on the minds, hearts and bodies of students, quality work is even more vital. In these moments, quality is not found in managing, containing or moving past difficult issues, but dwelling in their midst, opening them up and exploring their complexities. Or, in the words of Gloria Anzaldúa (2007: 100), "it is not enough to stand on the opposite river bank, shouting questions." To create quality, community-engaged projects, we must leave our opposite banks and stand on both shores at once.

How do we do this? How do we maintain this kind of border-crossing quality when we find ourselves on complicated personal and political terrain? In McAllen, I learned how not to do this. I chose to not come out during this project, because I thought it would help me do a better job. I thought it would improve the quality of my teaching by keeping me from that exhausting, watchful place that coming out in a new environment takes me—that place where I measure others' words and actions for signs of discomfort or support, discrimination or acceptance, and all the spaces in between. What I didn't expect is that this watchfulness is doubly present when I remain silent. It is directed both outward and inward; in addition to others, I monitor myself— my own thoughts, words and actions. In policing myself, I divided myself. I drew a clear line between my inner and outer selves, only allowing certain parts of my deepest self to cross over to the public (school) side. Because my best teaching rises up from this self, it is that much more difficult to maintain the quality of my work when she is under surveillance. And the quality of my work has direct bearing on the quality of students' experience.

Which brings us to this essay's final question: how do we use our unique position as Teaching Artists to impact the quality of student experience? As a visiting artist—someone students sometimes see only a handful of times—it's easy to think that our visitor status means we have little impact on students' overall experience. But this temporary, out-of-the-ordinary quality—the fact that we are not part of the institution—is precisely where our impact lies. As Teaching Artists we are truly on both shores of the education system; we are within it just as we are outside of it. Inhabiting this liminal space personally and professionally, we also create it in the classrooms in which we work. Just as we reconfigure desks to make room for pedagogical practice that falls outside of its physical confines, we create critical-creative spaces to explore questions, ideas and issues that don't fit into institutional curriculum or culture. After we are gone, the activities we introduce and the dialogues we facilitate may not be revisited, but they will always now be a possibility in the minds of the students.

In too many places in our country, counteracting queer bullying is still something that doesn't fit into curriculums and accepting queerness is still not a possibility in many folks' minds. Instead sexuality-specific bullying is met with silence, suppression and fear from teachers and administrators, even as nine out of every ten queer youth experiences it, even as queer youth are four times more likely to commit suicide than their straight peers, even as children as young as 11 are taking their own lives. There is a culture of silence around queerness that is pervasive, dangerous and, at times, deadly. During this project, I participated in this silence by sidestepping important conversations. While writing this essay, I've reimagined the conversations that could have been many times. Sometimes the students bring up queer bullying on their own. Sometimes I bring it up myself. Sometimes I come out; sometimes I don't. There isn't one right way to have these conversations, just as there isn't one way to work across any personal/political divide. When Anzaldúa tells us to leave our opposite banks, she doesn't give us a road map. Whether we know how to reach the other side or not, we'll never arrive without taking a first step.

Note

For more information about Drama for Schools, visit http://www.utexas.edu/finearts/tad/graduate/drama-schools.

Kati Koerner

BALANCING ARTISTIC AND LANGUAGE-LEARNING GOALS IN LINCOLN CENTER THEATER'S LEARNING ENGLISH AND DRAMA PROJECT

It was September 2011 and Lin Peng, a recent immigrant from China, missed home. He was misbehaving in class and seemed resistant to the idea of learning English at all. Even so, his English teacher described him as a good-natured and popular student who was active in his high school's Chinese culture club (Akiyama 2011). Later that semester, Lin Peng participated in Lincoln Center Theater's (LCT) Learning English and Drama Project (LEAD), a teaching artist residency that uses theatre to support English language acquisition. In LEAD, Lin Peng collaborated with his classmates on an informal in-class performance of John Steinbeck's novel *Of Mice and Men*, after which he noted, in a post-residency reflection, that "I found my confidence. This experience means a lot to me and my life."

Contained within Lin Peng's simple response is much of what is important to us in LEAD. Our understanding of quality practice is grounded in our work as theatre artists. From the outset, the building blocks of theatre became the means for English Language Learners (ELLs) to build proficiency and confidence in speaking English. We challenged ourselves to identify processes that are central to our work as theatre artists and that could be used to provide a diverse range of ELLs with immersive and supportive structures to help them learn English. Further, we sought to apply the process of inquiry that we might use to create a piece of theatre to the ongoing development of the program itself. We looked at how to create opportunities to fold the interrogation of our practice into the design of the program and then be flexible enough to shift what we're doing based on the results of that collaborative inquiry process.

What began as an intuitive understanding of the applicability of theatre to language learning crystallized into a basic program structure with the help of three veteran LCT Teaching Artists and three teachers of English as a Second Language (ESL) from existing LCT partner schools. As Director of

Education, I invited them to come together in 2004 to design a program that would use theatre to transform the English learning experience of struggling students like Lin Peng. From the outset, our understanding of quality program structure has rested in LEAD's teacher and Teaching Artist partnerships. Quality for LEAD has always been measured in its ability to balance arts and language learning, as well as to align the teaching and assessment practices that could most effectively deliver those outcomes. Now in its eighth year, the LEAD Project has grown to encompass fifteen 18-session residencies in ten project sites and reach more than 700 students a year.

My interest in starting LEAD was sparked both by the urgent needs of ELLs in New York City's public schools and my own personal history. I am the daughter and daughter-in-law of immigrants and spent a number of years living, attending school and working abroad. Many of the ELLs with whom LCT works, in grades six through twelve, have been in the United States for less than one year and are overage and under-credited for their grades. These adolescent ELLs are at a particular disadvantage as many of them will age out of the school system long before they develop academic proficiency in English. In 2011, the four-year graduation rate among ELLs in New York City public high schools was a dismal 46 percent. While motivation and engagement are key to the academic success of all secondary school students, these qualities are even more critical for ELLs for whom the barriers to academic success are particularly high. LEAD allows ELLs to develop a deep understanding of a text and lays the groundwork for the transfer of that knowledge to such formal academic structures as written essays and standardized tests. LEAD exists as a framework within which our students can move toward being more articulate, expressive and comfortable in their new language and culture.

LEAD facilitates a year-long, in-depth partnership between a classroom teacher and a Teaching Artist and allows each to bring his or her own area of expertise to bear on classroom instruction. The quality and impact of LEAD is entirely dependent upon the success of this partnership. One of LEAD's measures of quality is the extent to which that partnership succeeds at developing a common understanding of its students' language learning challenges—be they social, academic or cultural—and how theatre can help to address these challenges.

In creating LEAD, I made collaboration, which is at the heart of theatre, the central organizing principal of the program. The Teaching Artist and teacher co-develop the content of each residency. There is no uniform curriculum, which permits each residency to work with the text that best responds to the needs of its students. In the planning session that follows each teaching session, teachers and Teaching Artists engage in structured dialogue about individual student performance, the specifics of the next lesson's activities and the goals of the overarching residency. These meetings set the standards of quality for each individual residency. One criterion for the program's overall quality is the extent to which each individual residency structure is customized to fit the needs of each group of students. The planning meetings frame a common sense of inquiry that drives each residency, as well as LEAD's overall evolution.

LEAD's professional development reinforces our understanding of the criteria for quality collaboration. All classroom teacher training takes place with our entire faculty of Teaching Artists present. While some teachers have experience with team teaching, they mostly plan and teach alone. So one of the central challenges of LEAD has been to help us as artists arrive at a common understanding of collaboration together with our classroom partners. This is a skill that requires ongoing practice and is, perhaps, redefined and challenged by each partnership. Some LEAD teachers have been part of the project for years; others are involved for a single year. When the LEAD training calendar begins in October, veterans and newcomers alike role-play planning meetings and practice using the multiple-planning templates provided to them in the LEAD handbook. In order to sustain our vision of quality, we believe that the collaborative muscle needs to be exercised on an ongoing basis. For Teaching Artists, it is a reminder that each teacher and each group of students must be considered anew. For teachers, it is an opportunity to make the structure of the residency transparent and accessible.

Our common training typically offers participating teachers and Teaching Artists a scaffolded series of representative dramatic activities based on a specific text. These activities are chosen to introduce project participants to new classroom drama techniques, such as ways to use choral speaking, or how to explore character and context through the construction of simple paper props. Subsequent training at mid-year focuses on an area that teachers or Teaching Artists have identified during the fall residencies as being of particular need or interest. In June, teachers and Teaching Artists report from each project site by sharing videos of their in-class performances or by demonstrating key activities. Our understanding of quality practice challenges us to respond to the needs of our residencies as they emerge, increase everyone's arsenal of techniques and, most importantly, create a mutually supportive community of practitioners.

Learning in the LEAD Project occurs at all levels and on an ongoing basis. Quality practice is fully informed practice, and one of the central training challenges for LEAD's Teaching Artists has been to gain a working knowledge of ESL pedagogy. At times, this has forced us to redefine and justify our artistic work against a backdrop of seemingly competing ELL priorities. Oral production is pitted against written language; generic academic vocabulary against the specific vocabulary of the text being dramatized; the desire to have students respond spontaneously against the need to structure their participation. Sifting through that knowledge and applying it meaningfully to our work continues to be a challenge. The flexibility of LEAD's program structure has allowed us to adjust our instructional practice based on what we have learned and what new questions that learning has generated for us.

I have often likened the experience of working on the LEAD Project to feeling like Alice standing along a corridor in Wonderland, where opening one door only leads her to another door and so on. In the LEAD Project, as we were opening one door after another down the corridor of language acquisition, we became troubled by the notion that we had lost sight of the artistic integrity of the program. Even as we embraced the notion of the LEAD Project as applied theatre, in the service of the arts as well as language learning, we questioned our own integrity as artists in this work. While we felt good about facilitating opportunities for students to speak individually or chorally, to what extent were we structuring an authentic, quality engagement for them with the art form? To what extent did this work still excite us as artists?

By 2009, feeling limited by what seemed to us like an increasingly stale menu of classroom drama techniques, the LEAD Teaching Artist team explored ways to increase the theatricality of our work by making it more visual and character-driven. Embracing costumes, props and masks, which in LEAD are often made of newspaper and tape, and moving away from the recitative use of text toward simple dialogue or monologue structures injected new life into our work. This in turn excited our partnering teachers. Our standard of what constituted a quality theatre experience in the classroom had changed. Creating a concrete manifestation of character or plot in the form of a costume or prop infused our work with fresh theatricality. It gave students the chance to be articulate about their creation and provided them with yet another opportunity to activate their English speaking skills.

Our understanding of quality in LEAD has always been shaped by its dual focus on arts and language learning. When it came time to decide how we were going to measure student learning, we struggled with whether to place our focus on assessing our students' theatre or language skills. The solution was found, as at other moments in the program's history, within the collaborative inquiry structured into LEAD. We engaged participating principals and teachers in many discussions about what student learning outcomes they most valued in LEAD. Student speaking skills emerged as something schools wanted help with and was also authentic to theatre. We weighed our school partners' goals against our own artistic values and arrived at a framework that redefined our program.

Once we had settled on speaking skills as our key student-learning outcome, the challenge emerged to devise a project-wide structure to assess those skills among students with a broad spectrum of language proficiencies, from absolute beginners to those with near-native fluency. Further complicating the task were the many cultural factors that effected how comfortable students felt in speaking solo in public. What assessment activity could possibly be generalizable across our many residencies? Because each residency decides on its own text and sharing structure, it sometimes felt as if we were running many LEAD Projects instead of a single unified program.

Starting in 2006, we developed a student assessment protocol, involving a pre- and post-residency on-demand performance task that looked specifically at the development of student speaking skills. The assessment tool, which focused on vocal projection, articulation and communicating expressively, showed that LEAD had a positive impact on students' speaking skills across all proficiency levels and cultural backgrounds. It served as an invaluable curriculum framing and goal-setting device for all stakeholders in the LEAD Project, as well as an affirmation of quality teaching and learning. The assessment framework ensured that every student, teacher and Teaching Artist knew from day one the three areas of speaking skills we were all working on and could then apply that lens to all their subsequent work in the residency.

Although productive in many ways, our long-developed and highly polished assessment protocol soon began to show its limitations. The administration of our pre- and post-test gobbled up two days out of a nine-day residency. The on-demand speaking task often revealed itself to be more a test of students' skills at delivering a cold reading than of their true expressive abilities in English. Students would show themselves to be highly expressive actors in the final sharing and then freeze up on the assessment. The protocol was structured so that if students scored too high on the pre-test there was no way for them to show the growth of their speaking skills over the course of the LEAD residency. The text we used as the basis for our individual and dialogue speaking tasks were always either too easy or too difficult or, for repeat students, too familiar. Our assessment protocol ultimately collapsed like a house of cards.

We have returned to the founding values and the inquiry process structured into LEAD to guide us in our next steps. We've landed back in that corridor in Wonderland. We can look back and see how far we've come. As we look ahead, we know more doors remain to be opened. We've held on to our goals even as our understanding of quality practice has evolved. We are taking this year as a research year and an opportunity to once again ask ourselves foundational questions: what do we need to know about our students to inform our teaching and how can we best gather that data? What student outcomes will we use to gauge our effectiveness and how will they be measured? How will we balance critically important social outcomes for young ELLs such as engagement and self-efficacy with learning outcomes in theatre and literacy? How can we shift the focus of our inquiry to include the carefully nurtured collaborative relationship between teachers and Teaching Artists?

I am occasionally panicked about the fact that I am still asking myself these questions after all these years. At the same time, I find asking them exciting and oddly liberating. Thankfully, I am privileged to work with an extraordinary and expanding group of practitioners who are willing to ask them with me.

Chapter 5

Artistic Perspective

At the very least, participatory involvement with the many forms of art can enable us to *see* more in our experience, to *hear* more on normally unheard frequencies, to *become conscious* of what daily routines have obscured, what habit and convention have suppressed.

(Greene 1995: 123)

Artistic Perspective encompasses three 'A's' of theatre: *artwork, artistry* and *aesthetic perception*. The term synthesizes the characteristics of an artist: the technical skills of creating art; the dispositions and habits that form and inform personal artistry; and the ways in which the artist perceives the purpose, practice and impact of her work and the work of other artists. Artistic perspective embodies an artist's propensity to observe, engage with, analyze, interpret and express opinion about the world around him. Intrinsically motivated to give voice to his insight or inspiration through his art form, the artist persistently and reflexively experiments with, explores, revises and refines his art, his approach and his understanding of the possibilities of artistic expression.

This section centers on ways that the 'A's' of artistic perspective can, and arguably should, be integral elements of drama learning experiences, individually and/or collectively. Artistic perspective promotes participants to think and act as artists, who value and seek out creative pursuits that encourage risk, question pat answers and provide unique insight into their learning and personal artistry. Lee Humphries (2000: 1) notes that

Although aesthetic in nature, [the artistic process] is not confined to the arts, nor is it always present in them. Artistic process transcends subject area. Apply it to any endeavor and that endeavor will *become* an art—a vehicle for awakening insight.

In other words, when participants learn to think, act and respond as artists, they develop greater ownership of their experiences.

A Teaching Artist nurtures artistic perspective by guiding participants to reflect on how they build skills in creating *artwork*, develop personal *artistry* and/or cultivate *aesthetic perception*, the capacity for appreciation and interpretation of artwork. Making drama/theatre is, of course, an essential part of this training, yet it is not enough for participants to simply create. They should also have ample opportunities to reflect on how and what they accomplish, as well as share with and respond to others' work. By activating reflection on their art-making and/or viewing experience, the Teaching Artist cultivates participants' thorough understanding and appreciation of the art form and/or their personal artistry and offers them agency within their learning. The core question of artistic perspective, then, is: how do participants become astute, informed artists as part of any drama learning experience?

HOW DO PARTICIPANTS BUILD AN UNDERSTANDING OF CREATING THEATRE?

Guiding students to understand the elements and principles of performance and to develop the skills of a theatre artist is an undertaking that drama/ theatre teaching-artist well understand. Yet Teaching Artists can improve the process, and possibly our field in general, by codifying specific skills and criteria that will guide participants to not only create effective and engaging artwork, but to also gain understanding of and proficiency with the creating and performing processes, the latter being essential to continued growth as an artist. Many techniques already exist that define a specific artistic skill or approach. Linklater's voice work (2006), the physical training of Viewpoints (2005), Keith Johnstone's improvisation work ([2007] 1981) and Stanislavski's actor training methods ([1988] 1936) are well-established examples that permeate artist training because they are well defined by the practitioners through their previous explorations.

When working with the novice or beginning artist or in a drama-integrated learning experience that includes nonartists who need access to the most basic of expressive skills, how are such skills and their criteria defined and made accessible? Dan offers the following insight into what he titles the V.I.B.E.S.

I initially developed the V.I.B.E.S. chart to help classroom teachers integrate drama into their teaching practice. While many teachers could successfully facilitate simple drama strategies, they had no way to assess achievement. "What should I expect or look for?" they asked. V.I.B.E.S. defines a straightforward list of 'Tools of Expression': voice, imagination, body, ensemble and story. With each 'tool,' I synthesized a criteria list down to three or four points to help beginning teachers, Teaching Artists and participants take their first steps in developing or facilitating the development of the skills of a Theatre Artist. To define an accessible, tangible set of criteria for each tool, I drew from a variety of sources and synthesized them into novice-friendly vocabulary. For example, with voice, I started with elements from music such as pitch, tone, dynamic and timbre. Knowing I wanted these to be understandable to and useful for both young and inexperienced participants, I challenged myself to group and rename them into three categories. I came up with *Power*, *Pace* and *Passion*. Now once I introduce these basic criteria areas of the voice, I work with my students to define the ways we can vary the power of our voice, the pace with which we speak and the way we use passion to express the mood or emotion of a character or scene. Students help extend the vocabulary by identifying criteria they discover within each category, such as descriptors for volume (loud, quiet, silent) or pitch (piercing, mellow).

Experiment
What techniques defined your early training as an artist? First, write down specific skills you developed. Second, redefine one skill in language accessible to a 7-year-old, or a new acting student in eleventh grade.

By sharing and then expanding on a common vocabulary with participants, Teaching Artists offer their participant collaborators a way to understand what they are doing when creating, what specifically to reflect on in order to revise and improve on their work, and begin to define their own process for working.

HOW IS PERSONAL ARTISTRY REALIZED?

[A]sk someone what students learn in art classes, and you are likely to hear that they learn how to paint, or draw, or throw a pot. That's true, but it only tells us what they do, not how they learn to think [...] Does experience in the arts change students' minds so they can approach the world as an artist would? Students must be given the opportunity to think like artists.

(Hetland et al. 2007: 4)

To cultivate personal artistry, Teaching Artists can engage participants in reflecting on and building the artistic dispositions, or habits, of accomplished artists and learners as a part of each drama learning experience, either as the central or an auxiliary focus of the experience. This may contribute to participants becoming more informed and aware artists and also potentially develop them into more skilled learners, capable of transferring these habits of artistic practice to other aspects of their lives. By employing processes outlined in this book's sections on *intentionality* and *quality*, the reflective Teaching

Artist, their colleagues and participants can work together to identify specific artistic skills or behaviors that relate directly to their particular learning experience, which is essential to defining personal artistry.

Although no specific list of dispositions exist for the theatre field, the following examples do have application to drama/theatre learning experiences. Visual art-related habits identified through Harvard Project Zero's Studio Thinking resulted in a book of the same name by Hetland et al. (2007). The text contends that studio-based visual art experiences induced participants to, "Develop Craft, Engage & Persist, Envision, Express, Observe, Reflect, Stretch & Explore, as well as Understand the Art World" (6). Eric Booth (n.d.), inspired by the multiple habits of mind work, has developed his Habits of Creative Engagement, which include: generating multiple ideas and solutions, sustaining inner atmosphere of exploration, using one's own voice, trusting one's own judgments, formulating good questions and problems, improvising, finding humor, crafting, making choices based on a variety of criteria, inquiring skillfully, persisting, self-assessing, reflecting metacognitively, thinking analogically, willingly suspending disbelief, observing intentionally, going back and forth between parts and wholes, trying on multiple points of view, working with others, and tapping and following intrinsic motivation.

The arts education field has also made great efforts to connect to the Partnership for 21st Century Learning Skills (2011) movement in education, which highlights a select list of cognitive, behavioral and affective skills that are closely aligned with artistic practice: communication, collaboration, critical thinking, and creativity.

When rehearsing a play with young actors, the Teaching Artist can guide participants to reflect on the skills of performance and the choices they made when expressing a particular moment. They can also investigate the content and context of the play itself. What do participants understand about the time period, the setting, the cultural elements of the story? How does each aspect influence the way in which the characters respond or act? What are the deeper motivations and goals that shape the emotional life of the character, the physical interaction between characters and the flow and pace of a scene? Developing the actor's critical interpretative skills will influence how, when and why they apply their performance skills in a Triple-Loop Learning moment. They may also learn to apply and transfer these skills to future drama learning experiences and to life—to expand their ability to understand the perspective of others and to explore effective and efficient ways to dramatically express their understanding.

Look inward
What habits have you developed as an artist and how did you develop them?

HOW IS THE AESTHETIC OF DRAMA/THEATRE EMBEDDED?

Aesthetic perception comes from the Greek *aisthetika*, meaning 'perceiving through the senses.' For our purposes, we focus tightly on interaction with exemplary artwork, through which viewers learn to discern and make sense of how theatre works on the senses. Ideally individuals have opportunities to not only attend theatre but also to contemplate, discuss and trade opinions about their viewing experience. Whether a Teaching Artist arranges for her participants to attend a performance, attends the performance with them or simply benefits from being around when they attend, the Teaching Artist should consider questions for participants to consider as they are watching the performance. Preparing participants to engage in performance helps them to focus their viewing experience: "What do you notice about the way the actors use their bodies to give you insight into the characters' emotional state?" "How does the tempo of the actor's movement and speech help establish the mood of the scene or play?" After the performance, the Teaching Artist can revisit the questions with the participants and guide them to apply what they discovered to their own work. These experiences potentially help them develop greater insight into art and art-making, to better understand their own emotional and intellectual reactions and to better recognize and appreciate the place of theatre within their lives and society.

While the entire theatre field advocates that everyone should have regular access to quality, live theatre, this is not always possible. So how can a teaching artist introduce exemplary performance to students? Eric Booth (2009) proposes that the Teaching Artist should provide the exemplar, becoming a model for students' understanding of what constitutes engaging, effective art. As the exemplar, a Teaching Artist can both inspire students as well as present artwork that demonstrate specific skills or concepts students will explore and develop. A Teaching Artist sharing her own personal artistry can heighten participants' excitement and make the experience more personal and insightful.

Consider
What questions might you ask students before a performance to increase their enjoyment of the experience? What questions might help them closely consider the artistic and aesthetic choices in the play?

Reflection plays a key role in developing aesthetic perception. As a Teaching Artist guides students to analyze what constitutes an engaging and effective production, they will gain awareness of what defines an aesthetic. Students can then begin to fashion a personal aesthetic, learning to interpret material, take risks with their ideas and choices, and become sensitive to the effects on others of their choices.

HOW MIGHT THE THREE 'A'S' EXIST WITHIN A DRAMA LEARNING EXPERIENCE?

The Create–Perform–Respond cycle is a simple cyclical process that engages participants in the basic tenets of art-making to feed the developing artists' understanding of artistic practice, develop capacity for personal creativity, and gain appreciation for the benefits of participating in theatre and drama experiences. The cycle can be used with a creative experience of any size, from single tableau built as a part of studying historical events, to monologues shared between peers as they develop their presentation, to scenes and whole plays tested with preview audiences. Each of the three 'A's' of artistic perspective can be the focus of the cycle, as Teaching Artists guide both the participant artists and the audience to focus on, analyze and discuss the choices made by the performers or demonstrated through their presentations. In integrated experiences, the reflective focus can be shared between the content being studied and the creative form through which the participants share their learning.

When designing a learning experience, one that involves theatre making of whatever size, scope or purpose, a Teaching Artist might reflect on the following:

Create

- Who are the principal creative forces?
- What power and responsibility do participants have in the creative process?
- Does strong external direction feed creativity or stifle it?
- How much responsibility is given to a novice who has yet to develop and/or understand his own creative process?
- At what point during a generative, creative process does reflection, performance and responding play a role?

Perform

- How can 'perform' be an embedded part of the cycle of developing work, be it a single image created around a specific prompt or the creation of a fully realized piece of theatre?
- How does sharing ongoing work between and with participants throughout a process strengthen artistic skills and increase an understanding of how performance is viewed and understood?

- How do you determine when a sharing or performance will be most useful?
- What are the goals of a sharing/performance and how are they defined and shared?
- How is/are the audience/observers prepared for what the sharing/ performance will be?

Respond

- When is sharing structured as self-reflection and when does it include peer feedback?
- What is the protocol for sharing ongoing work and how can it serve both performer and observer?
- How do you balance opinion ("I think you should...") and suggestion ("If you are trying to achieve _____, maybe you might try...")?

A classroom of fifth grade students studying preservation of local wetlands faced an in-class debate on preservation versus human expansion: "Should the land remain for the wetland creatures or be made available for building homes?" Students shared their argument in the guise of tableaux, demonstrating the pros and/or cons of particular actions that they supported or refuted. Through this experience, the students had the opportunity to engage in the full cycle. They created the tableaux expressing their opinions, shared the creative work with their peers and responded by both interpreting the choices of their peers and providing feedback on the effectiveness of the creative choices in clarity, artistry and perceived audience engagement. By identifying both *what* their peers created and *how* they realized their choices, the students developed a heightened understanding not only of the subject matter but also of how the theatre can be an effective means of communicating ideas.

AND CONSIDER...

Drama learning experiences provide opportunity for developing a range of skills and habits related to and stemming from art and artistic practice, *if such skills are specifically targeted and cultivated through practice and reflection.* A thoroughly beneficial learning experience consists of developing specific, personally relevant skills; an awareness of how the skills work and how to access them; and the desire for and appreciation of what can be achieved with these skills.

When Teaching Artists speak of the purpose of their work, a single, powerful argument is the cultivation of this intrinsically engaged artistic nature. Developing the facility, skills and habits of *artistic perspective* will support *intentional, quality* practice, which can lead to artistically satisfying achievement whatever the focus of a drama learning experience may be.

TEACHING ARTISTS CONSIDER MULTIPLE ASPECTS OF ARTISTIC PERSPECTIVE

Through the case studies included here, writers from diverse settings and pursuits examine how to support the development of artistic skills and attitudes in multiple ways. Jo Beth Gonzalez probes how theatre as a metaphorical tool helped both her and her students gain tangible insight into abstract science concepts. Marsha Gildin examines the basic tenets of creating artistically and socially satisfying relationships between youth and elders in a personal story-based performance program. Andrew Garrod considers how bringing together culturally diverse youth from a war-torn area to stage a Shakespearean play offers opportunities for insightful interpretation of the playwright's intent. Carol T. (Jones) Schwartz and Kim Bowers-Rheay-Baran jointly unpack how a program focused on teaching dramaturgy to students helped them gain greater understanding of their work while deepening students' experience as artists and audience members. Finally, Karina Naumer deconstructs how art-related skills and attitudes contribute to the efficacy of a character education role-play residency and challenge her to closely examine her own artistic perspective.

Artistic Perspective Case Studies

Jo Beth Gonzalez

DEVELOPING 'DRAMATIC METAPHOR' TO TEACH CONCEPTS OF SCIENCE

My brain thinks in images. I can't help it; images pop up by themselves, unannounced. I see in story. I learn in movement. When I am engaged physically and imaginatively, I comprehend. Metaphor is my cognitive companion, and so I use metaphor comfortably and naturally in the classroom; in rehearsal; when understanding human, theoretical and factual relationships; and when interpreting emotion.

Crafted carefully to illustrate complexities in abstract processes, physicalized dramatic metaphor can instruct various types of learners in all kinds of contexts. Because metaphor activates the imagination, embedding metaphor into learning challenges students with suppressed imaginations to activate them, and stimulates others with active imaginations to learn through less conventional methods. Through funding from two different granting agencies, I created and taught expanded metaphors that introduce science concepts to fifth and ninth grade students.

When I was a public school student, science classes were not my forte, neither was I a fan of math. I did not learn well by lecture, yet most of the junior and high school math and science instruction I received was delivered that way. I earned consistently mediocre grades in math and science classes, my lackluster performance fueled by a belief that I was 'dumb in math and science.'

In 1990, while teaching at Texas A & M University, I applied for and was awarded a two-year Space Grant from NASA. Through the grant, pre-service elementary teachers and I devised astronomy lessons for fifth graders using drama as a teaching medium. For one particular lesson, we developed a metaphor to demonstrate how and why hydrogen transforms into helium.

Kids participated in a square dance set to words and using movements that simplified the process into a series of eight steps—and voila! I too understood the principle. Not only did I understand, I was enthused to study science. Unlocked by metaphor, science held intrigue. For the first time in my life, I experienced a connection between my creative spirit and science content. Metaphor was the key. For learners like me, consuming science is both meaningful and fun when served on a plate of drama.

As an art form, drama relies upon metaphor to communicate essential components about human nature. When an opportunity presented itself to co-teach science lessons through drama at the high school in which I currently teach, I wondered: "Could I continue to unleash the spirit of my imagination to process scientific theory? And if my imagination would help me understand science theory, could I shape those images craftily enough to effectively devise correct science lessons that would also be intriguing to 15-year-olds?" In the exploration that follows, I consider the integration of metaphor and science lessons in relationship to artistic perspective. I investigate how metaphoric thinking, as a component of artistic perspective, is useful as a way of teaching and what this understanding brings into focus about student learning.

According to *The American Heritage Dictionary,* metaphor is, "a figure of speech in which a term is transferred from the object it ordinarily designates to an object it may designate only by implicit comparison or analogy." Among other elements, artistic perspective includes metaphor, a construct that integrates the following elements to make connections that form knowledge and understanding:

- Imagery
- Creativity and imagination
- Insight into and recognition of the self, the world, ideas and human nature

I discovered the potential of metaphor to make powerful associations as a student in the MFA directing program at the University of Minnesota. In one course assignment, I had the task of devising a metaphor that would illuminate Lady Macbeth's objective during the monologue in which she asks the spirits to unsex her so that she might have the steel to assist her husband in the murder of the king (Shakespeare 1:5). I was making the mile-long trek on a very cold morning from my apartment to campus mulling the Elizabethan notion that women, unlike men, lack the visceral fortitude necessary to commit murder, when my imagination sparked the image of Lady Macbeth getting buff in a men's gym. For the class presentation, I delivered the monologue as Lady Macbeth: changing out of heels into tennis shoes, tossing a tampon out of her gym bag as she searched for a sweat band, lifting imaginary dumbbells. Feedback from the professor and classmates assured me that the comparison successfully reinforced and augmented Lady Macbeth's goal. That metaphor has stuck with me so strongly that I perform the monologue for my own students when I teach *Macbeth*; I even performed it for other theatre teachers at the 2009 International Thespian Festival.

What caused this image to pop into my head, and why was this metaphor so effective? First, walking is a stress reliever, so as I walk, I relax. Walking to class freed my mind to wander among possible interpretations, and I dwelled upon the meaning of the speech. Physical and emotional relaxation and time to dwell on an intellectual challenge are two ingredients necessary to shaping a metaphor intended to communicate an abstraction or complexity. Second, the Lady Macbeth metaphor works because it effectively transfers common understanding (lifting weights) to unknown knowledge (de-sexing): the image of Lady Macbeth pumping iron to increase her masculinity creates a visual impression that captures the essence of her speech, supplying information important to the speech within a context familiar to audience members who might be otherwise befuddled by Shakespeare's language and milieu.

Over the years since my graduate school days in Minneapolis, I have directed dozens of plays and relied upon metaphor to assist actors with character studies, to form stage pictures, and to conceptualize designs. If I can help my theatre students understand the abstractions and complexities of challenging plays by tapping metaphor, why couldn't I apply this same metaphorical thinking as a teacher to the study of science?

To understand for themselves, and to communicate to others, artists and scientists both form connections between the known and the unknown. A scientist at NASA once told me that a graduate student had been nervously explaining a complex math equation to an audience that included Albert Einstein. At one point, Einstein raised his hand and asked the student to slow down, because he couldn't keep up with the pace of the delivery. Einstein's ability wasn't to process rigid information quickly, but to make creative connections between ideas.

Maxine Greene is convinced that quality art can move one to "summon energies as never before to create meanings, to effect connections, to bring some vital order into existence—if only for a time" (1995: 98). Imagination, opines Greene, makes metaphor possible. When channeled to teach new material, teachers make practical use of imagination and metaphor. Without engaging in the domain of imagination and metaphor, Greene asks, "How else are [students] to make meaning out of the discrepant things they learn? How else are they to see themselves [...] working [...] in an often indecipherable world?" (1995: 99).

A 2010–2012 grant from the Ohio-based Martha Holden Jennings Foundation allowed me to co-develop and teach five ninth-grade science lessons in our school's auditorium. During each lesson, I introduced the concepts using dramatic metaphors, my physics colleague taught the concepts, and our technical theatre director demonstrated hands-on application of the concepts accessing theatrical equipment. All five lessons challenged me to understand the physics theory embedded in the science concepts before outlining dramatic metaphors that would connect the familiar knowledge to the new. This process required hours of self-study, and fortunately I had the relaxed pace of summer in which to (re)learn basic physical science concepts of color, optics and forms of energy. I conferred often with my science colleague and was surprised to discover that I had been holding many incorrect preconceptions about science.

Once I understood the science concepts correctly, I studied pages of physics notes and my imagination oriented to transferring theory into concrete metaphor. It is important to note that my imagination conceived of metaphors *as* I was learning, not devised and applied *after* I understood. Greene asserts that metaphor belongs less to inspiration than to memory (1995: 99). Knowledge recall, supported by metaphor, reinforces the value of imagination as a prime tool for learning. Given the powerful ability of metaphor to stimulate recall, we did not want the metaphors to teach 'wrong' science. Therefore, when we integrated the metaphors into the lessons' activities, my science colleague evaluated them for correctness and suggested refinements. We were ready to teach the lessons.

Gripped to a clipboard, stared at by 15 pair of eyes, tongue-tied, how do I attach four light fixtures to a twofer? A twofer allows for two fixtures, not four … Then I recalled my science colleague's reminder that a twofer makes more pathways for electrical circuits—just like opening up the gates in the rock concert metaphor we created. Yes! To attach four light fixtures to a twofer, we need to connect two twofers to a twofer. Meaning we need three twofers. Right. I paused, waiting for the knowledge I knew I'd gained to emerge from the temporary fog formed by the pressure of teaching. I recalled the story about a rock concert that we had presented at the lesson's start; images from the story reappeared, and I latched onto its metaphorical meaning like a buoy. Confidence restored, I demonstrated how to connect the twofers together for safe circuitry, incorporating key points of the metaphor to reinforce cognition.

The rock concert metaphor was my life vest in the sea of science concepts. How did I get to this metaphor? Science teachers use the words 'pressure', 'flow', 'resistance', 'friction', 'power', 'potential energy' and 'overload' to explain relationships among the electrical terms ohms, watts, volts, amps, electrons;

these words also describe human interaction. These are words I don't use when directing a play or teaching improvisation, but I was preparing to teach ninth graders about electricity. As I sat at my own desk studying the physics of lighting to prepare to teach, the image of pathways and gates emerged and memories of my youth flooded in: as a teenager I attended rock concerts throughout the summer with friends at Blossom Music Center in Akron, Ohio. I remembered waiting in lines, anxious to get through the gates. I remembered feeling herded, mincing my way with hundreds of others toward general admission lawn seating. As I reread the science explanations, I shaped the metaphor into a story. My colleague later refined lines to clarify specific phrases in the story to more clearly communicate scientific theory.

Though we use electricity constantly in our daily lives, the process of electrical circuitry is both invisible and rapid nearly beyond comprehension. The rock concert metaphor creates *entry* into knowledge acquisition of abstract science concepts by making the process of electrical currency human-sized and tangible, reducing its speed to a rate that can be digested in steps. The story that follows was staged by senior physics students for the ninth graders. It integrates seven science concepts related to electrical currency that capture, through metaphor, the science behind the fact that electrical circuits trip when current is allowed to move too quickly.

A huge hubbub (1. Potential = The *difference* in the charges between the two bodies—positive and negative charges—or 'buzz' about the show; anticipation) was afloat throughout the entire country. The greatest rock 'n' roll band ever was getting together for one final tour before they would break up (2. Source = What produces the voltage, or the show itself) forever. Tickets were sold out within hours and scalpers made out like bandits. In Ohio, the concert was held in an outdoor amphitheater and the highways were packed full of fan-laden cars. Hours before the concert was to start, those with lawn tickets began lining up in order to snag a place with an excellent view of the stage. As the late afternoon wore on and more and more fans (3. Amps = Measures *current*, or fans who want to enter the amphitheater) arrived, the excitement grew. The amphitheater could accommodate 50,000 fans. But this tour was extraordinary, and 20,000 more energized fans arrived, hoping to buy tickets from scalpers who were tripling the cost. The gates (4. Ohms = *Electrical resistance*, or gates) opened at 6pm, and the security guards (5. Circuit Breaker = Device that detects amps, or security guard) stepped up to the entrance in order to resist the flow of fans, eager (6. Volts = Voltage, or amount of *desire* the fans have to see the show) to enter swiftly so as to stand close to the stage. The gates of the main entrance were wide enough to allow 100 fans to enter every minute. The security guards had a hard time maintaining order because the fans' flow was so great (7. Watts = The *power* equal to one, or how much energy fans use per second to travel toward their seats). They were worried that the fans would trample each other trying to get in. To avoid this potential danger, this *overload*, the security guards opened the two side gates. This allowed the fans to enter at an even faster rate. Even more fans were scrambling to find good seats on the lawn. It was decided that the increased flow was too dangerous, so the security guards decided to shut down all of the gates. No one was allowed to enter until the fans began waiting patiently for their turns to enter the gates. They knew if they didn't, the security guards wouldn't admit them at all. Soon, the energized fans formed ordered lines, the guards opened only the main entrance gate, and back into the amphitheater flowed the fans, 100 per minute. A reviewer who was on the scene said this concert would go down in history as the greatest reunion concert ever because our excitement was *astronomical*. The entrance of all us fans alone was a *powerhouse*. And once the concert started—you could feel the energy! It was electrifying!

I am a theatre and English teacher; I do not profess to know how to teach science. However, I recognize that creating metaphors that illuminate science concepts helps me understand the complexities of scientific theory, and remember them. If it works for me, I am certain that the process can likewise be effective for students whose creative spirits pulse more firmly than the spirits that drive their left brains. These days I step into our auditorium eager to discover the science just waiting to be explored. Last year we had the chance to fly actors for the first time on our stage. As the students practiced pulling the ropes laterally, one of the flying actors glided back … and forth … and back again. I turned to our flight director and remarked, "There's science in action up there." He replied, "Yep. Pendulum motion."

Marsha Gildin

THE ART OF RELATIONSHIP: INTERGENERATIONAL THEATRE

> Life is not what one lived, but what one remembers and how one remembers it in order to recount it.
>
> (Marquez 2003)

> It is the function of art to renew our perception. What we are familiar with, we cease to see.
>
> (Anais Nin, writer, diarist)

I watch an elder place his hand on the shoulder of the student next to him for balance as they approach the microphone to speak. Another elder gets cued by her young partner, moving into place for their scene. A quartet of intergenerational players delivers a raucous dialogue on the power of imagination. When an audience member gasps at the gestures and others wipe tears away, I realize that our theatre aesthetic is serving not only to frame the meaning of the stories we have shared, but also the authenticity of the process we are in. Our performance becomes a metaphor for relationship building, connecting generations and the caring cultivated throughout the year. This insight influences my staging and direction choices. I know the magic is in the art-making. Yet, I never know what our piece will truly communicate or how it will be received. In a final student self-assessment session, young Michael says, "We did a fantastic show. But the most important part for me is the bonding we make with the seniors. That will last us a lifetime."

I work as a Teaching Artist in Flushing, Queens, one of New York City's most culturally diverse neighborhoods. The "History Alive" program is a partnership between Elders Share the Arts (ESTA), the local senior center and a class of fifth graders from the nearby public school. ESTA is a Brooklyn-based community arts organization dedicated to transforming memory into art by engaging generations, cultures and communities in collective creative expression.

My cultivated teaching artist practice is seated in the art of relationship building. Listening and celebration, empathy, respect and inspiration are all key factors. I am drawn to consider ways to bring people together that optimize receptivity and creativity. Within this context I ask myself: "How can I encourage an authentic open exchange between my multigenerational, multicultural students to build relationships both on and off stage that serve their art-making and their lives?" Our art-making is based on moments of meaning that come from our experiences and lives within the spectrum of the human heart. I feel called in my work to tend to an environment that balances the willingness to share with the vulnerability that accompanies opening the heart to remember. In this process I have seen children inspire fearlessness while elders inspire trust. This is a kindly chemistry for artistic exploration and interpretation generated through listening.

We are living history. As listeners, we bear witness to one another's experiences and simultaneously to our own. Perhaps we get to see ourselves anew in the retelling. I watch elders and children build interest and curiosity in one another through a lens of caring and affection. I have seen this affection evolve into respect, and respect into admiration, or, as my centenarian grandmother liked to say, "a mutual fan club." I have viewed the development of oral history interviewing-skills as gathering information from the *outside in*. Yet, witnessing my students' transformations, I recognize what matters to me most in the conversation. It is that we develop connections that stimulate our understanding from the *inside out* – to propel our learning, to feed our confidence and to magnify our generosity. My hope as a Teaching Artist is that from the understanding that arises through dramatic, embodied learning and the joy of ensemble building, my students' lives are touched by one another in an artistic process that sends them on life's journey informed by compassion and enhanced in their humanity.

I have developed my approach to intergenerational theatre work through ESTA's living history arts methodology, a unique blend of oral history, storytelling, reminiscence, reflection and art-making. This methodology compliments my teaching sensibilities and the value I place on the power of engaging personal story through the arts to transform individuals and communities. I enter an ESTA program with the intent to create a reciprocal exchange and inclusive performance experience for youth and elders that informs and inspires their learning artistically while generating community within and beyond the program walls. Within a fluid oral history and creative drama context, I hope to guide my students to reflect on the paths they've walked, recollect and recount memories, share feelings and impressions, dramatically interpret one another's stories and culminate with an originally devised theatre piece in response to their discoveries and experiences together.

> Why is being heard so healing? I don't know the full answer to that, but I do know it has something to do with the fact that listening creates relationships [...] There is no power greater than a community discovering what it cares about.
>
> (Wheatley 2009: 166)

I have discovered that for it to be worth it to open up, we must first feel an interest in one another. I wish to cultivate story sharing for my students from a natural place. Where can we begin? What can we all speak of? Perhaps the story of one's name; places these feet have walked; what my eyes love to see ... My students have shown me their love of sharing family photographs as a way of introducing themselves to one another. The stories behind the photographs have led us to lively preliminary tableau work, exploring the body as compass for feeling and the group in creative play. They have inspired me to design circle games that get us moving, playing, observing, strategizing and laughing together. In the process my students identify their own inner and outer qualities and I watch these elements draw group members to one another as commonalities and differences are revealed.

Early on, the children let me in on what they notice. Who of the elders is missing this week, who has returned, who is new? Their powers of observation surprise me and offer me indications of connections being made. I see the elders register recognition and feel valued for their presence. I feel encouraged and awakened to their awareness of one another. Something shared has left an impression. They are entering into one another's memory.

> The stories people tell have a way of taking care of them [...] Sometimes a person needs a story more than food to stay alive. That is why we put these stories in each other's memories.
>
> (Lopez 1990: 48)

Bill, a member of the intergenerational theatre group and a Holocaust survivor, shared a memory, as a boy of 17, of his first night of escape from four years in a slave labor camp. "Run for your lives," the Hungarian guards had told them. "The Nazis are retreating, but they will still chase you down." Bill ran and ran for 50 miles until he came to a wide open field seven kilometers from his village. Exhausted, he hid atop a tall haystack and rested. A full moon rose over the night sky and he felt a breeze caress his face. Was this 'freedom'? A unison call fills the air as the players on stage hold hands high, chanting, "Hope. Hope. And never give up hope!" This motto—lived and lauded by Bill—culminates the show as 45 children and elders take their bows showered in a sea of applause.

In the evolution of an artistic process rooted in listening, I contemplate what enables my students to connect most compassionately to the meaning in another's story. I am struck by the power of empathy to evoke understanding. In 2008 when Obama first ran for president we found ourselves exploring the themes of change/turning points/the unexpected. Bill's story of freedom emerged out of this, as did stories of love, work, social change and childhood. When an extremely shy student, a new immigrant, wrote in her ESTA journal about The Waiting Place, of how she stood nightly by the window in the darkness of the early morning hour watching for her father's return home from his new job as a dishwasher, I saw how her personal understanding of change enabled her to understand it more deeply in others. She wrote in her journal about Bill:

> When I read the book *When Hitler Stole Pink Rabbit* I thought it was false. How could that be true? I just could not imagine it. But then I was surprised to learn from Bill that it *was* true. It happened in his own life. When he first told us his story I felt like I was in his shoes in that terrifying scene. Thank you for sharing your memories, Bill. I learned so much.

I was touched by the tenderness of her words. I wondered whether she would speak publicly. I approached her and offered her the opportunity to express her own story in performance, and to the great surprise of the classroom teacher and myself, she said yes. We worked to strengthen her articulation and courage and she rose to the occasion for herself and her family in the audience, inspired by Bill.

> The arts are a gentle and true guide. For both the children and ourselves, it is a good reminder of our inner riches.
>
> (Irving, 92-year-old participant)

Few of my students think of themselves as 'artists' in their daily living yet through our weekly ventures into building a drama aesthetic and ensemble, they bring stories alive and witness their own unexpected capacities to listen from the heart and co-create artistically. I watch them come to know one another and depend on one another in their creative explorations. It is important to me to illuminate the strengths they have to offer one another in building performance. I wish to support the development of their creative choice-making and group problem-solving while honoring the relationships and leadership that have evolved between them. I highlight their compassion and connectivity. I made a discovery one day after extending the components of a traditional mirroring exercise to include their reflections on the experience. Their expressed understanding became a living metaphor for ensemble work. They provided the definition and the guidelines. "We became like one … It was calming … We were a team … We were fun and creative … My partner and I were concentrated with one another!" In taking this embodied camaraderie with them on stage, the performance itself revealed their connection. The power of this surprised me, along with the audience.

Elder Carl joined the group at a time when his memory was 'shaky.' He loved his involvement with both the kids and his fellow senior center community members. After confusing the scheduled day, I began to call him with weekly reminders. He started using our wake-up call to give me 'director notes' on creative choices he noticed the children making. Carl's observations grew in detail. In shaping the show, I offered Carl a main role as the jokester. I thought he could handle it. I assured him that, of course, he could and should use his script. His student sidekick had learned her part (as well as everyone else's) by heart. She so impressed Carl that he decided he was going to memorize his lines, too. Carl was inspired, enlivened and engaged, not to mention hysterical in the comedic timing of their repartee. They brought the house down. He discovered motivation and joyful determination within himself that defied forgetfulness. I watched how he dispelled the limitations put on him by others, myself included, no matter how subtle they may have been. Carl's response gave me pause to see my own assumptions and consider ways I compromise the flow of creative capacity within my students by letting my ideas get in the way.

Admittedly, as a Teaching Artist, groupings, clusters, and partnerships and how they serve the art of relationship building have intrigued me. I have seen intergenerational interactions form gracefully through serendipity, spontaneously assigned in process or planned in collaboration with the classroom teacher. Whether an elder and youth are inexplicably drawn to one another, like Michael and Kevin immediately adopting Irving and Doris as their grandparents while watching out for their safety on stage, or are randomly placed, like Rose and Jasroop, who became inspirational partners in a state of reciprocated support and enthusiasm, they have shown me that a depth of connection takes hold through the attention they give to one another. I watch them enter into one another's stories. They learn to listen incrementally, wholeheartedly, with curiosity and without judgment. That is the gift and the glue.

I now find myself contemplating the art of facilitation as the art of *getting out of the way*. While I recognize the value I place on relationship building, I also question how involved I need to be. I wonder what connections inherently form and grow between the elders and children as they step into the artistry of co-creation and communication together. Can I be less obtrusive? I challenge myself to consider how I can make my presence as facilitator less known while still guiding the process. I also consider my own capacity to trust, both artistically and relationally.

I recognize that the children and elders will experience the artistry of discovery both in and out of the rehearsal room. Inevitably they share with me stories of meeting one another on the street, in the bus, the supermarket, and introducing schoolmates and family to their 'friend' from the senior center; some even delight in the discovery that they are neighbors living in the same building. I look to evolve in the role of facilitator, as space holder, touchstone, reflection and container. I work to explore and be in service to the art of convening a generative space of exchange where we discover the best in one another. After all, I remind myself, everyone brings his or her life experience to the conversation, be it ten or 80 years on the planet. I meet the invitation to experiment, step back and trust. I welcome the artistry of the process to renew my perception of what an intentional relationship can be.

Andrew Garrod

BRIDGING THE DIVIDE WITH SHAKESPEARE: THEATRE AS MORAL EDUCATION IN BOSNIA AND HERZEGOVINA

What is the merit for me of directing a Shakespearean production with students, particularly in a bilingual, Bosnian context? Are there particular plays that are more conducive than others to fostering students' understanding of themselves and their culturally divided world? Is a single production (or series of productions), directed by an international organization, capable of enacting social change that outlives the life of the production?

The evening sun slowly sinks behind Hum Hill, the mountain that looms over the southwestern part of Mostar in Bosnia and Herzegovina. The crumbling outline of the city's old university library courtyard—bombed into ruins during wars in the Balkans in the early 1990s—is a darkening blue. Suddenly, a hurricane unleashes itself with thunder and lashings of rain—a tossing boat full of desperate mariners, lurching now left, now right, is visible among the bolts of lightning. Cries of *"Razbismo se! O Razbismo se!"* ("We split! We split!") rend the air in the gathering tumult. Then, silence. Absolute. A pinkish dawn light floods the stage area and a frantic young girl races toward the audience—her face aghast at the horrors she believes she has witnessed. An older man, cloaked, stave in hand, comforts the now kneeling girl and caresses her with his right hand:

Umiri se!	Be collected:
I ne boj mi se, nego milosnom	No more amazement: tell your
Svom srcu reci da baš nitko nije	piteous heart
Postradao.	There's no harm done.

The Tempest—with 21-year-old Bosniak (Muslim) law student Harun Hasanagic as Prospero and 14-year-old Petra Knezović (the child of a mixed Serbian-Orthodox/Croat-Catholic marriage) as Miranda—was the fourth multiethnic, bilingual Shakespearean production I have directed in Mostar.

I found that I could achieve my goal of helping the reconciliation process in the troubled and divided city of Mostar by building friendships across ethnic lines and fostering community cohesion through these plays.

There is now a tenuous calm in Mostar, but peace is by no means assured in this country, and ethnic enmities in no way erased. The ongoing trials of General Ratko Mladic and the political leader of the Bosnian Serbs, Radovan Karadžić, at The Hague keep the horrors of the war fresh in Bosnian minds. Overwhelmingly, Croats (Catholics) live on the west side of the city and Bosniaks (Muslims) on the east, the Neretva River serving as an approximate dividing line. There is little commingling between these groups, and some Croat teenagers will tell you that they have never crossed the reconstructed Stari Most bridge to the east side of the city for fear of encountering violence. The Mostar Gymnasium—considered by many in Bosnia and Herzegovina to be the most progressive school—has different curricula for Bosniak and Croat students. Incredibly, the two student bodies never socialize and are never taught together. As one student explained to me, "How can you be taught in the same classroom if you are sitting beside a boy whose uncle murdered your father?"

The merits of Shakespeare and *The Tempest* in a Bosnian context

"Why Shakespeare?" a skeptic might ask, particularly since Shakespeare is seldom studied in the country's schools. "Why not a Bosnian-written play?" The answer is simple—Shakespeare is what I know best, deeply love and, most importantly, what I believe has the most potential to effect moral change in young actors. For me, part of the allure of *The Tempest* was the relevance of its themes to the Bosnian context, along with the beauty and challenge of its language, the diversity of character, tone and mood, and the opportunity to employ a large cast on stage and numerous helpers backstage. I knew developing an interpretation of the characters' motivation with the actors would not only be intellectually stimulating but that it would also require countless conversations and interactions with the students.

There is much a country wracked by ethnic and religious strife can connect with in *The Tempest*. Through Prospero the play explores themes ranging from the relative influence of nature and nurture on human development to—most significantly for our context—the conflicting impulses surrounding vengeance and forgiveness. For our student actors, Prospero's stance that "the rarer action is in virtue than in vengeance"—that it is, in fact, nobler to forgive than to seek vengeance—offered a salutary message (Shakespeare 5.1.27–28). In a memorable group discussion, our young student actors also pondered the rights that the natives of Prospero's island, Ariel and Caliban, had in relation to their foreign master.

The experience of Ilija Pujic, a 19-year-old Croat actor who played Ferdinand, comes to mind in addressing the value of performing Shakespeare in a Bosnian context. When asked how his character could justify falling in love with the daughter of his father's enemy, Ilija explained that the play's themes of forgiveness versus vengeance confirmed his own social interactions in Bosnia–Herzegovina:

> Children from a young age are taught to be what [their parents believe] they represent nationally and to hate others who are different. But I think the new generation can start over a new world and I want to forget the past … if I have a good friend on the other side, I should feel free to pursue that friendship.
>
> (Personal communication, September 16, 2012)

By generalizing Ferdinand's dilemma to his own social circumstances, Ilija related a lesson he translated from the play to his own life—that children should not be trapped by the errors and enmities of their parents, or allow the past to dictate present and future relationships. Rather, Ilija espoused the theme of reconciliation that is central to the play.

My approach to directing the play

My intention was never to parachute into Bosnia–Herzegovina with an international team (mostly American, Canadian and British) to put on an isolated production that could not sustain reconciliation beyond the limits of its own duration. To that end, I made a conscious choice to also recruit heavily from the local population (educators, artists, etc.) as producers, choreographers, composers and costume designers. I hoped this would increase the likelihood of sustainability for future local productions, not only with younger Mostarians who recognize the social value of theatre in their community but also among older people equipped with the technical skills to help mount a production.

The auditions were carried out in two languages—English and some variant of Serbo-Croat. Language is one of the many politicized elements of life in the country, and now the government recognizes three distinct 'languages'—Croatian, Bosnian and Serbian. We made a conscious decision to enroll about 40 actors in the cast and worked to 'reach' as many students as we could from all sides of the community and from the outlying area. The international directing team led and participated in the daily exercises, games and improvisations with the cast, and each director helped analyze the text and block the scenes. I saw the youth of the four junior team members—all in the age range of 21–23—as a critical part of building bridges between the team and the local students, who were between the ages of 14 and 24, and as a model for promoting friendships across ethnicities. These 'bonding' experiences were further enhanced by two full-day trips to the Croatian coast for swimming and by multiple pizza parties. However, the greatest sense of camaraderie was developed during an extensive performance tour to sites within Bosnia–Herzegovina, Croatia and Montenegro, during which the student cast members were required to spend many hours in buses together and to share hotel rooms. We were always conscious of the social relationships we aimed to enhance.

None of the directing team was confident in any of the local languages, so it was imperative for the actors to speak a common language in rehearsals so that we could discuss character, relationship, motivation and plot lines (most of the cast spoke good English and understood instruction in English). Once the themes had been reviewed, the local version of the play— in this case a Croatian text—was handed out and those passages that were to be spoken in Shakespeare's language were highlighted. Overall, perhaps 85 percent of the text was in a variant of Serbo-Croat and 15 percent in Shakespeare's iambic pentameter.

Can theatre work as a form of moral education?

One of the challenges I faced while directing *The Tempest* was how to encourage the students to develop their own interpretations of the play's moral 'message.' None of our actors had previous professional drama experience and few had studied literature critically in school so it was hard to know if it was realistic to expect the student actors to participate in the creation of the play's meanings or if my directing team would need to impose our own understanding of the play on them.

In our cast discussions, we subscribed to Carr's (2005: 148) dictum that "much great art and literature is concerned less (if at all) to pass direct moral judgment, or to identify clear-cut moral imperatives, and more to call our established normative and evaluative assumptions into question." Calling this into question in itself offered extraordinary opportunities for the actors to develop personal insight and moral growth. Reimer, Paolitto and Hersh (1983) show, from a cognitive developmental point of view, how students challenging each other's justifications and moral reasoning can lead to important growth.

"In the taking of another's perspective one becomes aware of the inadequacy of one's own reasoning. Confronting a more adequate stage of reasoning begins the search for a new balance of thought" (219). It seems self-evident that an art form whose essence is role-taking—the assuming of a character with a past, a set of relationships and a range of feelings that may be quite unlike that of the actor herself/himself—will encourage deeper self-understanding and expand the moral imagination. Scholars such as Jonathan Levy have explored the relationship between theatre and moral education and theatre's capacity to educate feelings from different perspectives. The best way for human beings to gain self-knowledge about our feelings, Levy (1997: 72) argues, is

> through the exhibition of those feelings, in all their depth, variety and nuance in the theater, the theater being the best 'species of moral writing' for instruction in feeling because of the combination of the natural desire we have to look into the thoughts and observe the behaviors of others and 'the sympathetic propensity'—that is, the propensity to feel with others— that all human beings share.

Therefore, Levy concludes, "the theater better than other means, perhaps including actual experience, can educate us in feelings" (1997: 72).

The Tempest lends itself particularly well to this form of moral education, as it is susceptible to multiple interpretations and close interrogation. My directing team thus took the opportunity to engage our cast in finding answers to numerous questions:

- Is Prospero a kind old man who has been brutally wronged or a colonial oppressor?
- Is Prospero's magic malign or benevolent?
- Is Caliban an ungrateful and resentful would-be rapist and monster or a brave rebel, or some mixture of these?
- Is Ariel inwardly contemptuous of Prospero but outwardly compliant because he has learned that compliance is more likely to help him eventually earn his freedom?
- Is Antonio a more reprehensible villain than Caliban? If he represents only the brute forces of nature, why does Shakespeare give Caliban so much of the play's finest poetry?
- Is Prospero's forgiveness of the 'three men of sin' a failure because two of them—Antonio and Sebastian—do not accept it?
- Does the end of the play represent a modified triumph for Prospero, who can claim the faint strength that he now possesses as his own, or does the end suggest an old and broken man limping off to isolation and death?

In a letter Ilija wrote to me following the production, he talked about the personal transformation he had undergone through playing a Shakespearean lead, going so far as to claim that he was leaving our production with a deepened belief that he could now more fully "play the role of Ilija in real life." He claimed that the experience of embodying Ferdinand had brought him to a fuller understanding of himself and inspired him to go about his daily interactions with a heightened sense of personal responsibility. This sense has since led him, a year after our last production, to plan a theatre production for young homeless children (many of them Roma) in Mostar, with fellow members (both Bosniak and Croat) of the cast of *The Tempest*. I was pleased to also learn that, despite his love for acting and being on stage, Ilija and other former members of the *The Tempest* have gained a greater appreciation for the altruistic and compassionate aspects of our production project than a personal love for performance.

Conclusion

After two performances in the ruins of the old library in Mostar—just yards away from the former battle lines—the production toured to Stolac, a highly segregated community south of Mostar, to Niksic in Montenegro, and then to the capital city, Sarajevo, and finally to Srebrenica. By far the most controversial of these play sites, in both the eyes of the actors and of the actors' parents, was Srebrenica, the scene of the massacre of 8500 Bosniak men and boys by the Bosnian Serbs in July 1995. Some of our cast had been protected from all knowledge of the massacre by their parents and questioned our reasons for selecting this site. My firm intention in all the cities we toured was to showcase the talents of Mostar's youth, thus encouraging children and teenagers in other communities to aspire to greater heights, while at the same time enlightening my actors about the history of their country. Although our audience in Srebrenica was small, the trip to this community was justified in my mind by the profound reaction many of the students experienced to our visit to the memorial cemetery. Thousands upon thousands of graves lined the hills and the valley and the horrors carried out in the adjacent battery factory could be viewed on film—all of which was described dispassionately by our guide, whose twin brother and father had been murdered in the genocide.

As *The Tempest* approached its end, I wondered if the deep-rooted divides that led to such horrific violence could ever be truly bridged. It is the young generation—the Mirandas and Ferdinands—that gives me hope that ethnic tensions and segregation will one day be a thing of the past in Bosnia and Herzegovina.

Carol T. (Jones) Schwartz and Kim Bowers-Rheay-Baran

DRAMATURGY BY STUDENTS

"Dramaturgy by Students," a program of the Alliance Theatre, partners Teaching Artists with second grade through to twelfth-grade classroom teachers and students, the latter who serve as 'Jr. Dramaturgs' for an Alliance Theatre production. Students experience firsthand the work of a dramaturg, with a focus on:

- Text analysis and research
- Director/dramaturg/playwright relationships
- Audience education

Through this, the Jr. dramaturgs create 'real world products' for the theatre, including Audience Guides, director's research notebooks and notes for the actors, and Dramaturgy Boards displayed as lobby 'program notes' for the audience.

FIFTH GRADE JR. DRAMATURG:	I didn't know so much research goes into doing a play.
CAROL JONES, PREVIOUS DIRECTOR, INSTITUTE FOR EDUCATORS AND TEACHING ARTISTS:	I initially wondered—how might we better connect students with our artistic work at the Alliance Theatre? How could a program challenge students to think critically and creatively, enrich their collaborative and communicative skills, and contribute to their development as empathetic and emotionally aware people?
THIRD GRADE JR. DRAMATURG:	This was exciting because we were able to be a part of the play. When we saw the play, we knew details no one else knew and saw some of our ideas in the production!
KIM BOWERS-RHEAY-BARAN,	I didn't even know what a dramaturg was when I first observed this unique integration of classroom

ALLIANCE THEATRE
TEACHING ARTIST:

curriculum with artistic work. But as a resident Teaching Artist and a professional actor myself, the program was a perfect fit for me.

CAROL:

At an early 1990s' Southeastern Theatre Institute for Arts Education, the presenters demonstrated how to attend to the seven strands of National Standards for the Arts in Theatre through a Discipline-Based Arts Education approach: directing, acting, playwriting, designing, audience, criticism and research. The seminar prompted me to reflect on one artistic area that I had not previously considered— dramaturgy. How might a dramaturgy-based program purposefully build students' *artistic perspective*, increasing investment in and understanding of the process of staging a play?

I met with the Alliance Theatre dramaturg to better understand her artistic process. She described vetting scripts, working with the director in rehearsals with script structure, writing playbill articles, giving preshow audience talks and nurturing new playwrights. She produced an enormous notebook of script research. I noticed that dramaturgy research and writing paralleled work students do in class. If presented in a relatable manner, students might find dramaturgy engaging. The dramaturg and I explored how to present a dramaturgical challenge in a manner that would encourage students to drive the research.

THIRD GRADE
DRAMATURG:

Being a dramaturg felt more like getting to know a friend and introducing him to other people than doing research on a subject and presenting a report.

KIM:

I love inspiring children to engage in and appreciate art and artistry. It is enlightening when they find crucial connections between their research focus and the play that opens a discussion of how the art of creating theatre is a complex process of scaffolding one art form on another—acting, directing, designing, composing, choreographing. I often want to follow my students down the proverbial 'rabbit hole' when they find something of great interest during their research, even if not directly related.

However, at those moments I have to say, "That's great, but what does this have to do with the play and the dramaturgical research you are doing?" I have to balance student-centered inquiry with the need to produce a functional, professional product.

For example, when a group of fifth grade Jr. dramaturgs created an Audience Guide for *Honk!*, one fledgling playwright in the class was determined to include a short play in the guide. But the guide could only be eight pages long. We needed to find a compromise. With guidance she concluded that she could inspire the audience to write their own play based on the play's themes. She self-selected a short part of her play as an example. She learned how to fit her artistry into the intent of the Guide.

Throughout the Dramaturgy by Students program's 12-year development, we have learned to help students sift between research and opinion to find the best of both. Some of the most powerful work I've witnessed with the students is the emotional impact of considering major themes. After reading *Honk!*, the students embarked on a lengthy discussion about the violence of a gunshot that was to be used in the play production. The group disagreed with each other about the use of a gun shot so passionately that it became an outright argument. My partner teacher and I had to rein in emotions to determine the core issue. In the end they concluded: "Keep one gunshot in the play. It might be violent, but it's important to the plot. It tells the audience that the character of the Cat is REALLY bad." The Jr. dramaturgs defined the moral lesson the gunshot implied and suggested the dropping of a single feather falling from the fly space and change the lighting to soft red to symbolize a character's death. When the students saw the play and how their suggestion directly impacted the final production, they felt their artistic voice was validated.

CAROL: In the beginning, the Alliance dramaturg and I crafted a basic plan for student dramaturgical research using *Anansi*. I felt fortunate to have a subject that might intrigue fifth graders—the origins and meanings of African trickster tales, which was part of the language arts curriculum. We designed two classroom workshops based on 16 research questions about *Anansi* tales, posed by the play's director.

We presented the workshops to 22 gifted and talented fifth graders at a local Title One school that attends Alliance Theatre productions. They first giggled at the word 'dramaturg' and stared with awe at the thick research notebook. We read an excerpt from the script, explained the director's request for help to research information about *Anansi* tales and presented the questions. We told the students that the director believed she would receive useful answers from students who are familiar with trickster stories and who also attend plays at the Alliance Theatre. Before the teacher could finish assigning 'dramaturgy groups,' two students jumped out of their seats and ran to the computers. At that moment I knew we were going in the right direction. The enthusiastic students accepted the role as 'experts' and seemed determined to prove that they could find answers needed by the director.

The class produced a detailed and well-organized Research Notebook for *Anansi,* which included information that surprised the theatre dramaturg. The students discovered one of the tale's origins that even she had not located. The teacher reported increased student interest in attending the play.

Through the Dramaturgy by Students experience, students devise work plans using resources including the Web, printed materials, primary materials from former productions of the scripts and interviews with playwrights and artistic staff. The classroom teachers notice that students identify and use critical thinking skills, collaborating to edit and revise their work and making considered choices—the heart of the artistic process.

The depth of the student work developed our awareness that the teacher can employ the full spectrum of Bloom's Taxonomy as students apply their previous knowledge and organizational skills, analyze their research, evaluate and prepare their project components, and create the final product.

KIM: Each year, projects evolve based on the Alliance Theatre season and the particular research requirements of a targeted play. As the themes and topics of the play changes from year to year, I rely on the Understanding by Design structure as a Teaching Artist to keep me focused on the 'Big Idea' of research and theatre and the essential question: "How can I provide an audience, director and actors of a play vital information based on my researching components of the play?"

With regular deadlines looming from the theatre company, we often ask if there is time for the students to make sense of and own the material they research without simply delivering a product for the theatre. We must give students time and space to effectively gain the insights and skills of an artist and to develop their own artistry. As a Teaching Artist, my job is to keep the lines of communication between the classroom and the theatre open and moving, juggling the demands of researching, creating, writing and the expectation of a final product, to insure that student learning is standards-based, that the Alliance Theatre deadlines and needs are met, and that the audience also benefits from the students' work.

Celise Kalke, Director of New Projects and Literary Manager, recently noted that the Theatre for Youth and Families plays had not had a Dramaturgy Board in the theatre lobby for some time. This new project raised theatre's connection level up through the education and artistic departments to the marketing department. A new group of third grade Jr. dramaturgs took on the project. Two students shared a vision for the

CAROL:

dramaturgy boards and the staff and I worked with a graphic design team to interpret that vision.

The original program was facilitated by professional dramaturgs, but other Theatre Artists, working collaboratively with the Alliance literary department have also facilitated the program with great success. The commitment and participation of the classroom teacher is crucial to the effectiveness of this program, since it requires much student work outside of the time the artist is present; the teacher is the primary guide for the work in between teaching artist visits. This has turned out to be a key element, which has helped us strike a balance between the desired student learning-process and the required theatre deadlines.

KIM:

One of my favorite aspects of this program is working with the partner teachers, through which we develop lesson 'pathways' that offer possibility for expansion. The students themselves make amazing connections and decide how to improve upon the original plan that we as adults never could have imagined. The balancing act between encouraging exploration, maintaining focus, enjoying the moment and working toward a deadline is all a part of the process.

The connection between the artistic staff and the Jr. dramaturgs also plays a crucial role in deepening the school/theatre partnership. Before a new production begins Rosemary Newcott, the Sally G. Tomlinson Artistic Director of Theatre for Youth, sends me her guiding questions for the Jr. dramaturgs. Her desire is to receive a 'child's eye view' of the play. For the play *Charlotte's Web*, Rosemary posed the question, "Who is the Charlotte in your life?" It not only framed the student's thinking about the characters but also stimulated deep reflection about family, friends and teachers' impact on their lives. Such a process connects the students to their own selves as much as to the play. Students commented that, "she took notes to remember my ideas, because my opinion

CAROL:

really matters." The affirmation of knowledge keeps them engaged in understanding and appreciating art and artistry, and in their own learning as well.

On reflection, I realize that Dorothy Heathcote's concept of 'mantle of the expert,' in which students assume roles in a drama and problem-solve through research and collaboration influenced me in the early stages of development, even though I was not fully conscious of its potential. Heathcote's approach has been described as "creating meaningful, purposeful and deeply engaging contexts for learning." Her drive was to radically alter the commonly held view of education from one that held it as a preparation for future need, to one where children's learning is not defined by their lives as adults, but by the value of what they do collectively in the classroom today.

KIM:

Working so often with students who have never seen a live performance, the theatre-to-classroom integration makes theatre come alive for these students, developing greater interest in and appreciation of the work of the artist. I recently had a student tell me that her work as a Jr. dramaturg has inspired her to "think and create my own art, like acting, music and drawing."

Influenced by the professionals gathered around them, students cultivate their ability to think and work like artists. One of my favorite days with the students is when we read the script that will be produced on the Alliance Theatre stage. This alone connects them intimately with the production and starts the conversation of 'who' their audience is for the project. The reading begins their journey together as creative and critical thinkers as they look for vocabulary to define for younger audience members and work to discover themes and topics that will be part of their research.

CAROL:

This project helps students make connections with, and become part of, the artistic processes of professional theatre, heightening their understanding of the artist's craft. The students

KIM:

appreciate theatre through their direct connection to the theatre.

When the Jr. dramaturgs see the play, they walk in as 'experts.' They see their artistic work on display in the lobby and finally witness what they envisioned. With *Honk!*, a third grade Jr. dramaturg researched frogs, based on a character in the play. He discovered that many make the sound "Jagarum!" He included this in his report to the actor playing the frog. At the performance, when the frog entered, he croaked, "Jagarum!" The young dramaturg sported the biggest grin when he heard 'his word.' The pride he felt in that moment exemplified his ownership of the artistic process.

CAROL:

As the program continues developing, we see significant connections to the Common Core Standards in Reading for Information and Literature, Writing, Speaking and Listening. And we ponder new questions: can we extend to other grade levels and student populations? How does the dramaturgy program support the changing standards and demands in other academic subjects? What kinds of assessment tools can support the claim of student achievement in this project? What professional learning does the classroom teacher need to be a successful partner?

Yet our original core question continues to motivate us: how does this program challenge students to think critically and creatively, enrich their collaborative and communicative skills, and contribute to their development as empathetic and emotionally aware people?

As I visit classrooms, view student videos, read research reports and study guides, and talk with both students and teachers, the evidence is clear that a high-level of critical and creative thinking are taking place in the classroom. I have watched student communication skills grow in just a few weeks; less confident children fill with enthusiasm as they share what they have learned and how they feel about the plays they are supporting. Heathcote stated that, "The Mantle of the Expert is about community." We in the field of theatre education realize that authentic engagement with our communities—with the audience—is the reason for our existence. When we can bring the community of learners together to become part of the artistic process, I believe everyone benefits. To me, Dramaturgy by Students is one of those elegant ideas that creates its own path because it manifests the truth of the art form as collaborative, complex and embedded in humanity.

Karina Naumer

WHAT'S HAPPENED TO QUEEN FANCY FISH? DECONSTRUCTING AN APPLIED THEATRE LESSON FOR THE EARLY CHILDHOOD CLASSROOM

Silence filled the classroom. Twenty-five first-grade 'fish friends' had just received a glittery invitation to Queen Fancy Fish's palace, and their body language communicated emotions ranging from complete puzzlement to thoughtful anticipation. The Teaching Artist, in role as a rather absent-minded Messenger Fish had just delivered the invitation; however, as they prepared to leave the safety of the ocean cove for a swim to the palace, Messenger Fish abruptly sat down upon an 'ocean rock' with a disgruntled expression and said nothing. After a few moments, one of the fish friends in the group said, "You have forgotten the way to the palace, haven't you?" Messenger Fish looked up and replied, "Unfortunately, yes. Now I am not sure what to do."

The fish friends, not letting this stop them, launched into an elaborate problem-solving sequence about how to get to Queen Fancy Fish's palace. One fish friend had a compass. This led to a discussion about identifying a compass and explaining how one might use it. Another fish friend had a map. Several remembered that they had been to the palace in the past and could find it again. So, they all began their journey to the palace keeping in mind the many dangers that they might encounter along the way.

The previous description is part of the arts-based humane education lesson, "What's Happened to Queen Fancy Fish?" that I teach for HEART (Humane Education Advocates Reaching Teachers). I designed and teach two eight-session kindergarten through third-grade programs for HEART, which use role-play, choral speaking, puppetry, storytelling and pantomime in service of HEART's unique three-pronged approach to human rights, animal protection and environmental ethics. "What's Happened to Queen Fancy Fish?" is the sixth lesson of the program titled "Protecting Our Planet."

HEART's mission is compatible with my philosophy to provide opportunities for young people to make their own educational discoveries as well as to develop life skills not necessarily represented within the standard educational curriculum. As Meena Alagappan, HEART's Executive Director, writes on the teachhumane.org website:

> There is a growing movement among educators and administrators to include character and humane education in their school curricula as a way to teach students respect, responsibility, and empathy, and to help them develop critical thinking and decision-making skills based on compassion, tolerance and integrity.

Implementing each drama lesson for HEART 15 to 20 times a year has afforded me tremendous opportunities to evaluate my work as a Teaching Artist. I am continually adjusting the lesson based on student participation, responses and classroom teacher feedback. And over time I have developed a set of evaluative criteria that both informs and guides my curricula development and teaching practice.

Specifically, the lesson What's Happened to Queen Fancy Fish? asks children to notice the litter that they see around them, to consider how it might affect sea life and to think about the choices that they make regarding trash disposal. The lesson also reinforces environmental terminology such as recycling and reusing. However, as a Teaching Artist I also have goals to engage the children as imaginative, co-creators of an undersea world. I want them to be able to inhabit it from the point of view of the characters— distanced through a theatrical lens, yet able to experience and problem-solve the dilemmas firsthand.

The first step is to design a narrative structure that will fulfill HEART's curricular content goals, yet be open-ended enough that the story can be co-created by the students. I ask myself: "Is my narrative structure for this drama compelling enough for the children to participate with commitment? Is it open-ended enough for the children to be able to contribute their ideas? Do the story dilemmas parallel real life enough so that the outcomes can be genuinely solved?"

Jerome Bruner informs my own thinking about the powerful connection between narrative and learning when John Crace (2007: 1) quotes him in writing:

> If pupils are encouraged to think about the different outcomes that could have resulted from a set of circumstances, they are demonstrating usability of knowledge about a subject. Rather than just retaining knowledge and facts, they go beyond them to use their imaginations to think about other outcomes, as they don't need the completion of a logical argument to

understand a story. This helps them to think about facing the future, and it stimulates the teacher too.

What makes a narrative compelling? I notice that children become excited when their imaginations are central to the experience. We will accept the idea that fish talk and there is a palace under the sea and whatever we contribute will enhance this world. Also, I find that young people find dramatic narratives particularly appealing when they unroll in real time. When we are propelled forward through certain given circumstances in community with others, compelled to make discoveries and solve problems that affect us, we commit to the experience and want to demonstrate the skills to be successful players.

One of the reasons that I think video gaming is so successful is that these games are set within fantastically alluring settings; there are built-in rewards for successful action and kids want so much to 'get to the next level' that they fully commit to the experience and work to develop the skills necessary to do so. Developing the skills seems to be the means to an end—not the end in and of itself.

What's Happened to Queen Fancy Fish? follows a similar narrative structure:

- *Given circumstances*
  Messenger Fish, a bumbling but well-meaning character, arrives and delivers an important message to the fish. The fish friends have been invited to Queen Fancy Fish's palace, but must figure out how to get there as Messenger Fish has forgotten.

- *Playable action/gaining mastery/discovery*
  After working together as a community to navigate dangerous waters, confront and overcome many dangers, they arrive only to find that Queen Fancy Fish is not there to greet them. (Note the fish friends fill in many holes here as they must determine how to find the palace, what the palace looks like—not only what dangers they will face in their journey but also how to overcome them.)

- *Dilemma/opportunities for problem-solving*
  When Queen Fancy Fish does appear, she is trapped in a clear plastic six-pack holder. The fish free her and Queen Fancy Fish brings out other items that she has collected on the ocean floor that the group also identifies as litter. This propels them into a serious discussion about the effects of litter and pollution. In order to educate the people, the fish problem-solve what and how to communicate them.

- *Resolution*
  In a closing narration, the people receive information about littering that asks them to re-examine their behavior, and they acknowledge that the fish have taught them an important lesson.

Though the narrative structure is extremely important, I believe it is my facilitation that ultimately 'makes or breaks' the experience in the classroom. Thus I am constantly evaluating my choices and making adjustments before, during and after each lesson. I think about how my role-play facilitation enhances and/or hinders the children's ability to commit believably, build relationships with the other characters and/or express their ideas. I also think about how the structures that I create in-role support and/or hinder children's ability to engage safely with freedom.

In What's Happened to Queen Fancy Fish? I play two roles: Messenger Fish as well as, later on, Queen Fancy Fish who is a puppet. Messenger Fish is the main facilitator of the drama and appears as soon as the 'fish friends' enter the drama. Here is the setup: the children close their eyes as I get into character. Message in my pocket, I cover myself with post-it notes, and don a green fish hat. When in-role, my voice takes on a raspy quality, lowered in pitch. "On a count of three you will open your eyes and be in that ocean with all of the other fish and Messenger Fish."

MESSENGER FISH: Hello fish. Thank you so much for meeting me here on my rock. It is good to meet you (*I shake fins with a few and wave to others*). Oh, yes. I see that you are looking at all of these yellow sticky papers. This is my way of making sure that I remember everything that I am supposed to tell you. (*I pull off the sticky notes and begin to read them one by one.*)

Did I introduce myself? — Oh yes I did that already — Did I tell you who I am? — Oh good, I did this too — Did I tell you my job? — No? Well I am a messenger. Do you know what that is? — Thank you for that explanation. It is a VERY important job — Did I tell you whom I work for? — No? I work for Queen Fancy Fish. She is Queen of this part of the ocean. In fact, I am supposed to deliver a message to you from Queen Fancy Fish, but, oh no, where is that message? I know I brought it. (*The children discover the message, which is in Messenger Fish's fish pocket.*) There it is! Good thing I didn't lose it.

The previous sequence is one that I rehearse. It takes time to implement but I see it as an important step in establishing the artistic frame—setting the stage in the classroom. The clear 'status' shift from teacher to a character with foibles gives the 'fish friends' permission and hopefully compels them to offer ideas and take on leadership roles. Also, I believe that the introduction helps the fish friends and Messenger Fish build their relationship and care about each other.

Once I establish Messenger Fish I use a series of questioning techniques that ask for both verbal and physical responses to create opportunities for freedom within a specific structure. I gauge children's commitment based on many factors. Are they listening—bodies engaged? Are they contributing with energy and excitement? Are they willing to speak even if they have not raised a hand? I find that often shy and/or quiet children will contribute when they find the questions engaging or know they can't be wrong. From the safety of the dramatic frame, Messenger Fish asks with trepidation, "What dangers might we encounter on our sea journey?" The answers come fast and furiously: "A giant squid, a Portuguese Man of War jellyfish, many kinds of shark such as the hammerhead, the nurse and the great white." Messenger Fish exclaims, "You have actually seen a great white shark and lived to talk about it! What might WE do to stay safe?" The fish friends contribute what they know about sea life verbally and physically, "We have hidden in beds of seaweed, ducked into dark caves, camouflaged ourselves or have become frozen—completely still."

When I first implemented this lesson, I unconsciously called only on excited, very vocal boys to contribute. Then one day I noticed that very few girls were raising their hands. From that moment, I questioned girls, too—hands raised or not.

I have found that the open-ended nature of the role-play allows all of the players to step outside habitual roles and see each other in new ways. For example, in one class, a first grade boy labeled as a troublemaker by teachers and classmates (his desk was literally separated from everyone else and turned toward the wall) volunteered to be the fish leader and kept us all safe from a giant squid. The other fish followed his lead. His two teacher 'fish' watched him work as a committed and able member of our team.

I have also noticed that when children feel safe, supported and are having fun they are likely to take positive risks. Last spring, one small group of second grade afterschool students spontaneously jumped up and created a scene of the fish friends interacting with the people. Before our eyes, they negotiated their parts as the fish versus the people and improvised their lines. Two fish friends confronted the people about their littering behavior; the two people demonstrated their remorse and asked for advice.

And yet, for all its success and rewards, role-play facilitation has many potential pitfalls. I look to a set of criteria as questions to keep myself grounded:

- Are my characters believable and human?
- How do my characters communicate just enough information to provide the structures for the children to fill with their own experiences?
- How do I remain true to the imaginative environment that the group is creating together?
- Am I communicating real emotion in a way that offers children opportunities to believably buy into the experience?
- How am I facilitating learning goals so that we stay on track with the objectives set for the lesson?

When playing Messenger Fish, I work to find a balance between adding humor and being serious about the dilemmas posed. I make character shifts based on how the young people react to me. For example, sometimes the children still take the drama seriously when Messenger Fish indulges in humor—so fun! However, when I notice the children's silliness factor rise, I may be overindulging in 'humor' and not allowing the seriousness of the dilemma to land with enough weight.

Also, if I focus too much on my own acting, I may lose the co-intentionality of the experience, sidelining the children as spectators. If this happens, I right the situation by pausing and changing the tenor of my character. At times that this has not worked, I momentarily step out of role and layer in a narrative that describes consequences of the dilemma (e.g. trash was still piled high up within the beautiful coral reef) to get us back on track.

I have on occasion allowed the teaching to overpower the character work by unintentionally dropping my role and losing my emotional connection to the material. Or I have kept the problem-solving sequence going too long without resolution. When these happen, the young people lose focus and/or the drama takes on a flat or even preachy quality. Getting the balance right between teaching and acting is actually one of my great challenges.

Ultimately, I strive for drama experiences that feel honest. Though imaginary, they still contain the tenor and feel of real-life experience. I think that I can only make this happen when I am true to the artistic and educational criteria that I have set for myself, so that when I am in the classroom I am able to facilitate a co-constructed drama with the young people.

Note

Andrea Dishy and I first created a version of The Queen Fancy Fish story for a role-play workshop for classroom teachers that we designed and taught together for the Alliance Theatre in Atlanta, Georgia. When I joined HEART, I adapted that story to meet my own programmatic goals.

Chapter 6

Assessment

Assessment is 'any of a variety of procedures used to obtain information'.
(Linn and Gronlund 1995)

There can be confusion about the role of assessment in drama/theatre teaching-artist practice. For some, assessment is solely the language of education; by forcing the arts into rubrics or scales, the unquantifiable value of the arts is potentially lost or misconstrued. Additionally, the language of assessment is often linked to social-science research paradigms, which have a complex vocabulary of terms and practices. For those not trained in quantitative assessment methods of measuring and analyzing numerical data, phrases like Likert scales and T-tests are a foreign tongue. Qualitative assessment that involves recording and analyzing words, images or objects can feel more familiar to Teaching Artists, but can still feel like the work of someone who is outside the actual practice. It's no wonder that many Teaching Artists glaze over when the conversation turns toward assessment. *Isn't that work best left to the researcher, the evaluator or the program coordinator?* They might say. *I'm a practitioner, teacher and an artist, so what does assessment have to do with me?* The final core concept, *assessment*, is dedicated to exploring and challenging this thinking.

Take a moment to consider
How does assessment function in my process? When and why do I assess someone? Who assesses me? How am I assessed? Why am I assessed?

How is assessment relevant to the reflexive Teaching Artist? In our discussion, we hope to move the conversation of assessment beyond a clinical examination of shifts in knowledge, skill or attitude as a result of a specific experience. In this chapter, we will suggest that assessment is about *advancing individual and group learning* through feedback and reflection. Again we return to the power and potential of Triple-Loop Learning, which includes reflection, reflexivity as well as a deeper understanding of how to apply our learning in new situations. In this way, assessment functions not just as an ending but also as a beginning point and an ongoing touchstone, which spurs new action, new learning and better understanding throughout a drama/theatre learning-process.

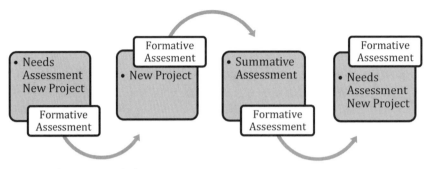

Figure 6: The Assessment Cycle.

Assessment is an active ingredient in each of the other core concepts discussed in this book. We assess goals when intentionality is a part of reflective practice. Quality reflective practice suggests that we develop and apply our assessments in conversation with our participants and stakeholders. We assess our knowledge and application of aesthetics through the consideration of an artistic perspective. Praxis requires that we assess, then act, then assess the impact of actions, so that we may act again based on prior learning and reflection. Despite its ubiquity, assessment warrants its own chapter and focus due to the specificity, rigor and intention it brings to reflective practice.

In this chapter, we will explore the potential of assessment to serve multiple purposes. First we discuss how a needs assessment can be used to begin a program with a clear intention. Next, we look at how assessment functions as part of praxis throughout a program. We look at how formative assessment can engage the individual and group in ongoing reflection on the quality of the artistic process. Last, assessment is considered in its summative form as way to end a program through reflection on the potential impact of specific activities and learning objectives reflected in and through the final product/s. This final reflection, ideally, concretizes discovery so that related future efforts benefit from past learning.

NEEDS ASSESSMENT: WHERE DO I BEGIN?

For the reflective Teaching Artist, assessment takes many forms. In the ideal drama/theatre learning-process, information has been assessed about the instructional context (the people, the space, the goals) *before* the teaching artist work begins. We assess a community or classroom before partnering on a program to better understand and define participants' needs and interests.

This type of needs assessment can take many forms. In an arts-integration residency in a school, the Teaching Artist and the classroom teacher might participate in a professional development experience where they train together and consider what they will need to be successful in their upcoming residency. They might collaboratively fill out a planning form where they set goals, define a process, and articulate how they will assess the impact of their partnership.

Or, as part of an audition process for a youth theatre ensemble at a professional theatre, a Teaching Artist might conduct interviews with teens to explore what they want to get out of the performance process and why. Through pre-assessment, the reflective Teaching Artist is able to learn from and with his community to better prepare for the work ahead. This type of assessment is directly related to establishing reciprocal, intentional practice for all participants. Although needs assessments offer valuable information, it is important to consider the symptoms of needs, what are the larger issues at play that make the 'need' feel important to an individual or a group. This often relates to systems of power or inequity that stem from a variety of factors. We often can't change these larger systems but having awareness that they are *present* is a productive way to begin to acknowledge the factors that shape our lives.

ONGOING ASSESSMENT: HOW CAN I EMPOWER PARTICIPANTS TO DEEPER LEVELS OF LEARNING AND GREATER RESPONSIBILITY THROUGH A FORMATIVE ASSESSMENT PROCESS?

When we assess in and through the arts we can measure different types of learning, skills, knowledge and attitudes related to a wide range of factors. As articulated in a prior core component, part of quality reflective practice for the Teaching Artist is working with participants to define the factors that determine growth and learning. When skill, knowledge or attitude 'success' is determined by the group, all participants are required to have an understanding of what they are doing and why. The group determines the criteria for artistic perspective, what quality work looks like and how it can be achieved. Through praxis they reflect upon or assess their progress and then make their next choice or action based on this reflection.

Formative assessment is a process where feedback is given along the way about how the process itself is occurring. An essential part of the formative process is involving students in their own learning. When issues arise, as they inevitably do, students can problem-solve solutions together.

For example, a play-building residency with a fifth grade class might involve students taking on specific roles within the discipline of theatre: director, actor, playwright, designer, stage manager and/or dramaturg. For further information on discipline-based approach to theatre education see Joan Lazarus's excellent text *Signs of Change* (2012), which explores this concept in full. Each student or group of students define how their role contributes to the final play product and how 'success' is determined for their related tasks and contributions throughout the process. Students are asked, periodically, to assess their success. *Are you doing quality work? Why or why not?* The teacher offers her thoughts as well, in a descriptive, detailed format. This ongoing assessment allows for immediate self and group redirection. More importantly, students are building the life skills of organization, goal setting, responsibility and perseverance. This type of ongoing assessment becomes a form of activated praxis. Students are asked to pause their action and reflect on their progress toward the larger goal, and then use this individual and group reflection to define and refine the next task. In doing this, they recognize their power and contribution toward the final outcome and their ability to challenge, change and act when problems arise.

> **Take a moment to consider**
> How can I use formative assessments to involve students in their own growth and learning process? How can I involve students in each other's assessment? How might I add formative assessment to my reflexive practice?

SUMMATIVE ASSESSMENT: HOW CAN I MEASURE MY ABILITY TO REACH MY GOALS? WHAT DO I DO WITH THIS INFORMATION ONCE I HAVE IT?

The most common form of assessment, summative assessment, often occurs at the end of a project. Summative assessment often measures changes in knowledge of arts and nonarts content, skills and attitude and is linked to the project goals. For example, a summative assessment might look at change in the knowledge and understanding of collaboration and group work from the first day to the last day of a drama program for second graders. A Teaching Artist can assess a fourth-grade participant's tableau skills, an individual or group frozen picture created with the body, and whether the participant includes multiple levels, full body engagement and a clear point of view. An assessment of attitude might look at refugee students' shift in the language used to describe who they are before and after creating an original play on the theme of home. At the conclusion of a drama/theatre learning experience, a summative assessment gives a Teaching Artist multiple ways to consider impact and change from the beginning to the end of the program.

The very nature of teaching-artist practice suggests that education and the arts are working together. In the arts, we often assume that the experiences we provide students are both engaging and beneficial. The field also likes to make causal claims, meaning: *I can prove that this caused that* when the data often suggests a correlation at best, meaning: *I think this could have something to do with that.* Can Teaching Artists truly make claims about the impact of their work? The challenge is that there is an ephemeral quality to much of what we hope to achieve in our practice and participants are also impacted by a wide variety of variables outside of our work.

For example, it's not uncommon for an arts organization to claim that high-school students will have higher self-esteem or will be more likely to attend college after participating in a summer playbuilding program. Or third graders will end bullying in their school after seeing an interactive play that teaches them how to be a courageous bystander. These are challenging impacts to measure and frankly inappropriate claims to make. It is impossible to measure long-term impacts like 'college attendance' or 'ending bullying' without doing a very costly longitudinal study (a type of study that covers many years to measure long-term impact or change). Changes in self-esteem require surveys before and after the drama/theatre experience. It is essential to document where something started if the goal is to measure whether change occurred based on some sort of new experience, through what researchers call an intervention. Plus to have any true weight the measurement tool should be validated, meaning others have used this survey in rigorous research study and found it to be accurate. Once data is collected, statistical analysis is typically needed to find out whether findings are 'statistically accurate,' which means enough things changed to count as a significant finding. Finally, any sharing of outcomes should account for factors, or limitations, that might also have shaped the results. For example, students in an English Language Learning classroom working on a playbuilding residency with a Teaching Artist might show improvement in their speaking skills due to the theatre program AND because their English teacher is using a new literacy curriculum AND because their parents are receiving coaching on literacy from the school through a Saturday program. All three interventions should be shared in findings; the theatre residency can be discussed as an important factor in a holistic intervention approach, which includes home, teacher, and student intervention.

All of this academic language can be distancing for the Teaching Artist who just wants to do good work and make a difference. This text isn't suggesting that all Teaching Artists need to immediately enroll in a statistics seminar or learn the skills of program evaluation. However, we hope Teaching Artists will consider how to use simple arts-based activities to assess usable, practical information to understand what is happening in the work and from the work to make the work better and how to share this information, accurately, with others.

So, for the third graders watching a play on bullying, a Teaching Artist might create a post-show workshop to observe if and how students remember and apply language from the play. Are students able to transfer what they learned from the play to another type of scenario presented in the workshop? What is exciting about this type of arts-based summative assessment is that the measure does not need to be, nor should it be, a survey. This type of question and assessment requires the best of what the arts bring to the field of educational research. This is an opportunity for embedding summative assessment thinking into arts practice.

For example, after the aforementioned play on bullying, a Teaching Artist could use drama to invite students to make connections between the play and their real lives. Students are invited to share stories or brainstorm anonymously about a time they saw or experienced bullying in their school. Then they create short scenes to activate the stories. The Teaching Artist could ask the students to freeze the scenes and offer advice or to step into role as courageous bystanders themselves, rehearsing the language of change to use in the situation. This isn't work that is looking for a single 'correct' answer from students. It focuses on students finding the language to intervene and the recognition of the complexity of the decision to intervene.

We can see the impact of our work in the language students use/don't use from the play when exploring the content afterwards. We can accurately share this story as part of a larger picture with our funders and the school to encourage them to offer time and financial support for this essential arts-based extension and assessment.

However, the true 'proof' of learning won't come until days, weeks or years later when a student chooses to make a different choice in a challenging situation, outside the artifice of the classroom, long after the original performance and related programming has ended. Part of successful summative assessment is naming what learning is truly possible to measure in and through the arts and accepting the limitations inherent in assessment done without the support of a larger evaluation or research team.

> **Consider for a moment**
> How can I embed multiple forms of evidence gathering into my work in and through the arts? How can I share an accurate story about my work with others?

TEACHING ARTIST ASSESSMENT IN ACTION

This next set of case studies offer examples of how reflective practice uses assessment to engage in questions of intention, quality, artistic perspective and practice throughout the artistic process. Teaching artists working in a variety of contexts across the world reflect on how assessment functioned in a specific case study. First, Ryan Conarro reflects on his assessment intention and choices in a rural Alaskan Native interview-based project. Stephanie Knight and Heli Aaltonen consider the larger implications of assessment methods in applied theatre practice in their European university programs. Tracy Kane interrogates agency and power in her discussion of student-driven assessment tools in the theatre classroom. Cory Wilkerson and Jennifer Ridgway discuss how reflection served as a bridge between program design and practice in a literacy project for early elementary students. Finally, Bridget Kiger Lee explores what is lost and gained through the use of arts-based assessment tools in a professional-development program for K-12 in-service educators.

Assessment
Case Studies

Ryan Conarro

CAPTURING THE STORY: A TEACHING ARTIST'S ATTEMPT TO ASSESS A DOCUMENTARY THEATRE PROJECT IN RURAL ALASKA

I have a photo album from "Village Stories," an interview-based drama residency I facilitated in a Yup'ik village on the Yukon River. I was the Drama Content Coach for the Alaska Department of Education's State System of Support (SSOS), a team providing professional development for teachers in struggling rural schools. In one image, students participate in a movement activity. In another, a teacher wears a costume, testing an in-role lesson. Outside the building, a tuft of autumn tundra berries waits for picking. Boats rest on a frozen winter riverbank. A teenage boy, Ronald, passes on his snow machine.

Village Stories engaged students in interviews with community elders; then, the youths performed interpretations of those stories. This village, like most Native settlements in Alaska, was affected by decades of cultural change brought on by non-Native influences and the influx of a cash economy. I hoped that our work could offer an alternative process to the strictly mandated classroom learning routine, inciting relevant discussion among students about cultural memory and identity. I sought—in the words of ethnodramatist Johnny Saldaña—to engage students and teachers in "exploring, restoring, achieving dignity, and asking questions" (2005: 9).

For me, these intentions were the heart of Village Stories, but when the project ended I felt I didn't have enough to show for it. The assessments I'd conducted didn't reflect the vibrancy of those photos. My favorite images in the album are the smiling portraits of the elders we interviewed, and the children and teachers engaging in those dialogues. It's their discoveries—the students, educators and community members—that my assessment efforts didn't quite represent. Village Stories taught me three fundamental questions I now ask myself when I assess drama education projects in order to best capture the stories of the participants in their process.

Defining intentionality: Why am I here?

I arrived at the village in August. From the plane, I watched skiffs heading up the wide Yukon River, hunting caribou. I reminded myself that I was an outsider in this place, a white guy from a far-off city. When I met the principal—a non-Native man beginning his second year in the community— he outlined the challenges I should expect. Some villagers might view me with skepticism. Some teachers, whose attention was fixed on raising student standardized test scores, might be irritated by my disrupting their classrooms with time-consuming 'extra' drama activities. Some students might be disengaged or defiant. The curricula, designed far away in a language that didn't originate here, sometimes insinuated that leaving the village could offer a better future than staying home. Many youths quietly rebelled against this notion, taking interest only in the caribou and the berries outside the window, or in the cell phones and iPods in their palms.

I was also an outsider in the halls of the Department of Education. Some administrators there took little interest in the arts as agents of school improvement. But one arts advocate at the Department had battled to represent drama and visual arts as 'content areas' on the SSOS. So—in addition to my contractual mandate to offer in-class support to teachers—I hoped to use this residency to demonstrate the potential impacts of arts-integrated learning, and to present our outcomes to the skeptics: Department of Education policy-makers, district administrators and community stakeholders.

I pitched the idea of Village Stories to the school staff. In this first week, I would share fundamental drama-in-the-classroom strategies. In February, I would return to guide students and teachers in practicing their listening and questioning skills. Each classroom would conduct an interview with an elder, focusing on a subject of their choosing under the topic of 'life and history in this community.' I would model academic lessons based on the interviews, so that teachers could witness how students might engage in standards-based learning through the project. Each class would also create a simple interview-inspired performance piece. In April, during my third visit to the school, we would host a performance event. With my insistent optimism, all but one of the teachers agreed to participate in the project. I pledged that Village Stories would have a positive impact in their classrooms.

Here was a problem: I set out to prove a point rather than to learn from my collaborators and make discoveries with them. While I touted a shared process in which teachers would work alongside me to realize the outcomes of Village Stories with students, I didn't allow adequate time for us to "work together to define the most practical and doable ways for" our collaboration (McIntyre 2008: 15). I printed deadlines on a calendar, and I subtly pressured teachers to agree to it. I was preoccupied with future-oriented goals (Moffit 2003: 68). I wanted to prove that students could successfully engage with the community in deep questions through the arts; that they could learn academic knowledge through arts integration; and that they could interpret their experiences in performance. My expectations for teachers occasionally forced me into the role of project taskmaster. Teachers didn't experience their participation 'as a choice'; at times, it may have felt to them more like 'an imposition' (McIntyre 2008: 15). In retrospect, I might have initiated an open-ended discussion with teachers that first week, sharing my intentions with them and listening to their ideas, concerns and proposals for a mutually agreeable plan.

Designing assessment: How do I establish appropriate markers of success?

When I returned to the village for my February residency, the Yukon River was frozen hard. My progress with assessing the project felt similarly stuck. The Department of Education's standardized site-visit form limited me to checking boxes and typing brief statements about schools' adherence to their districts' Improvement Plans. For Village Stories, I wanted an assessment approach that would capture a more holistic story, including the perspectives of students and teachers involved in the project. I attempted to arrange a formal case study or an external evaluator, but district administrators and SSOS leaders were loath to commit their resources to this goal. I worried that if I evaluated our work myself, I'd have trouble establishing a researcher perspective as I "move[d] between multiple identities" (Silverman 2007: 2)—designing lessons, mentoring teachers, teaching students and facilitating community interviews. But I saw that I had no choice but to deploy two assessment strategies of my own.

I circulated a survey featuring Likert scale measuring students' reactions to the arts sessions, like: "When I am doing drama, I feel (circle one) Happy. Okay. Frustrated. Embarrassed." My aim was to demonstrate that students liked arts activities in school, and that the Village Stories experience was positive for them. I also conducted interviews with the teachers:

- Have you addressed the goals we set in the fall for using drama-based teaching strategies? If so, how?
- How have the Drama Content Coach visits helped, hindered or not affected your instruction?

I assured teachers that my questions were not intended to evaluate their participation, but to gauge my impact as a Content Coach. I hoped that teachers' answers would show the Department the positive impact of arts-based instruction on student engagement and teacher self-efficacy.

I found it difficult to circulate surveys and keep interview appointments in the midst of my other residency duties. More challenging than my limited time and energy was my realization that my data wasn't capturing the stories as I'd hoped. The students' answers to their surveys seemed narrow. Many of them apparently did not take the survey seriously; they expressed apathy that did not reflect their evident enthusiasm for the activities. The Likert scale itself didn't measure students' feelings on a clear continuum. I'd borrowed the scale from a colleague, and I hadn't taken the time to critique it before distributing it.

The teacher interviews yielded richer answers that told a more multidimensional story about their experiences in the process. But I began to suspect that if I took the time to organize and present qualitative data from the teachers, presenting data beyond what was expected from the standardized reporting form, state administrators wouldn't pay attention. I buried the transcribed texts in a folder in my laptop, and I never shared them.

I'd succumbed to a positivistic perspective of educational research. I wanted hard numbers linking students' improved attitudes and attendance to this project, and I naively limited my data sharing to this quantifiable material. I fell into what Philip Taylor calls the "game of scientism," "reducing the arts to a measurable cohort of scientific experiences" (1996: 7). When I processed students' answers into numbers and graphs, the data felt—as Jonathan Carroll describes—"dead," lacking "the human and artistic interactions that gave the drama value in the first place" (1996: 72).

My motivation to present the surveys and interviews flagged, and I invested in concerns that felt more compelling, including the ongoing challenge of persuading the high school students to participate with me in the drama sessions. One high schooler, Ronald, showed high engagement. He was the first to volunteer for the Sculptor & Clay Game, a Boal-based introductory exercise. His classmate Alexis refused to join our circle, but Ronald slowly coaxed her into the activities. After we completed the high school interview, Ronald led the group in creating a series of tableaux based on their elder's story.

If I had interviewed Ronald about his experiences in Village Stories, or documented Alexis's journey into the circle, that material might have demonstrated the project's impact more meaningfully than any Likert scale tabulation. If I had shared the teachers' complex answers—if I had asked elders to describe how they felt about coming into the school and talking with students—I might have better showcased the nuances of Village Stories. My effort to compile quantitative data was misdirected because it wasn't measuring the project's true intentions. And my attempt to arrange an external evaluator—what Taylor (1996) calls an "interventionist" approach to assessment (31)—may have been misplaced. Education theorists posit that data is most trustworthy when it is observed and reported from the outside (4). But teachers and teaching artists can also function as reflective practitioners, embedded in the process we're assessing, rather than looking "to an outsider, a stranger to the field, who will conduct this function" (31). We can facilitate reflections between all the players in a project, and we can engage freely in those conversations rather than attempting to produce results that mask our roles as both facilitators and researchers. We can challenge policy-makers to consider nontraditional means of data presentation. Such participatory assessment practice can multiply the exploration, restoration and achievement of dignity that projects like Village Stories intend to foster.

Determining aesthetics: How do we work together to establish shared standards?

When I first pitched Village Stories, some teachers responded with doubts about the idea of a public performance. "Our kids can't perform in front of an audience," they said. I'd met similar skepticism in other schools, and I'd found that students often surprise teachers with what they can achieve. With the benefit of four weeks at this site, I was confident in my ability to guide these students. I resolved to craft an event that would meet high aesthetic standards, showing teachers and the community that their youth could use their bodies and voices to tell their stories.

In April, the final week of the project, the village was shrouded in a storm. The still-frozen banks of the Yukon were barely visible from the school. Inside the gym, I was leading rehearsals for a prologue featuring all students onstage. I knew from past projects that such a gathering of students could be powerful, but I hadn't properly gauged the readiness of these teachers and students to take on this task. Several class groups lacked behavior routines for such an overstimulating activity. Meanwhile, I found that some teachers had not rehearsed their class performance pieces as they'd pledged to do. The high school group particularly disappointed me: Ronald and one of his peers were away for a student leadership gathering. No one had told me they'd be absent. Without Ronald's example, other students refused to perform. Frustrated, I assembled a digital story using photographs of the teenagers' tableaux, so that their effort could still be represented in the show.

On Friday evening, the gymnasium was bustling for Village Stories, but I felt that the event was riddled with mishaps. The prologue lacked the ensemble focus I'd hoped to conjure. There were technical difficulties with the high school video. Some students were distracted and off-task.

After the show, we offered framed photo portraits to each interviewee as a demonstration of thanks. They beamed. A few elders approached me, saying they were gratified and pleased. In spite of my personal aesthetic critiques, these community members were genuinely happy about Village Stories. They were moved by what they saw. Perhaps, as Jim Mienczakowski suggests, "the audience and performers [left] the room or the auditorium changed in some way" (1997: 166).

When I first resolved that the production would meet 'high' aesthetic standards, I hadn't clarified whose standards I intended to use. I brought to the school a set of decontextualized expectations, and I'd forgotten that "the artistic project is not only aesthetic, it possesses 'emancipatory potential' for motivating social change within participants and audiences" (Saldaña 2005: 3). The transitions might not have been crisp and clean, but there was a different sort of beauty occurring in the room that I neglected to enjoy: the community was gathered at the school, listening to its young people tell stories of their own heritage.

Next time …

Since my experience with Village Stories, I take care to interrogate my personal and professional intentions in drama education projects. I strive to create authentic assessment tools to reflect those intentions. And I work to ground my aesthetic expectations in those intentions and those of the participants. These three concerns are intertwined; each affects the others.

One of my favorite photos from my time in the village captures a moment from the February potlatch, a traditional festival of Yup'ik dance in which neighboring communities trade gifts and subsistence foods. Ronald is there, dancing. Alexis is dancing, too, demonstrating a confidence she never showed in the classroom. I realize that in the context of the community potlatch, both young people 'achieve dignity' with ease and strength. I believe that a project like Village Stories might offer them some similar sense of identity and independence, right inside their school. Perhaps it's not so important that Ronald and Alexis missed the April performance event. They participated in a process. Ronald practiced leadership; Alexis followed and grew. They each transformed a bit—exploring, restoring, achieving dignity and asking questions.

Heli Aaltonen and Stephanie Knight

THE APPLICATIONS OF THEATRE AS PEDAGOGICAL AND RESEARCH METHODOLOGIES: SCENES AND WAVES OF INVESTIGATIVE DIALOGUES ACROSS THE NORDSJØEN (NORTH SEA)

Scene One: Prologue

Heli and Stephanie are introduced and discover common themes and interests in their applied theatre work. They are devoted to investigating theatre's applications and its effectiveness in doing the job it has to do. They live in different North European countries, on either edge of the shared **Nordsjøen** (North Sea). As reflective Teaching Artists, applied theatre signifies an umbrella term for theatre practices with theoretical and practical connections to critical pedagogy, community-based and political theatre.

Their work is based on related ethics and principles, yet the applications are varied and contextual. Reflective Teaching Artists are expected to be remarkable artists and work in complex contexts requiring knowledge of other sectors. It is because of their creative education and flexible thinking that these other competencies can be accommodated within arts practice.

Heli and Stephanie discuss the key areas of effective applied theatre—participation, aesthetics, ethics, safety and assessment. They agree that assessment is contextual and closely interwoven within the realities of the project, and the investigative nature of applied theatre.

Teaching Artists are expected and prepared to work in many contexts, some challenging, some dangerous, yet remain passionate and committed due to their belief in justice and democracy, and the political and cultural rights of every citizen. It is the political belief in democratic rights and social and environmental justice that contributes to ensuring that the critical space in participatory arts practice remains one of the few uncensored spaces for education.

Heli and Stephanie also work in universities, teaching under- and postgraduates. Their students work in participatory projects, and sometimes are co-intentional learners and researchers in the theatre projects Heli and Stephanie develop. Because of the context in which a project takes place, it will be different every time it is run, thus reflecting the reality of the professional world in which the students work, within a framework of critically engaged education. This means that assessments have differing layers to meet the needs of the participants as well as the students.

They leave this first meeting and agree to keep in contact through Skype.

Scene Two: The Skype dialogue

HELI: Hi Stephanie, I have been thinking about the interesting comparisons and similarities of our work. I find the most rewarding work is when all the strands are consciously interwoven. How do you keep applied theatre work and assessment separate from each other?

STEPHANIE: I don't see theatre and assessment in applied theatre as some separate activity; this would be a contradiction. I try to focus on eliminating contradictions that may undermine the principles of critically engaged practice.

A simple example of a contradiction: it's easy to talk about wanting to empower participants. Such a statement is based on the assumption that power is ours to give! This reveals a need for greater analysis of the participants' critical engagement, which leads to empowerment.

It is important to think through the politics and ethics inherent to applied theatre; if not, they can subvert and discredit the work.

This understanding of ethical practice then informs assessment that is defined by the context. Once a contextual analysis of the intended project is underway, I design the assessments required. As a Teaching Artist, if the project is in compulsory education then assessment will be defined by the formative and summative assessment procedures already in place, and the requirements of the program that is being taught. Additionally, there are always processes that I prefer to assess, as I believe that it deepens the quality of the learning experience and the quality of the art production. I endeavor to assess the quality of my reflective thinking continuously. This includes the interrogation of the ethics that are underpinning the work.

When I am working in informal education contexts, the contextual analysis informs my approach to assessment. Very often this work will include participants' aspirations and activism, where theatre has a job to do beyond making art. For example, ten years ago, I did a project with survivors of forced marriage, developing a piece of theatre as an education tool for the communities involved. It required intensive contextual analysis and ethical conduct, especially as I was working with participants who were survivors, and yet traumatized by their experiences.

So, when working in a context with participants and students, I create a framework for the project and include the students' course intentions. I reflect and assess whether this framework is generating all the knowledge and creative productivity that we believe are in the potential of the work.

To witness the awakening of a sense of curiosity and fun about learning and creativity has to be one of the greatest rewards for a Teaching Artist!

HELI: I am inspired by Nancy R. King's 'Critical-thinking-working-structure' (1981: 3–11). She was my teacher in Stockholm 30 years ago, and I still think her work is exemplary. One chapter in her methodology book is titled 'Self-assessment'; here she guides the actor to develop self-knowledge. Many things she writes are nowadays considered to be part of reflective practice. She considers that critical thinking will be developed when we assess our work on different levels: private, semi-private, semi-public and public. This offers us peer-learning, possibilities for sharing, describing, showing and suggesting alternatives.

However, these principles need to be connected with the different phases of the devising process. We have to focus on the phase we are working on, and in the here and now! Otherwise the peer-assessment produces comments that do not help others to continue. One way to keep focused is to comment on basic dramatic material of the performance. Chris Johnston (2009) suggests five headings that are useful in peer assessment: theme, world (aesthetic), narrative, imagery and relationships.

When I encourage university students to share their creative work with each other, I am conscious of how demanding it is for them to give feedback. The meaning of feedback, as Phil Race suggests, is "to help learners to *make sense* of what they have done." He uses the term "feed-forward" for "pointing towards improving and developing future work" (2005: 95).

Currently, I encourage participants to use visual methods (Mitchell 2011), and to learn to consider the environmental costs of their artistic production (Garrett 2012). For example, with a youth theatre production that included some university students, the students gained more understanding of reflective writing when they went through their captured visual evidence. In the next youth theatre productions, the students are required to think about sustainability and use "Green Theatre Choices Toolkit" (Mo'olelo Preforming Arts Company 2007). The website Julie's Bicycle: Sustaining Creativity has resources on environmental aspects as a part of its assessment criteria. I believe this influences the participants as they work alongside the students.

What do you think about this? You use every opportunity to investigate your own practice, how do you document the working process?

STEPHANIE: Reflecting back to early influences on my theatre practice, once I began to think through these areas, it made such a difference to the quality of my work. For my generation the work of Freire, Illich and hooks had strong pedagogical influences on our practice, and I was hungry and curious to try these out.

As I began integrating them with my practical theatre work, I saw the potential and continued to develop these critical pedagogies with other influences as they emerged, and hopefully inspired passion and curiosity in other people to do the same.

The importance of ethical engagement was profoundly illuminated when I had the privilege of working with Anna Halprin in San Francisco, California in 1990. The project was with Positive Dancers and a scrupulous analysis of the care and conduct was required to ensure effective work. It reinforced my hunger to develop my professional practice, my ability to self-assess. The Positive Dancers participants were men living with HIV/AIDS and in 1990 there was still only short-term life expectancy if HIV became AIDS. As an artist involved with the project, the reflective process demanded I was clear and thoughtful about my role, acknowledging that I was a visitor to their culture and I had a lot to learn from being involved. For example, if I had brought any judgmental observations from what some mainstream commentators were saying at the time, then this would have been detrimental to the work and the trusted relationships. It would have undermined the intentions of the project and the distinct culture of the participants.

The documentation of which you speak is defined by the knowledge that is generated by the participants and the intentions and aims of the project, and ensuring these are captured. This is crucial evidence.

HELI: Critical pedagogy is a part of applied theatre, but what you are suggesting is quite revolutionary! It's so interesting to mix practical theatre work with critical pedagogy, and question even the learning frameworks.

I would love to know more and find ways for constant reflection and assessment of my own working frameworks. I am interested in action research methodology, but I have never used it in connection with applied theatre work. It sounds interesting. How do you make it happen in practice?

STEPHANIE: Come back to Scotland, Heli!

Scene Three: Glasgow, Scotland in January

Heli has an ERASMUS university exchange with Stephanie at the University of Glasgow. Stephanie and her colleague Prof. Martin Beirne (2007) designed and deliver the Programme of Applied Theatre Investigative Workshops for Master's students in International Management. It includes international leadership, diplomacy and the analysis of organizational behavior. This programme's pedagogical methodology is applied theatre and works in physicalizing critical dialogues within problem-solving improvisations, and this learning informs investigations, assignments and professional knowledge.

The international students form Communities of Practice (Wenger 1998), and each community has people from each continent of the world. This develops intercultural understanding and collaborations. Each community makes a presentation about its critical approach to international leadership. This presentation incorporates theatre conventions and film, illustrating their understanding of critical, nonoppressive leadership and ethical management for empowerment and innovation. Each presentation is assessed through critical self-reflection, group reflection, and peer and staff feedback.

Heli investigates how storytelling can be integrated into these students' learning and presentations. During Heli's visit, she visits Stephanie's home, giving the opportunity for Heli's questions to be discussed.

STEPHANIE: What I find exciting about assessment in our work is when it awakens a sense of inquiry and curiosity for everyone involved.

For the students this encourages them to develop the skills of continuous professional development, and learning through reflective practice. From here they can develop toward the competency of reflexive practice (Rifkin 2010).

So, apart from formal assessment for students, assessment can include journal work and

188

documentation, and also mark the stages of progression in a project (including stages for any funders who are investing in the project)—depending on the project's aims.

There is the requirement to assess whether it is ethical for higher education students to participate in the applied theatre research projects that I do. I also have to think carefully as to how appropriate it is for the criteria of their course. The context of the work is very important to consider. What takes time and careful planning is making sure that every assessment point is woven into the design of the project. It is crucial for the project to be reflexive practice within an action research framework. Developing the professional skill of self-as-instrument takes time and honesty for everyone concerned. It ensures that I have enough knowledge of self, so as not to cause harm to others and myself, and have a negative affect on the culture in which I am working.

In the end, Heli, it's the big question you mentioned, 'whose story is being told?' and what is the quality of the collaborative art being made?

HELI: I am astonished that some students from traditional education systems do not have the confidence to work with their autobiographic material. People make sense of their life by telling stories and simultaneously become conscious of the power of storytelling. Applied theatre has an important task to discover counter stories to the grand narratives told by using enormous economic power. Every nation and generation has its grand narrative and unheard and untold stories. The question is, obviously, who is telling them? I use storytelling based on life stories, and applied theatre projects become deeply interesting when practitioners use storytelling approaches.

Yes! Actually this is what we are doing at the moment! We share our stories with different scenes and tell a story about assessment!

Scene Four: The Skype dialogue before Stephanie goes to Norway

Conclusion and reflections

STEPHANIE: How appropriate is your last comment, Heli. I have been thinking again of how the process of assessment in applied theatre requires the theatre convention of 'being in the moment'—the here and now that you mentioned before. This ties it in with contemporary concerns of 'mindfulness' that resonate with reflexive practice. I am thinking of the integrity of the story and the disdainful attempts to bend these not just for grand narratives, but for the outcomes promised to secure funding. We are back to the concern of ethics and transparency in applied theatre practices.

HELI: So must begin another dialogue! Stephanie, come to Norway in the autumn.

STEPHANIE: What a lovely invitation! I will.

Tracy Kane

ENGAGING THE OUTLIERS: ONE THEATRE EDUCATOR'S JOURNEY TO REACH HER MOST CHALLENGING STUDENTS THROUGH CHOICE, RIGOR AND EMPOWERMENT

I can recall the glory days when I worked as a Teaching Artist for Honolulu Theatre for Youth and Hartford Stage Company. My arrival at schools was greeted with enthusiasm from teachers and students alike. Even though I typically taught in a regular classroom with desks pushed to the side, the respect and reverence shown toward me made up for the less-than-ideal space. I never connected the need for a visiting theatre artist to the low status of drama in public education. If theatre had been a priority, schools would employ full-time theatre teachers to deliver instruction all year, just as they tended to employ music and visual arts teachers. No wonder when I started teaching full-time in public school, the space assigned for theatre always paled relative to the space for other arts. This reality rang true once again when I began teaching in an urban magnet school with extensive arts programming. In addition to fewer faculty for theatre than other arts, the school lacked space; it was expanding from a middle school to include high school. Suddenly, the building, which to this point had given teachers the infrastructure they needed, fell short. My status as new to the school didn't help. For more than a year, I taught in a center hallway, where traffic passed every few moments. Even worse, an elevator emptied into the space and the waiting area for an Assistant Principal, who dealt with discipline problems all day, was right there. His floor-to-ceiling glass windows enabled my students and I to observe the goings-on inside. Ironically, the intense dramas there were more theatrical than theatre class, and this reality made it difficult for students, even easy-to-manage students, to concentrate.

This problem of space exacerbated the challenge of working with some of my students who, like theatre, had outlier status. Even though some groups of students were easy to engage and motivate, many struggled. Their challenges fell into one of four categories: poor concentration; apathy and low motivation; mean-spirited behavior toward peers; insubordination and disruption. Sometimes students were so apathetic, they preferred leaning against a wall over joining the theatre circle to participate in theatre-game favorites such as "wax museum" or "name showdown." Of course, getting on each other's nerves affected their motivation; 'shut ups' flew across the space like shrapnel. What was most upsetting was when some students seemed determined to disrupt the entire enterprise—running around, throwing things, refusing to respond to simple requests. Not every class was like this. Throughout the year students produced work of impressive sophistication. But I encountered enough negative behavior that I left school exhausted and drained many days. Sometimes I felt like a failure.

It was hard to fathom such lack of cooperation in this nationally recognized magnet, which promoted kindness and bonding with peers through required service learning-hours and overnight field trips. I started to question long-held assumptions about drama and its value for all kids, especially those who felt disenfranchised from those subjects considered core to the academic program. The work I was asking students to do was challenging. It required deep collaboration, perseverance, creativity—skills and habits of mind necessary for success in the twenty-first century. Maybe the tasks were too challenging? Maybe drama was not appropriate or engaging for all students? Maybe students unconsciously sensed theatre's outlier status and behaved accordingly? Most disconcerting, maybe the outlier status of theatre in school programming was justified? In the meantime, I was lucky enough to be in a school that hired me to create and implement a sequential theatre program. That reality made me determined to improve the quality of experience for students and teachers.

As I contemplated these questions, two books by Allan Mendler stood out: *Motivating Students Who Don't Care* (2000) and *Discipline with Dignity* (2008). In these works, Mendler identifies lack of power as a root cause of many behavior problems. Rather than insisting on obedience, which teaches nothing about choices and consequences, he advocates finding ways to empower students to make positive choices. The need for power felt palpable with some of my outliers, who tried to control class by disrupting a vocal warm-up with shouting, for example, or by getting the group off beat in a rhythm game. I tested Mendler's assertion by relinquishing power every now and then. I'd ask an outlier to lead a warm-up exercise or assume leadership of a theatre game. Sometimes the strategy seemed to work.

At this juncture, I should offer a glimpse of what I was asking students to do. My instruction addressed many topics and theatre standards because I taught several grade levels. For the purpose of this essay, I am going to present only the content of the first unit in the curriculum for students in grades seven and eight. More students interacted with this unit on staging than any other; therefore, it provides the best window into the nature of the tasks. Using the Understanding by Design (Wiggins and McTighe 2006) model of curriculum design, I developed an essential question and guiding questions to frame the learning experiences:

Essential question:

How can I make staging choices to create clarity and interest for an audience?

Guiding questions:

1. What makes an effective tableau?
2. In staging, how can we use areas of the stage, levels, body positions and facial expression to create emphasis?
3. When staging a tableau, how can furniture effectively be used to convey meaning?
4. When is it effective to use a full back position?
5. What makes an effective transition?
6. What does it mean to polish a performance?

After a series of lessons through which I introduced and modeled staging concepts, students had structured opportunities to explore and mess about with staging. Eighty-eight-minute blocks frequently had a similar format, moving from a warm-up and games to a review of an old concept and the introduction of a new concept. This was followed by a rehearsal, during which small groups created staging to reflect the new concept. Finally, students either wrote a reflection about their learning/experience and/or shared their work to receive feedback from peers. These activities were low stakes. The work at this stage was not assessed for quality, but rather students received 'productivity points' for attempting the tasks. Ultimately, I expected students to synthesize concepts by creating and performing a story for Share Day, which had as its audience peers in other arts classes. The task was presented in this way: "In a small ensemble, communicate a story to an audience through a sequence of seven tableaux and transitions." To get them started, I asked students to consider what story would be worth developing over four or five classes, and sharing with an audience. Because choice is empowerment, it was crucial for performance ensembles to generate story ideas. Using a protocol for brainstorming and consensus-building, groups settled, as one might expect, on a range of subjects. Some topics, such as bullying, were serious. Others were more fanciful: 'Aliens Attack' was the title of one group's piece.

Another point that Mendler makes is that no one looks good when a teacher and student enter a power struggle, not the teacher and not the student (2000: 115). If a teacher is successful in getting a student to obey, the student still learns nothing about making positive choices. I tried changing my 'teacher talk' when confronting low motivated and disruptive students. One instance, for example, was when Jose M., an eighth-grade boy, sat on the floor rolled up in a ball during rehearsals. I imagine some teachers would have insisted he participate. Such a demand would certainly escalate, which then would require an office referral. Because students learn more by being in class than not, as long as a student was not interfering with teaching and learning, I worked hard to keep my outliers in class. Rather than making demands, I said:

> Jose, I know theatre isn't your favorite class, but I am glad you are here. If you don't want to be in every tableau, that's okay. You can choose to have a smaller role. The rubric says you can be in as few as three out of the seven. But your group will need your commitment for those three.

I then turned to his group, encouraged them to let Jose know they needed him, and walked away. Eventually, I *would* observe Jose cooperating. Frequently I worried about this approach; without a rationale for my conscious choices, some teachers might have thought me too lenient.

I experimented further with choice and empowerment by exploring group roles for collaboration on the performance: leader, stage manager, recorder and feedback facilitator. The *leaders* were to communicate my instructions to their small performance ensembles, monitor time and review rubrics. Because I had groups rotate rehearsal stages (as a way to more deeply ingrain knowledge of and skill in using areas of the stage), the *stage managers' job* involved orienting the group to upstage, downstage, stage right and stage left. Stage managers also took charge of setting up and breaking down stage cubes and props. The *recorder* took responsibility for writing down scene ideas or drawing pictorial representations of staging ideas. Finally, *feedback facilitators* called on members of the audience to evaluate the works-in-progress by saying something about the performance they 'liked, noticed or wondered.' This strategy both empowered the feedback facilitator to manage class discussion while peers evaluated staging using constructive language.

Rather than assigning roles, I provided groups with job descriptions. I empowered students to consider and discuss the best roles for each ensemble member. In most cases, students felt equipped to make these decisions. If the group elected an unfocused person to lead, I intervened by saying, "The leader's job is to keep everyone on task. Since I noticed you were off task during our warm-up, I'm wondering if leader is the right job for you." In some instances, after a few rehearsals, a group would approach me and ask if they could switch roles because a leader became distracted. This initiative to change leaders showed reflection on the part of my middle school students.

Another way I sought to empower students was to employ an assessment-for-learning framework. Instead of using rubrics at the end of a unit to evaluate work, I provided students with rubrics at the outset of the task. From the start, students knew targets and the requirements to achieve three levels of proficiency: awesome, acceptable and attempted. They then utilized the rubric to monitor progress and achievement by applying criteria to practice work, their own and that of their peers'. They also used the rubric to make choices about how ambitious they wanted to be. Along the way, they could elect the number of tableaux, the variety of stage composition, and the creativity of transitions. Because this was a first theatre experience for many students, the rubric ensured that as long as performers tried, the grade could not fall below *attempted*.

I wondered whether a rubric for participation could improve the ensemble dynamic. During the first semester, in a panic, I created a participation rubric as a strategy to manage difficult behavior. Looking back, I see how punitive the rubric was. Second semester, when receiving eight new rosters, I decided to take the assessment-for-learning framework further by making students partners in their own assessment. Rather than writing a participation rubric, I asked students to collaborate. I sought to establish a positive, theatre culture by posing an essential question: what does a productive theatre ensemble look and feel like? Since tableaux were a staple of my staging unit, I asked groups of students to create two: one depicting a productive theatre ensemble, the other an unproductive ensemble. Students enjoyed creating contrasting stage pictures. In the off-task tableaux, students presented what one would expect: gossiping, slouching, use of cell phones, gum chewing and mean-spirited behavior. The images of productive ensembles showed the opposite: concentration, focused eyes, cooperation and engaged body language. These tableaux provided a springboard for generating a list of positive behaviors necessary for a productive theatre ensemble. The list was developed into a *participation rubric*, articulating what productive participation looked like at various levels of proficiency: awesome, acceptable, attempted, absent. As multiple classes contributed to the rubric, each developing and revising the work of the previous group, I informed students that at two points during the marking period their participation grade would be the average of my assessment and their self-assessment. Despite this empowerment, throughout the process, I felt frustrated that few students took interest in the analytical work necessary to create the rubric. Here I was giving them a voice in how participation should be assessed and who should assess it, and many students did not seize the opportunity to provide input. Despite the unevenness of collaboration, the student-generated participation rubric ultimately had five targets: risk-taking, cooperation and concentration, respect for others/being an audience, completion of tasks, and preparation.

Now at the beginning of my second year, still teaching in the center hallway for another month or two, I continue to explore strategies for engaging all students, even those outliers, who are hardest to reach. One example is the pact I made with myself to call two parents each day, at least one of which must be to say something positive. I might say, "I am enjoying having Thomas in theatre class. He is always respectful," or "You should have seen Greshka's excellent facial expression in her pantomime." Parents love receiving these calls, and I love making them. These small actions go a long way toward building a positive culture. As I continue to reflect on my choices and teacher talk, I know that I am on a circular journey that will never end, one that will have high points and low points, one that requires constant reflection. My responsibilities as a public school teacher are different from those I had when I was a Teaching Artist. Instead of teaching in a new school every week, now I remain year after year as students progress from middle school to high school. Even though I will never reach every kid, I have a moral imperative to try and hope that this year I might reach an extra few.

Cory Wilkerson and Jennifer Ridgway

REFLECTION AS A BRIDGE BETWEEN PROGRAM EVALUATION AND INSTRUCTION

In late 2008, the Fulton Theatre of Lancaster, Pennsylvania began experimenting with the curriculum and methodologies of Neighborhood Bridges, a critical literacy program designed by the Children's Theatre Company of Minneapolis (CTC). This program, based on fairy tales, fables and myths, was modified for young learners to teach four Pennsylvania State Standards for Early Learning. Following educational best practices, evaluation tools and assessments of student learning were created to measure the outcomes and impact on the students.

During the subsequent four-year journey of creating and refining these tools it became clear that the assessment had become the backbone for reflection and discourse; it created a bridge between the Teaching Artists, the classroom teachers, the program administrators, Fulton management and even program funders. In an informal conversation, Jennifer Ridgway, Fulton Director of Outreach and Education, and Cory Wilkerson, arts assessment consultant, describe the experience of building the bridges that ultimately defined and shaped pedagogy and curriculum, impacted professional development and programmatic decisions, and transformed staff into reflective Teaching Artists.

CORY: Early in my career as a theatre teacher I had the good fortune of being chosen as Pennsylvania's representative to the National Arts Assessment Institute, where I was given intensive training in designing and implementing arts-assessment tools for assessing student learning in a theatre arts curriculum. At the time, I was employed as a theatre educator leading an afterschool drama program for approximately 100 middle-school students in a rural school district. Each year we did a spring musical as a summative performance-assessment task linked to Pennsylvania arts standards. This particular year we were producing a Japanese folk tale and I had carefully planned our production around the study of Japan's historic Edo period and kabuki theatre. A newspaper from a nearby urban area sent a reporter out to interview my students and me. I proudly described the student learning opportunities and shared our proof—student designed costumes, silkscreen scenery and kabuki influences in the production. As I stood beaming nearby, the reporter asked my male lead, "Can you tell me how it felt to be learning about kabuki theatre?" to which the young man responded, "What's that?"

Although it certainly burst my bubble, this incident marked the beginning of a shift in my teaching. I realized that although I could describe in great detail what I had taught, I had not created a tool that accurately assessed what my students had learned.

JENNIFER: I thought I had prior experience with assessment, but if the organizations I worked with used assessment, I was not directly involved, and never saw the results. My practice included providing the organization with the physical and verbal indications I noted regarding student mastery of program goals. This reflection became vital to my own teaching and learning process. But looking back, I realize the process and tools used were missing the student's voice, and there was a disconnect between participants—teacher, artist, student, organization and funder.

CORY: In my practice, I found myself disturbed by discovering a disconnect between my program design and what was happening in the classroom. Somehow I was out of touch.

JENNIFER: As an administrator, I coached instructors to reflect on their teaching. My own teaching experience proved that reflection after each lesson and within the lesson helped me to notice the small steps that students took to demonstrate program goals, and how the instruction techniques I used prompted specific learning from students. As I moved into administration, I further encouraged the reflective Teaching Artist in developing the practice of connecting their lesson reflections to their curriculum and instruction, and to the programmatic assessment.

CORY: Assessment has always been important to me because I see it as a form of communication between student and teacher. What I lacked was a tool to turn that communication into a dialogue. Assessments, guided by cycles of reflection and revising, became the answer. Separately both Jennifer and I were exploring how deep listening to what was happening with our students through reflection and sensitive assessment could transform our teaching. Our journeys were about to intersect at the Fulton.

JENNIFER: Fulton Theatre Teaching Artists were trained as a satellite site of CTC's Neighborhood Bridges program. Energized by the program mission, goals and instruction techniques, they passionately practiced the curriculum wherever they could. Through support from PNC Bank and its Grow Up Great fund, the Fulton began offering the program free of charge to a variety of area preschools, serving children living at or below poverty level.

CORY: Now a full-time arts assessment consultant, I was hired by the Fulton to help design a method of program evaluation that demonstrated the efficacy of the program to funders. Based on my experiences, I was convinced of the need to carefully design tools that would give a clear picture of what the students were learning.

JENNIFER: The biggest challenge was to create an assessment that was developmentally appropriate and scalable so that it could be given in exactly the same way in eight classrooms. In addition, since we were assessing emerging literacy, pencil and paper tasks had to be designed for nonreaders and it had to be

CORY:

streamlined so that 12–15 young children could complete it in under an hour. The Floyd Institute's Center for Opinion and Research at Franklin and Marshall College in Lancaster, Pennsylvania, would evaluate the data Cory collected.

I began by interviewing the Teaching Artists to identify the program's learning goals. Together we matched our targeted learning goals with the Pennsylvania Early Childhood standards. Next, I created a student assessment to measure student learning in the four main areas of literacy, creative arts, and social and emotional growth. After listening to a story, the children were asked to complete age-appropriate pencil and paper assessment tasks that tested understanding of character, setting and problem. Children matched drawings of the characters with emotion icons to identify feelings. In addition, the Teaching Artist interviewed each child to assess their understanding of the events in the story and their ability to imagine a different ending. Finally, both the Teaching Artist and the classroom teacher completed a checklist evaluating student social and emotional growth. Classes were taught for ten weeks in one and one half hour sessions and the pre- and post-tests were administered during the first and last sessions.

At this point the Fulton lost a Teaching Artist and I was invited to complete eight of the ten weeks of teaching and the post-assessment for two groups of children. From inside the program I felt frustrated. How could I possibly have expected a Teaching Artist to have a clear picture of each child's social and emotional growth when they were only spending an hour with the students each a week? It also seemed unlikely that in such brief periods of interaction with the children our program could justifiably claim credit as the sole source of growth in the many social and emotional standards we chose as targeted learning goals. When the program evaluation from Franklin and Marshall came back in the summer, the results bore out these initial impressions. Had the kabuki incident come back to haunt me?

JENNIFER: When I arrived at the Fulton Theatre in 2009, the staff was reviewing the first year's report and discussing the Bridges' second year. The work elicited several "Aha!" moments for me. The program was similar to my work as a Teaching Artist with Wolf Trap's Early Enrichment Program. While experiencing recognition, I had trepidations about the relevancy and effectiveness of CTC's copyrighted curriculum (designed for elementary and middle-school students) in an early learning environment with only minor curriculum adaptations. I shared Cory's concern that the 2009 program report identified too many program goals. I suggested the team narrow, or rather focus, its impact for the upcoming year. I was most concerned about the lack of emphasis on the dramatic arts. Had the program's emphasis on critical literacy diminished the importance and value for theatre education and outreach, which is integral to the Fulton Theatre's mission?

CORY: I remember one day after teaching a lesson, I found myself reflecting, "Didn't have time to get to the drama today." Had I fallen into the trap of forgetting that I was, in fact, a theatre arts teacher and not a language arts teacher?

JENNIFER: So, I stepped back, and observed each Teaching Artist, the entire curriculum and every classroom, while framing questions that ultimately served, in conjunction with the assessment data, as a basis for program reflection and refinement. I noted that while this theatre-based emergent literacy program was effective, and partnerships with countywide early-learning centers were becoming its home, the collision of these two worlds produced anxiety from all participants. Many of the Fulton's teaching staff were inexperienced in standards-based learning, lesson planning, classroom management and the early learning environment. The implementation of the curriculum required classroom teachers to assume the role of story-dramatization facilitators with no training, or prior experience. Additionally, the students struggled with the assessment activities, as well as with each lesson's length.

CORY: In the second year of the program I took over teaching in three classrooms. I had been teaching and consulting 15 years or more at this point, and had also been a trainer of teachers for years. Surprisingly, I found myself hesitant to embrace improvements in the curriculum that required a change in my teaching strategies; yet I was asking artists in the program to embrace a change to assessment and standards-based lesson planning. Looking back, red-faced, I must confess I was among those who gave Jennifer the push back.

JENNIFER: Looking back, and forward, alongside Cory and the entire Fulton team, those moments of push back were, and are, the foundation for our most productive reflection process. The conversations were opportunities to reflect, understand and refine. In its second and third years, the push back came from classroom teachers, students and Teaching Artists, and I believe our program is better for it. A dialogue evolved between artist and educator, administrator and artist, artist and student, student and educator, administrator and funder, curriculum and assessment, teacher and assessment, artist and curriculum. The conversations never ended, and they continue to multiply. Our artists, our teachers, our administration and our funders are consistently and continuously reflecting. In reflection, we assume the role of agents of change to the program, to its participants (teachers, artists, learners, administrators, funders), to the Fulton and to Lancaster County.

CORY: One of our initial changes was to overhaul the 12-week curriculum residency structure and support the Teaching Artists in the program with professional development workshops.

JENNIFER: The redesign of lesson activities came from the Teaching Artists themselves. This process helped the artists to integrate the best practices for curriculum development that Cory had shared with them. Following the post-lesson meeting with the classroom teachers, I requested that all of the Teaching Artists reflect, in writing, on the process of teaching and assessing, guided by prompts to help focus the free writing. Initially reflections were not always submitted, but I never stopped encouraging them. I always provided specific and detailed feedback and supports in response to reflections, and shared understandings with reluctant reflective artists. Reflections were an opportunity to continue our professional development conversation and a basis for sharing ideas and success stories. It was a process—and it took time and patience, but ultimately all participants engaged. Once engaged, motivation and understanding was immediately raised.

CORY: From the perspective of a Teaching Artist, I can attest that one of the most effective things Jennifer did was to provide a space for all of us to share knowledge and skills. Wearing my consultant hat I was thrilled that this sharing meant that our assessment and program evaluation had actually become a program-formative assessment in a model of continuous improvement. Key to this was the use of reflection to bridge the gaps between our program goals and the actual results. The assessment was instrumental to the process as a snapshot of student learning that provided the Teaching Artist with a vital feedback loop.

JENNIFER: Reflections became increasingly important. Teaching Artists and teachers reflected on the entire program and suggested improvements. Classroom teachers began to pose a reflective question as part of their morning meeting to clarify student learning from the previous lesson. Ultimately, this rich discourse became a formative assessment producing qualitative data that drove changes in curriculum and instruction, as well as the quantitative data collected from student assessment, which then produced measurable results in student performance.

CORY: The entire experience drove home what I had been teaching in my professional development workshops—how crucial assessing student learning is to being a truly reflective Teaching Artist.

JENNIFER: Yes, that was my big "Aha!" as an administrator. In my prior experience, assessment was a pat on the back. Fulton's program could have successfully run year after year with only minimal refinements, as the assessment showed significant student improvement. However, through the more effective reflective practice, our staff listened to each other, the teachers, the funders and, most importantly, the students. They analyzed and critiqued the relationships among texts (our assessment), language (our instruction) and power (our roles of teacher and student). The power relationship in the classroom was deconstructed, and the student began to teach the artist. All participants guided the journey, as instructors and learners, both providing and gaining information and knowledge. This year's focus will be an exploration of how to include parents and the community in both the program and the assessment. Previously classroom teachers noted that our expectation for parents to engage with student take-home worksheets and crafts, without the how's or why's of the value, unrealistic. They suggested parent workshops, and encouraged us to make program materials available to parents through a local book mobile. A tool to measure parent engagement is in the works. It is our hope that by enriching the child's home life that we will increase student learning. The process of assessment tools, combined with a reflective teaching practice, is our lens for seeing our program more accurately. Our lens is focusing the design of our curriculum and instruction, and our impact is rapidly mushrooming. Reflection continues to

CORY:

serve as a bridge between each aspect of the program, be it a person or material. Our philosophy of reflective practice provides every participant with a journey spotted with dazzling "Ahas!"

Ultimately, drama-in-education programs are a beautiful collaboration between the artist and the teachers, and the art form and the classroom curriculum. All collaboration hinges on clear and continuous communication. To me, assessment is not simply a test of what children are learning, but rather a method of communication between the child, the teacher, the artist and the program administrators. A good assessment is a living tool that is continually revisited and refined. This refinement can only happen through deep reflection, both during instruction and assessment and later as the data is shared. Without this reflection, the data is nothing more than a static moment in time. The "Aha!" I took away from my work with Jennifer was that reflection provides the vital lens for viewing the data and creates the context that makes the assessment a meaningful bridge between what is happening in the classroom and what is happening in program design.

Bridget Kiger Lee

NAMING OUR LEARNING ALONG THE WAY THROUGH ARTS-BASED ASSESSMENT

In my teaching artist work, I enjoy the process: creating art together, learning new material, and collaborating in a community. Sometimes I wish I could just stay in the process and say, "I'm still learning!" It's a comfortable place for me. In my teaching artist work, I find a different type of joy in the product: our final artistic creation, the skills and new content learned, and connections made with each other. Sometimes, I wish I could skip the process and get to the product and say, "Look what I've learned!" It's an invigorating place for me. In this case study, I discuss how *process*-oriented, arts-based strategies can be used as *product*-oriented, arts-based assessments for a community of learners. Our process becomes part of our product and our product becomes part of our process—learning, and naming what is learned along the way. Arts-based assessment uses the process of various art forms as a product to name the learning. This is the joy of arts-based assessment—a dependent relationship between process and product situated in the arts.

How I use arts-based assessment in practice

The Summer Institute: Activating Learning through the Arts was conceived and developed by faculty and graduate students in the Department of Theatre and Dance and the College of Education at the University of Texas at Austin. The research-based institute is a two-week intensive and immersive experience in the pedagogy and practice of drama-based instruction and learning strategies (DBI). Although primarily focused on drama, we facilitate strategies in other art forms as well. For the last three years, pre-service and in-service teachers, arts and nonarts educators, educational administrators, community-based teaching artists, theatre directors, undergraduate and graduate students, and educational psychologists have gathered to explore the potential for using

DBI in their individual contexts (e.g. the classroom, the therapeutic setting, etc.). For some, the institute provides an introduction to drama-based strategies; for others, it is a way to deepen their understanding of DBI educational theory and practice.

Arts-based assessment: Matriculating with 3-D models

At the start of the institute, participants synthesize or name what they already have learned or know about teaching by bringing a copy of their teaching philosophy and how it is (or how they hope it will be) operationalized in their individual contexts. This encourages participants to consider their current conceptions and beliefs about teaching. They respond to multiple writing prompts including: (1) how do you interact with students; (2) what are your core values as a teacher; (3) what is your instructional style; and (4) what might someone see if they entered your classroom? Some participants bring beautifully constructed philosophies, while other participants scratch a few ideas on a piece of paper. If the words are thoughtful and they are a representation of their philosophy, then both versions are acceptable and useful. The goal of the exercise is for participants to focus explicitly on what they already know and believe about teaching. This allows participants to reflect on these ideas throughout the institute.

On the first day of the institute, each instructor moves a group of participants through an arts-based pre-assessment by creating a 3-D visual representation of their teaching philosophies. First, participants silently read their philosophy, circling two to five words or phrases that sum up or are most vital to their philosophy. This is a time for *personal* reflection and assessment of their teaching philosophy. Then in small groups we take a 'tour' of all the art supplies at their disposal. Finally, we invite them to construct the 3-D model of their teaching philosophy—only including words that they circled on their philosophy. Upon completion, each group 'reads' the 3-D models. As a final step, the artists may discuss any intentions or clarifications of their ideas.

This process allows for a rich dialogue among participants and myself. For example, one student struggled with creating a visual representation of her teaching philosophy, claiming that she wasn't creative. Admittedly, her model was maybe not as dynamic as others in the group, but she spoke eloquently about her very structured, yet flexible, classroom. As she reflected on the activity, she realized how uncomfortable she was with so much freedom to create a model. I keyed in on this revelation for her and for myself.

In response to her reaction, I facilitated a group discussion loosely guided by these questions: what does it mean to us and our students to use arts-based strategies for assessment? How might students respond to the endless possibility of artistic expression through various materials? As educators and facilitators, what do we gain and/or lose by assessing our students through arts-based strategies? As I reflect on this discussion, I wonder how I can scaffold this process such that all students feel compelled to offer their best work. By doing this activity on the first day, I started a dialogue about how to scaffold student learning through arts-based assessment. I wonder what might have happened if I had not had this conversation. Maybe nothing would have been different. Alternatively, maybe this was the difference.

In the institute, we name our learning through the teaching philosophy and 3-D model representation; and then we deepen our learning by questioning and troubling this process. Participants synthesize their ideas by constructing a visual representation ('testing') of their philosophy. Additionally, they make specific choices in how to explain and represent their ideas to others and provide the rest of the group with their reasoning for those choices ('self-explanation').

During this dialogue with the participants, I struggled with how to balance the curriculum and its assessment. I know that assessment in some form is not only necessary but it's actually good for learning. Did participants learn one and half hours more information when naming or translating their learning through an artistic expression than they would have learned spending 30 minutes sharing their written teaching philosophy with a partner? I don't know. I like to think that they don't learn the same quality of information, but at this point, I can't be definitive in that answer either. How can I compare the effects of an arts-based assessment to another form of assessment? I can't. However, I can align the curricular goals and the form of assessment to meet the needs of my students. This means that I may have to take a little more time to have an in-depth dialogue about their 3-D models and forego the planned curriculum. For me, the product of the dialogue is necessary to the process of learning.

Why I do arts-based assessment

Even as I struggle through the process of incorporating arts-based assessment in meaningful ways, I use assessment often and in various forms throughout lessons. Educational research suggests that assessing a student's learning multiple times actually increases their retrieval of information and deepens their understanding of that information. Informally, people believe that rereading a chapter better prepares you for the upcoming test. In reality, a student who spends time taking a practice test before the actual test will outperform a student who spends her time rereading the chapter and her notes (Carrier and Pashler 1992). This 'testing effect' holds true even when the questions you ask are not the questions that are asked on the test. So what does this have to do with arts-based assessment?

Researchers have found that it isn't actually the form of the 'test' that increases chances for success; it is actually the process of recalling, synthesizing and making connections to previously learned material. Conceived broadly, this is what arts-based assessment does well. It invites participants to recall the learned material, and then synthesize and make connections between ideas to create an artistic expression to share with others. To go one step further, students who provide justification or self-explanation for their choices on an assessment show the highest level of success on future assessments (Chi et al. 1994). In other words, when I ask students to tell me *why* they chose to represent their ideas in a specific way, the students actually gain a deeper understanding of the material.

Arts-based assessment: Culminating with a Recipe for Me

Toward the end of the institute, participants 'name' what they have learned about the theory and practice of DBI, including potential opportunities and challenges with the work. One specific form of assessment is Recipe for Me. In this strategy, participants reflect on the 'recipe' for being an engaged and responsive teacher who uses drama-based strategies in their individual contexts. In small groups, they create a group recipe that incorporates each person's voice in some way. (See further for an example of a Recipe for Me group script.) This performative act is a type of formative evaluation of their learning. Again, this is a not a holistic picture of everything they learned— what assessment can tell the full story? However, this does allow for a snapshot of ideas that are resonating with the participants. In addition, it helps frame this work for people who have not been a part of our experience.

One cup of creativity and a dash of flexibility.
One gallon of compassion and a few tricks up my sleeve.
Add spices slowly and consistently as needed and required.
Bake until everyone reaches their full potential.
Serves 16 comfortably, up to 22 if spread thin.

(Recipe for Me, excerpt from group script)

To that end, for the final day of the institute, we invite administrators, colleagues, community members, friends and family for a peek into the work that took place over the last two weeks. This year, one group of participants shared their collective Recipe for Me. Referencing the aforementioned Recipe, as the group stated the line, "Serves 18 comfortably", the group was in a tight standing circle. Then they took three measured and slow steps out to widen the circle. In one resolute voice, the group stated, "Serves 22 if spread thin." When planning this part of the Recipe, the group almost deleted this line. But one participant spoke up, "No this *needs* to be heard. Administrators need to know what it takes to teach well." The challenge of ever-growing class sizes resonated with everyone in the room at that final sharing. Administrators and colleagues chuckled and nodded, as a way to acknowledge that they understood.

Through this assessment, teachers and Teaching Artists named and gave a voice to a real struggle in the classroom—much more impactful on my memory than reading a news clip about large class sizes. In the moment, I thought, "This is what arts-based assessment can do!" Participants recalled and *reflected* upon their learning, *synthesized* that learning into the structure of a recipe, and *made connections* to their prior conceptions of what effective teaching includes. They presented their 'product,' but because of this performative act, everyone in the room had a moment of empathy and connection to the struggles of teachers.

Nevertheless, even with all these potentially positive outcomes, some participants felt overwhelmed by using an unfamiliar art form for assessment. They had to create a script and stage a short performance with their colleagues highlighting the ingredients for effective teaching. I expected participants to learn new content, and then I assessed this learning in a new way (Perkins 1991). As an alternative, I could have offered a list of effective teaching tips and quizzed the participants on the content (something very familiar). However, I believe that this drastically shifts the learning and places a higher value on the instructors' experiences rather than the participants' experiences. In addition, the beautiful visual representation of the teachers 'spread thin' is more likely to create an episodic and meaningful memory than the image of participants reading a list.

Considering the participants' comfort level, I should not expect someone to do their best work when they are unfamiliar with *how* to do the work in the art form. To me, this is actually argument for *more* arts-based assessment. To this end, in the classroom I need to revisit arts strategies in multiple units of study, such that the participants no longer have to use valuable attentional resources on the art process of the assessment tool, but can focus on making connections to the newly learned content.

Concluding thoughts

As I plan future curriculum that includes assessment, it isn't a matter of tagging art onto the end of a lesson and presto—we have arts-based assessment. First and foremost, my learning goals need to direct my curriculum. (1) What do I want participants to be able to do by the end of our time together? (2) What are the steps to getting participants to that learning? (3) At which points should I assess their learning? (4) How do I need to scaffold the assessment such that everyone feels able to participate? (5) What forms of assessment most appropriately fit the learning goals? (6) How can we facilitate assessment that encourages participants to explain their learning and justify their choices? Then I can evaluate whether an arts-based assessment tool can achieve these goals.

I have read an abundance of advocacy and support for arts-based assessment; however, it isn't just the process of doing 'art' as an assessment that is effective. When using arts-based assessment, I structure assessments so that they include a space and place for practicing the process of recalling, synthesizing and making connections to previously learned material. Then I allow opportunities to explain what was learned, how it was learned and why it was learned. This is the product of arts-based assessment.

I assess what the participants have learned about drama-based pedagogy *through* their use of arts-based practices. Not only do I have a better and richer understanding of the participants' learning but participants also learn a way to conduct arts-based assessment. As participants in the institute, they 'try out' or 'test' their drama-based practices with other learners, and, in doing that, their learning and ideas about DBI are confirmed, created, rejected and/ or revised. As a community of facilitators and participants, we rely on the process and product of drama-based work to deepen our understanding of DBI through learning and naming our learning along the way.

Acknowledgments

I want to acknowledge my partnership and collaboration with Kathryn Dawson, Sarah Coleman and Stephanie Cawthon on this project. They, along with many graduate students and Teaching Artists, collectively contribute to the process and product of the Summer Institute. In this essay, I am representing my reflection on our work together.

Chapter 7

Praxis

Praxis is the embodied synthesis of theory and practice.

(Nicholson 2005: 39)

Praxis is a tricky word. In some circles—where watered down critical theory has been popularized almost to the point of commoditization—the word 'praxis' has been adopted as an easy, everyday replacement for the word 'practice' in conversation. "I have a student-centered praxis." "My praxis has really shifted over the years." "What type of praxis does she do?" These casual references, best heard in the university coffee shop and the academic conference session, where folks can try a little too hard to prove their worth, suggest that the speaker has begun to drift away from the true meaning of praxis. How, then, can we avoid pretension and reclaim praxis as a productive tool for the reflective Teaching Artist? In this chapter we offer a working definition of praxis and explore how the term specifically supports intentionality, artistic perspective and quality within reflective teaching artist practice. We consider how to apply praxis in a collaborative drama/theatre learning process. Lastly, we consider the unique role prior knowledge plays in the reflective praxis cycle.

Praxis comes from the Greek verb meaning 'to do.' The term praxis, in its twentieth and twenty-first century application, as described before, is not simply an easy replacement for the word practice. Praxis references an ongoing, reiterative cycle of reflection and action that moves the individual toward a new critical awareness. It *is* about what one does; but also, why one does it, and how choices reference and impact larger systems of power and the people/policies/structures within them. Paulo Freire, in his book *The Pedagogy of the Oppressed*, bases his definition of praxis on the writing of Karl Marx and Friedrich Engels. He suggests that praxis is an ongoing cycle of, "reflection and action on the world in order to transform it" (1993: 51).

For this reason, teaching-artist praxis aligns with larger discussions in this text about the relationship between reflection and reflexive thinking. Praxis, like Triple-Loop Learning discussed in Chapter 2, involves the recognition that reflective and reflexive thinking is part of how we reflect on experience

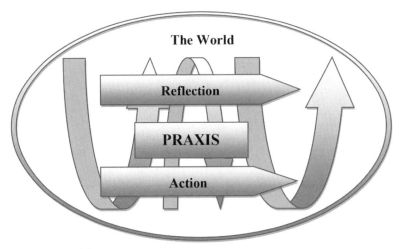

Figure 7: Praxis Model.

or action within the world and ourselves. The ongoing cycle of praxis suggest we move beyond simple reflection (*What happened?* and *What do I think about what happened?*) toward larger thinking about the impact of actions (*What is the impact of my actions on others?* and *How is my next action informed by my reflection on what I learned and how I want to impact others?*).

Friere's use of the term 'praxis' references how marginalized populations of adults learn to read and write as part of a larger call toward emancipatory pedagogical processes. In his text teachers are not asked to deny their own specific pedagogical intentions, skills or experiences but to build on the knowledge and experience of the learner. This aligns with our earlier discussion about intentionality in reflective practice and the balance between personal, participant and contextual intention in teaching artist practice. This argument can be furthered as we think about literacy beyond the understanding of mere words but rather 'literate' as an understanding of the relationship between word and action. This also references larger discussions about reflection on artistic perspective and quality within our work, as drama/theatre skills teach us to translate between word and body, internal emotion and outward expression. It isn't enough to just know what something means. We need to understand that words and images have power to express, to change and to transform when we share them with each other and in performance. For the drama/theatre Teaching Artist, activating *praxis* challenges us to be literate (within ourselves and with others) about the cycle of reflection and action during our artistic process and, when applicable, about the cycle of reflection and action within and around the sharing of our product.

WHERE DOES PRAXIS START? WHICH COMES FIRST THE ACTION OR REFLECTION?

Praxis offers a true chicken or egg scenario. Does praxis begin with pre-flection—the thinking before a Teaching Artist starts a new process/ project where he considers his intention and the intention of others—this thinking, then, shapes and informs the first action he takes? This type of pre-work reflection directly addresses issues raised in the chapter on intentionality by including all three forms of intentionality (personal, participant and context) prior to practice.

Or does praxis begin when a Teaching Artist pauses the action of her process at a critical juncture—to reflect and assess what has happened and the larger implications on her, her work and her participants—and then uses this reflection to re-engage in a new action, shaped by her reflection? Critical junctures are moments where process takes a natural pause. It is a moment defined by a shift in activity, approach, tone or goal during the artistic process. This type of mid-work reflection can occur just with the facilitator—as she mentally considers her next question in response to a dramatic learning moment—as well as in dialogue with the full group so all participants can fully engage in the reflective process that determines the next step.

Take a moment to consider
What is the balance between action and reflection in my work? Where do I support time to reflect on what I do and/or what we do together?

The reflective Teaching Artist ideally activates praxis throughout an artistic process. He reflects on intention *before* a new practice while being sure to reflect after critical junctures *within* practice to better determine the next action and at the *end* of practice to synthesize and connect the learning both in and through the art form to larger questions in the world. The reflective Teaching Artist makes praxis central to her personal growth and works to facilitate praxis with participants and stakeholders throughout the collaborative process.

HOW DO I ENGAGE PARTICIPANTS IN AN ONGOING, REITERATIVE CYCLE OF ACTION AND REFLECTION?

How can reflection with and by participants be linked to action throughout each step of the artistic process? If the project involves multiple sessions, ritualized moments can offer important spaces for individual or group thinking on an essential topic related to the common inquiry. For example, a simple check-in, "I'm feeling ____ today" (reflection), can be used to begin a session, giving time to acknowledge that participants arrived from other places and that their outside experiences shape the energy and attitude (action) they bring into the new collective space. For the Teaching Artist, a participant check-in provides essential information about participants' ability to work or focus and allows her to adjust her teaching to meet the needs of the room. For participants, a check-in offers an important reminder that quality work in and through the arts demands a specific type of focus and discipline, one that might need a conscious, articulated shift at the top of the working session.

A Teaching Artist might also choose to facilitate a ritual at the end of the session to encourage participants to reflect on their experience. Noted university professor and drama educator Megan Alrutz often ends her teaching session by asking participants to synthesize their experience into one word. Each member of the group completes the statement: "____ ... it made me think" (reflection). This becomes important information for the group and the facilitator as they consider potential goals for the next session (action). The same activity can also be facilitated through the body instead of relying solely on words. In this version, participants 'check-out' by sharing a single physical gesture that represents what they will take from the day (action). Whether shared physically or verbally, or both, an end of the session reflection requires participants to consider what they gained from the day's exploration (reflection).

Reflection can, and should, move beyond the beginning and end points of drama learning experience. As discussed earlier, reflection can be used throughout a process, at critical junctures, where the group reflects to decide on or to prepare for the next action. For example, in a devising process, when a Teaching Artist invites small groups to share their work with the full group for feedback, or when the full group moves through a portion of their collective work and then discusses how it might improve. Reflection is essential to quality practice.

Also discussed earlier, quality practice in drama/ theatre suggests that the dramatic exploration is framed through a larger inquiry. For example, when the reflective Teaching Artist facilitates an exploration of the folk tale *Rumpelstiltskin* with a group of fifth graders, he might use a guiding question, "How do words hold power over people?", to focus the exploration. Praxis is activated as students interrogate the intention of characters (reflection) through images sculpted in pairs (action). As each student group shares their image (action), the Teaching Artist facilitates a discussion to

Take a moment to consider
How do I use reflection to give participants further agency and to deepen their critical awareness of their actions within the world? How is power negotiated when reflection shapes action; whose reflection drives decisions and in what ways?

enable the group to process their observation and interpretation of what they see (reflection). The Teaching Artist uses questions to help connect student interpretations to the way power is exerted by various characters throughout the story (reflection). Then, at the end of the lesson, the students demonstrate their understanding of how power is represented within the story through the construction of a physical continuum (action). This marks a return to the initial inquiry about the power of words. Eventually this becomes a larger discussion about how power is exerted in larger systems (reflection) and what they can do about it in the future (action). Herein lies the power of praxis. Group reflection gives us a way to connect a larger idea or concept to our actions within our individual and collective world.

HOW IS PRIOR KNOWLEDGE ENGAGED THROUGH PRAXIS?

Helen Nicholson (2005) states that "Praxis is informed therefore by the creative and contingent mapping of different narratives—cultural, personal, social, political, artistic—and learning is negotiated and choreographed as encounters between the artistic practices of drama and theatre and the vernacular know-how of the participants" (45). Nicholson reminds us that praxis is multidimensional. When we engage together in praxis we connect our practice to our individual lived experiences through reflection and then negotiate new meaning and understanding when we take individual and/or collective action based on our reflection. This dual space of individual and group praxis invites each participant to make their own meaning as they accrue a better understanding of how others make meaning of the world.

For example, a role-play based on Robert Munsch's feminist reimagining of the fairy-tale genre, *The Paperbag Princess*, might include moments where the 7- and 8-year-old players are asked to take on the expertise of advertising executives. The drama picks up just after the narrative of the book ends, when the Princess realizes that the Prince doesn't appreciate the fact that she has saved his life. The facilitator steps into role as the Princess who is looking for an ad agency to create a new campaign about the powerful things princesses can do. The young players easily step into role and begin to give advice to the Princess. They offer examples of activities that might appear in print ads and commercials, which demonstrate the power of girls. Naturally, they pull these examples from their own lived experiences, punctuating their offers with stories

Take a moment to consider
How do I include participants' diverse experiences and encourage multiple ways of knowing through praxis?

about times when they helped someone else. Some students argue that in their experience girls can't do as much as boys and a lively argument ensues. Eventually the facilitator asks students to create an ad campaign with a slogan about what a Princess can do. Students are asked to synthesize their ideas into a phrase that represents their main idea; they are asked to take their reflection and turn it into action.

PRAXIS IN ACTION

The final collected wisdom features case studies from Teaching Artists activating praxis, both in their personal process and in their work in school and community locations. Each of the featured Teaching Artists critically engages with the relationship between reflection and action in their practice as well as the larger impact their action has on the world. Jamie Simpson Steele reflects on culturally responsive instruction in process drama, as a white middle-class woman exploring indigenous Hawaiian stories with native Hawaiian students. Gillian McNally considers how her developing skill set as a drama/theatre Teaching Artist supports and contradicts praxis for her nascent players in a devised theatre project. A digital storytelling residency provides Megan Alrutz an opportunity to interrogate how African-American student identity is represented and mediated in a US elementary school. Christina Marín learns with and from her Latina participants in an annual conference on Latina/o youth empowerment using Augusto Boal's praxical Theatre of the Oppressed techniques. The final essay takes us to New York City, as Teaching Artist Peter B. Duffy struggles to create praxis in a play-building process where presumed difference challenges his assumptions about a specific population and context.

Jamie Simpson Steele

THE VAGABOND'S DILEMMA: REPRESENTING HOST CULTURE AS A GUEST

The Teaching Artist is a vagabond of sorts—we drift from class to class, school to school, as an honored (but homeless) guest. We face mild discomforts from ignorance of where to park, use the restroom or eat lunch, but a more enduring anxiety rears when we realize how different our own history, class, color and language is from those eager students who greet us. This story stems from my belief that teaching through culture is an act of freedom and hope in our changing world (Freire 1993), but it also reveals how deeply rooted assumptions and presumptions can block that ideal. How do I provide my students with rich cultural experiences without misinterpreting, misappropriating or oversimplifying my representations? If it is true that 80 percent of what we teach is who we are (Booth 2009: 128), then how do I confront the invisible forces of my white middle-class privilege when I am teaching children who have not had the same advantages?

Huikau

Eleven years ago, I accepted a job with Honolulu Theatre for Youth and moved to Oʻahu, sight unseen. Prior to landing, I did not know indigenous Hawaiians existed. Having never met a person of Hawaiian ancestry, nor considered Hawaiʻi as anything more than an unaffordable vacation paradise, I truly thought Hawaiians were a sort of lost mythical tribe. I quickly learned: Hawaiians were thriving with sophisticated agriculture, religion and government prior to first contact with Western civilization in 1778, after which they endured a sharp population decline due to the massive influx of

Western disease. Hawai'i was a sovereign kingdom illegally overthrown by Americans with sugar interests in the late nineteenth century, eventually annexed and adopted as the 50th state little more than 50 years ago. Today, Hawaiians face substance abuse, poverty, domestic violence, suicide and incarceration rates disproportionally higher than the many other ethnic groups who now thrive in a place they call home (Clark 2003: 274–275).

The damage of colonialism cannot always be perceived through medical terms and social statistics; Osorio (2006) writes of *huikau* (confusion), a sense of Hawaiian disorientation in the face of Americanism and asserts that the modern school system participated in the humiliating process of separating Hawaiians from their identities (19–25). During the *hapa-haole* (half-foreign) era between the 1920s and 1960s, imported Caucasian teachers emphasized American virtues and patriotism in the classroom, repressing Hawaiian language and culture to encourage responsible and effective American citizenship (Fuchs 1960: 264–267). At the same time, paintings, literature, music and film created stereotypes that eroded the self-concept of indigenous people throughout the Pacific. Artistic representations—influential contributors of cultural knowledge and social values—are not innocent in the dynamics of oppression and colonialism (Hereniko 1999: 140–141).

Kuleana

Armed with this new knowledge, it seemed right to address the savage inequities (Kozol 1991) perpetuated in the schools of Hawai'i. I had lived here for days, countable hours really, but as an artist and an educator I felt double *kuleana* (responsibility and privilege) to incorporate indigenous Hawaiian culture into my work with children. I still believe it is the *kuleana* of both artist and educator to engage others in praxis, to ensure knowledge thrives as people explore and reflect upon how to be good human beings in a complicated world. My new world was Hawai'i and so it followed I would engage in Hawaiian history, practices and stories in my curricula. At that time, however, I failed to interrogate my place as a guest on indigenous soil, and today I am certain I assumed responsibility where I had not yet earned privilege.

E kala mai

In Hawai'i's past, when a person made a mistake the wrongdoer would apologize by presenting *kala*, surgeonfish, to the person wronged. Today, we might say "*E kala mai*" to ask for forgiveness, which seems an appropriate heading for this particular episode in my story. It is through the reflexive process I now look back at my theory in action to find it marred with insufficiencies.

My first residency featured the character Moki the Gecko and was inspired by children's literature written by Bruce Hale, a Caucasian from California who lived in Hawai'i for a period of time. In this process drama, young elementary students and I role-played animals of Hawai'i. We received a message from humans asking us to become their 'aumākua (spiritual guardians) and proposing to select animal 'aumākua with appropriate strengths and qualities to protect each family for generations to come. As we prepared for the "Aumākua Choosing," Moki experienced a range of insecurities and social mishaps as she learned to share, be true to herself and apologize to those whom she had hurt. The residency embedded social values and lessons appropriate for children between the ages of five and seven.

As teacher-in role, I played Moki the Gecko as a low status goofball needing guidance from her friends. I adopted traits of similar characters I had played in the past: for example, Moki was always little lazy and a little late. As a Teaching Artist on the continent, I noticed children loved these traits, laughing and correcting the silly behaviors, but it is one thing if a sorcerer's apprentice is late and lazy, another if a character placed in a Polynesian setting is late and lazy. I intended to play these traits with child-like naïveté as a strategy for engagement, but in hindsight, I wonder if I was participating in the reinforcement of a very well-established, damaging stereotype.

To my surprise, Moki started speaking pidgin (formally Hawai'i Creole English). A short background of pidgin may prove helpful to fully explain the impact of this development. Pidgin evolved as a result of English and non-English speakers working side by side during Hawai'i's plantation era, and was inspired by a conglomeration of Hawaiian, English, Chinese, Japanese, Filipino and Portuguese languages. The language includes slang, unique intonations, foreign words, nonstandard English grammar and transformed pronunciation of English phrases. Today, pidgin is often the language children speak upon entering public school and it can certainly help a teacher to know *shi-shi* means 'pee-pee' and *pau* means 'all done.'

Pidgin is a major signifier of *local* identity. The term *local* refers to decedents of the same ethnic groups of plantation workers who first developed pidgin and have a common identity with a shared past and commitment to Hawai'i's shared culture (Okamura 1994). A defining quality of being local is the contrast, or even opposition, to outsiders and oppressors who pose an economic threat, namely *malihini* (newcomers) and *haole* (literally foreigners, but commonly used in reference to Caucasians). Hence, a *malihini haole* speaking pidgin smacks of condescension.

As pidgin crept its way into Moki's speech, I wonder if she sounded patronizing, projecting a negative value judgment on local identity, trying to be someone who she was not, and undoing the very social lessons I endeavored to teach.

Finally, dramatizing the "Aumākua Choosing' was a questionable choice. Pukui, Haertig and Lee (1972), define 'aumākua as ancestral gods as deities who had once been alive but as departed ancestors had become advocates and protectors to their 'ohana (family) (123). 'Aumākua come in the forms of animals, plants and even rocks, appearing in dreams to help guide individuals, in human form to provide punishment or advice and sometimes appearing unsolicited to provide safe harbor or bountiful harvest.

Today, families may be able to identify the forms of their 'aumākua, but much of the specific information about the actual name, history and place it is from has been lost. Modern Hawaiian leaders see these losses as key links to past practices and places, and many believe restoring the role of 'aumākua in the life of a family and community might have a healing effect (Goldman 2010). In my drama residency, I made the assumption that the Hawaiian spiritual world was one of the past—the gods and goddesses firmly placed in today's world as figures of mythology and folklore. As a newcomer, I failed to see how some people still hold beliefs about the power of the natural world and are mindful of Hawaiian deities. I did not recognize the spiritual significance of an indigenous tradition nor handle it with appropriate dignity.

Imua

I began to hear the voices of respected Hawaiian educators around me, and weighed my Moki choices against assertions that Hawaiian culture is commonly trivialized in the classroom (Kaomea 2005). To me, praxis involves a cycle of truth-finding, critique and action. I took a close look at my choices, found them lacking and struggled forward—imua.

In a new process-drama for upper elementary grades, students played maka'āinana—common working people, living together on a slice of land stretching from mauka (mountain) to makai (ocean)—with specific, physically active and historically accurate, work groups. The dramatic conflict ensued when they stumbled across a sailor (fictional) accidentally left behind when Captain Cook (historical) set sail after he 'discovered' Hawai'i. The sailor did not know he was on kapu (forbidden) land, drinking kapu waters and using Hawaiian implements inappropriately. To make up for these offenses, the sailor attempted to make a deal with the maka'āinana to teach them a new language, easier ways of doing things and provide materials like tools and medicine, promoting his Western way of life. The drama concluded as students debated this choice, created physical images to predict what life might look like just five years later, and reflected upon the similarities and differences between these images and the world we live in today.

In contrast to Moki's adventures, I spent more time unpacking difficult concepts such as 'tradition' and 'culture.' I was also careful to address the line between fact and fiction, between creativity and accuracy. For example, in the work groups, students harvested *kalo* in the *loi* (taro fields), went fishing at night with their torches and nets, and wove *lauhala* (pandanus leaves) into fine mats. Through tableaux and pantomime, students explored the details of their work, imagining what life might have been like 300 years ago, observing the many challenges of basic survival. In this instance, students embodied details of life known from historical accounts. However, when the time came for us to establish our village traditions, I facilitated invention. I transparently framed this: "This is not a moment when we have to be true to history. Our village is an imagined place, and our traditions belong only to us." I was also careful to explain how *hula*, one of the traditions that truly would have existed in the past and still thrives today, should be taught by *kumu hula* (expert teachers) and rigorously practiced with respect to the source.

The other important difference in this residency was its open-ended culmination, not the recreation of an historic or cultural event. The class usually split on their decisions during the debate; some desired a life of ease with modern conveniences, wanting to build skills to help them survive in the changing world, and learn as much as they could to help them prepare for the possibility of more strangers landing on the island. Others vehemently argued that they would need to hold more tightly than ever to their own traditions in order to remember their ancestors and honor their past as the world changed. Many students fell in between these two extremes of the continuum and argued for a combined approach—survival would depend on learning new things, but also teaching Hawaiian ways to the newcomers. Throughout these debates, I strove to become invisible with only the occasionally probe: "What makes you say that?" In this instance, students became actively engaged in important and relevant questions about culture, reasoning their way through arguments with supporting evidence, fully immersed as movers and shakers of a culture in flux. The students became praxis practitioners, using the action of drama to test their theoretical positions, assuming the power to interpret their own pasts and determine their own futures.

Nānā ka maka; hoʻolohe ka pepeiao; paʻa ka waha

Observe with the eyes, listen with the ears, shut the mouth. (Thus one learns.)
To conclude my journey, I share a common proverb I have only recently come
to embrace. 'Shut the mouth' is a difficult proposition for people who come
from a Western discourse tradition; I fundamentally believe students must
learn to question and co-construct meaning through dialogue. But now I
understand how this proverb applies to my own praxis as I learn to be quiet
and observe before assuming the privilege of action. By listening first, I learn
about issues important to the people native to this place, and once I understand
that much I can scrutinize educational and artistic choices to make sure I do
more good than harm. 'Shut the mouth' also means leaving some things to the
experts and being transparent about what I do not know. This requires *haʻahaʻa*
(humility) to reflect on choices without guilt or ego and place myself
appropriately within the context of my surroundings. I consider taking action
more difficult after having listened and observed, much more so than my
previous head-long-dive approach. After engaging in praxis with a 'shut
mouth' it is easy to feel skeptical, as though this is all beyond my world and
because of my guest status I can do nothing that is *pono* (righteous). I find it
important to muster the courage to act, regardless of the potential for failure.
If I am committed to inciting people to challenge the circumstances of
their lives, then I must engage in the politics of place and the people who live
in it. If it were easy then it would not be necessary.

Gillian McNally

ACTIVATING COMMUNITY: PROCESS-CENTERED PHILOSOPHY IN A PRODUCT-ORIENTED WORLD

The idea of 'third space' invites us to focus on that which might, at first glance, seem to be invisible. It is the 'space between' teachers and learners, between the various individuals in a learning group, and between the learners, teachers and works of art. This is the space in which meaning that has been negotiated and constructed by the members of a group emerges. When students, teachers and others gather around a work of art created by an artist or a student, and they strive to understand that work—what they see, what it means to each of them, what it makes them feel—they not only make sense of the work, they build community and understanding among themselves. The beauty of the concept of 'third space' is that it helps draw our attention to a space that is essential to learning and the creation of community—the place where connections are made (Deasy and Stevenson 2005: vii).

This philosophy served as my core belief as I embarked on devising a youth theatre production of *I Come From...* at People's Light and Theatre near Philadelphia, PA in 2004. This collage-style play was created collaboratively with Teaching Artists from People's Light and Theatre and a racially diverse group of teenagers. This project will serve as a springboard to investigate the question, "In what ways does a Teaching Artist negotiate her approach to collaboration/co-construction within a devising process with youth?"

People's Light and Theatre, located in suburban Philadelphia, has a long-standing tradition of quality work with youth and communities. New Voices, a youth theatre program founded in 1989 by Artistic Director Abigail Adams, strives to create imaginative work with black urban youth from the low-income city of Chester, PA. Students from this economically depressed area are given full scholarships to attend classes, rehearsals and performances at the theatre. In the spring of 2004, I worked with a group of Teaching Artists to create an original piece titled *I Come From...* with youth from Chester and the nearby, predominantly white, suburban communities. This racially and economically diverse group of teenagers worked over the course of two months to create an original, devised play that explored their feelings of frustration and pride surrounding the themes of family home, neighborhood, mothers, grandmothers and community. Movement, music, poetry and improvisation were used as tools to devise the hour-long play. A team of six Teaching Artists with a wide range of skills facilitated the afterschool rehearsal process. David Bradley, Director of Education at People's Light and Theatre, served as the lead director of the project. He created the overall theme and vision for the nonlinear, collage-inspired piece.

Guiding philosophy

As a Teaching Artist, I came to People's Light with the firm belief that teachers are not all-knowing masters of information in the classroom, but rather co-investigators working with young people. In order to create an original theatre piece revolving around community, it was essential that our working environment embrace the 'third space' philosophy. Our piece delved deeply into issues of race, poverty and power. Our intention, as Teaching Artists, was to create a safe space where artists, teachers and students could question, discuss, interrogate, reflect and create original devised plays based on a specific theme.

Working as a Teaching Artist in a professional theatre allows for a completely different rehearsal atmosphere and set of goals for youth theatre. David and I were both passionate about using the arts as a means for diverse groups of young people to have meaningful dialogue around community issues. We agreed with applied-drama scholar and practitioner Helen Nicholson's belief that, "Drama provides a powerful opportunity to ask questions about whose stories have been customarily told, whose have been accepted as truth, and to redress the balance by telling alternate stories or stories from different perspectives" (2005: 63). Nicholson gets at the heart of our artistic philosophy: how can we tell stories from multiple perspectives to reflect our diverse students and communities? While I fully wanted to live out Nicholson's beliefs, devising an original youth-theatre play proved to be a process where strongly held beliefs had to be negotiated with the real-life action of performance and its related deadlines.

Working collaboratively as Teaching Artists

One of the reasons I enjoyed being a Teaching Artist at People's Light was that I had the opportunity to create projects with multiple talented artists.

The product created by our team reflected our philosophical belief that thoughtful art is created by many different voices, rather than one person's vision. We encouraged the students to work as a strong ensemble, and we needed to model that in our process of creating each performance piece. Our ensemble had to negotiate bumpy terrain, including our collective vision, the continuation of the students' growth in performance-skills training, time, money and logistics. Traditional, hierarchy, teaching methods were set aside, and a collaborative group-devised process was employed to honor our unique goal.

There were several benefits and challenges in working with a team of Teaching Artists while devising an original piece. The biggest benefit was adding multiple areas of expertise to the process. Because we worked on several projects together, Director of Education, David Bradley, assigned various roles according to our skills. In our team we had people who specialized in playwriting, music, movement, stage management, teaching and directing.

In addition to our teaching-artist expertise contributions, we were each challenged to work on an area that was not necessarily our strength. One of the things I most enjoyed at People's Light was that we were encouraged to grow and expand our skills on each project. For example, I was put in charge of a nonlinear, theme-based, devised section of the play. My brain works in a very realistic/linear manner, so working on this piece challenged me to work in new ways as an artist.

As a teacher and artist I felt both successful and challenged as a member of the production team. At two specific points in the process my beliefs in the 'third space', where art-making and meaning were co-constructed, were challenged by the practical realities of the production process. The first interruption came during the scene I was in charge of directing. In this scene, we developed unique neighborhood characters that struggled with conflicts large and small. The students eventually created a scene that explored what an ideal neighborhood could look like: where people connect with one another in meaningful ways. I set up an atmosphere where I felt like the students and I were making discoveries together about our theme. However, our process felt like a lopsided tennis match. I would set up an activity; they would respond with brilliant, thoughtful improvisations and ideas. Then it was my job to mold their ideas into the next stage of the devising process, but I was artistically stuck. What happens when you have a strong philosophical setup, but struggle to implement ideas in practice?

Our production date was approaching and I finally had to humbly admit that I was lost in the process. This took incredible courage for me. I was assigned one specific scene and I wanted it to be a piece I was proud to create. This was the one part of the show that I could officially say that was my specific contribution. The scene was created out of a simple machine game exercise. The beginning process of devising the scene was inventive and creative, but as we progressed, I had a difficult time with the nonlinear, nonrealistic structure of the piece. After many attempts to fix the scene, I had to do what was best for the performance and ask for help from my colleagues. Part of me wanted to stay in the brainstorming stage with the students because it felt safe and naturally creative. However, as one of the directors on this project, it was ultimately my job to make sure that they arrived successfully at the end of the production process. When I allowed my ego to get out of the way and focused on solving the problem, I realized that I had an entire team of amazing Teaching Artists at my disposal to help make the scene a success. What was it about the stress of a final production that stirred a sense of insecurity in me? Was it the fear that people would judge me as an artist? If you fail in the classroom, you often get another chance to make it better the next day. However, if a scene fails in a performance, judgment is often placed on the artists and the creative leadership. Perhaps, it was this fear of judgment that paralyzed my problem-solving. In the end, David helped to make a few adjustments and the scene, finally, worked.

The second time the 'third space' philosophy was difficult to embrace came further into the devising process. A challenge in devising is that it can be difficult to know when to transition from the brainstorming phase to the final decision-making phase. In *Making a Leap: Theatre of Empowerment*, practitioners Sara Clifford and Anna Herrmann encourage directors of devised work to purposefully and transparently transition between the brainstorm phase and the production phase of the rehearsal process (1999: 162). At one point in the process, I felt a strong sense that the ensemble was ready to move forward to the production process. The open-ended improvisation-based work was exciting to watch each day, but my question was: "To what end? What were we generating all of this material for?" I brought my concern up at one of our daily meetings. At the time, we were all working on multiple projects at the theatre and finding an extended amount of concentrated time to dedicate to any one project was nearly impossible. Our devised production needed careful attention and David took my advice and came back a few days later with a map that would guide us beautifully to our final performance. As soon as he created the outline of the performance I felt like we all had a clearer sense of where the piece was headed. The students and the Teaching Artists could finally collaborate toward a common vision. As a team we activated praxis in our work—the clarification of what story we wanted to tell, and why, enabled us to figure out how to move our play forward.

This moment was difficult for me as a member of the ensemble of Teaching Artists. Prior to my time at People's Light, I had always directed devised pieces by myself. I was used to being the director in charge of the entire production. Because I played a more supportive role in this process, I did not feel that it was my job to dictate the various stages of our rehearsals.

Why was I able to make this suggestion during our process? David was my boss, and the official director of the project. In a traditional production process, my role would be to follow the director's lead. As with any theatre production process, it is tricky to know when to take a leadership role and when to take a supportive role. It was only because of the ensemble-based philosophy at People's Light, and because we embraced the egalitarian nature behind the 'third space' philosophy, that I felt a sense of agency to share my thoughts on the process. David and I had a very open and honest relationship. Because of this trust, our discussions focused on the needs of the students or the goals of the project, and not on our own personal agendas. We had worked on several projects together and we had incredible respect for one another as teachers and as artists. Since my suggestion was not a criticism, but rather an observation of a need to clarify how to move the piece forward, David was receptive to my idea. I was honored that he took my suggestion and happy to see our play progress in a significant way.

The process of working collaboratively with a group of Teaching Artists is a roller coaster ride like any other production process. As an experienced Teaching Artist, I am strongly grounded in my philosophy that drama-based pedagogy is one of the best ways to create a democratic, egalitarian classroom for students to explore, discover and create. On the process/product continuum, devising demands that you honor both ends of the spectrum. As an individual and as a group of Teaching Artists, in this project, we collaboratively embraced the beauty of the process stage and returned to our core philosophies as we pushed towards the product stage. We discovered, through moments of frustration and clarity, how to unlock the potential in our students and in each other by being honest and supporting one another in moments of need. I collected notes from all of the Teaching Artists in a daily journal of our process. Each day we documented our activities, moments we wanted to keep for the production, thoughts on the students' progress, and ideas of where to move the process forward. This written dialogue on busy days forced us to stop, contemplate, analyze and make important decisions about the progress of the students, the production and how our work could best facilitate these needs.

Embracing praxis as part of our daily routine allowed this group of Teaching Artists the necessary reflection time to balance artistry, teaching and student development. What I learned in the process of *I Come From …* is that the moments of discomfort, when I felt completely lost, became the times that moved our process forward the most. I found that I did not have to abandon my process-centered philosophy in order to cross the bridge to final production. Moreover, my philosophic process-based beliefs were key to the collaborative creation of the final product. As a group of Teaching Artists we positioned students as collaborators in the theatre-making process. Their words, their thoughts, their movements created the final production. As *teachers*, our job was to create the atmosphere where this kind of magical exploration could happen. As *artists*, our job was to help the students mold their thoughts into a piece that could be shared with the wider community.

Megan Alrutz

PLAYING AT PRAXIS: LOCATING YOUTH VOICES IN HISTORY

> We hope to become better than our parents.
> Hope. Hope. Hope ...
>
> (Alrutz, Reitz-Yeager and Brendel Horn 2008)

This was only the beginning. And the lines repeated in my mind for months as I worked with a group of third and fourth-grade students to prepare, perform and produce a series of digital stories as an extension of their social-studies unit on African-American history. For this piece, a small group of young people sang their words into a microphone in our makeshift recording studio. The entirety of the recorded narrative later became the voiceover track for a digital story—in this case, a one-minute digital movie or performance collage for which students edited poetic, personal narratives with still photographs and background music.

My current work as a Teaching Artist combines digital storytelling (see Lambert 2009, 2010) and applied theatre in an effort to diversify the stories and experiences that get foregrounded in schools and communities. I've come to rely on digital storytelling as a tool for connecting with young people's interests in technology and inviting them to contribute, rather than simply consume, ideas about what it means to be a young person today. For this project, the Extended Research Classroom (ERC), I worked with a Teaching Artist team that included Traci Reitz, Elizabeth Brendel Horn, Jennifer Adams and Victor Randle. We combined creative writing, theatre devising and digital storytelling as a process for students of color to actively represent the past while constructing new narratives, with/in a social-studies unit on African-American history. As students researched the lives of prominent African-American figures, such as Rosa Parks, Martin Luther King, Jr. and Barack Obama, we used performance and media tools to explore not only what made these individuals significant from an historical perspective, but also to reflect on how these histories related to the students' lives. The resulting digital postcards, digital stories and recorded interviews became assets, or digital scenes, which we edited into a 30-minute digital video called *Hoping for a Better Future*.

While this project achieved many of our intended goals, it also raised questions about the various ways that our approach to praxis can help expand who and what gets valued in/by history. By inviting students' lived experiences into the classroom, and helping students place their stories in conversation with 'official' histories of famous African-American leaders, I believed I was changing the ways that young people participate in history. After all, we were democratizing the social studies classroom and curriculum, reflecting on notions of responsible representation and dialoguing about the content and quality of our creative choices. In (re)examining this project several years later, I am struck by some of the missing links in my approach to praxis within the ERC. Despite our commitment to reflective practice and locating youth voices in history, we did not always engage youth around larger contexts and systems that ultimately determine if and how they (and their experiences) count in/as history. With this essay, I reflect on several stages of the ERC project, looking to articulate a critically engaged approach to teaching artist praxis.

Playing at praxis: Action and reflection in teaching artist pedagogy

Applied-theatre scholar Helen Nicholson (2005) describes praxis as a dynamic process of integrating action and reflection, while educator Paulo Freire's writing (1993) emphasizes praxis as a process for transforming the world. As a reflective Teaching Artist, I work at my own pedagogical praxis, consciously reflecting on and revising my thinking (insight-building) and my doing (facilitation and performance-making) in order to improve my facilitation and, hopefully, to some extent, the lives of young people. Moreover, I aim to engage students in a manner that similarly supports their own active and reflective performance practices.

At the beginning of the ERC, I focused on developing an inclusive and engaged pedagogy. Our Teaching Artists team partnered with two classroom teachers. Together we worked to support students in reflecting on their lives, as well as their creative choices within a digital-storytelling process. To this end, praxis underpinned our pedagogical process. The Teaching Artist team engaged in a cyclical process of action and reflection, which kept our facilitation responsive to students' interests, experiences and studies. Most of our daily activities evolved in direct response to our experiences with the students. Throughout each digital-storytelling session, I kept mental notes on students' personal interests, such as family, cars and nature, as well as repeated themes in their work, including hope and the desire for a better future. I also reflected on how students participated in theatre games and warms-ups, such as where competition impacted (positively and negatively) student motivation and how the structure of various activities supported the students' storytelling and collaboration skills. As a team, our attention to students' ideas and skills allowed us to help students connect their personal stories and experiences with the history-based narratives they studied in school. Regularly reflecting on students' work and our own facilitation process directly shaped the projects we pursued with students, the content we explored in the room, and the ways we motivated and guided student participation.

Throughout the ERC, I remember feeling excited about our approach to teaching-artist praxis. I was inspired by the amount of time we invested in reflecting on our work with the participants and in developing and revising our pedagogy. Our intentionality around praxis also helped me feel connected and accountable to the students; they noticed when and how our facilitation responded (or didn't) to their ideas and they readily shared their thoughts about how we approached the creative process. Simultaneously, the students' accountability to the work seemed to shift. As the project progressed, they were more prepared for and invested in each session. They focused throughout the sometimes-tedious process of editing digital stories, and they seriously debated form and content issues within their projects. At the time, I was confident that our approach to teaching-artist praxis was responsive, responsible and engaged.

Supporting student praxis: Locating youth voices in history

I also began this project with an eye toward student praxis. I wanted to create a reflective and generative framework for students to locate—both find and place—themselves (their lives, stories, images, perspectives) in their school-based, social studies curriculum. Our Teaching Artist team guided the group through a reiterative process of creative action and personal reflection. We invited students to research and reflect on their history curriculum; relate that curriculum to their own experiences; and then create and reflect on a variety of artistic products, including digital photographs, embodied image work and written narratives. Specifically, students used their bodies to create physical images of their research on African-American leaders. They engaged in story circles and improvisation exercises to reflect on moments from their own lives that connected to their studies. Through these types of embodied and verbal-reflection techniques, students also considered and debated the qualities that make a valuable leader and what made particular individuals significant in history. Each of these reflective practices, many of which were simultaneously creative actions, led students to name and then visually represent major themes that guided our digital storytelling work. Thoughtful individual and group work underpinned the students' creative praxis. (See the following chart for a sample of how students integrated action and reflection within their digital-storytelling process.)

At this stage in our process, I was excited about our intentionality around student praxis. We were inviting students to create new work and to reflect on themselves and their creative practice within the context of history-based studies. Students were eager to participate in the work and they readily brought their personal stories, experiences and perspectives into the room. They reflected on parallels between their own lives and some of the more 'official' biographies from their school curriculum. As they developed original digital and performance materials, they documented school-sanctioned histories in a way that included their own lives. In my mind, students' praxis was working to broaden traditional approaches to history and curriculum; it offered a reflexive framework for young people to participate in history-making.

Elements of praxis in students' creative process	Description of the students' creative work
Reflection (with some creative action)	Using a variety of drama-based techniques, students analyzed and discussed themes running through their research and classroom studies on African-American history. From these reflections, students decided on a theme to explore in their first digital project: hope.
Creative action (with some reflection on self)	Students visually represented the notion of hope. They captured and edited digital images to signify one of their own hopes. Reflecting on their feelings about hope, the students created digital images of themselves in relationship to hope. These images included digitally altered photos of themselves in fancy sports cars, with family and religious figures, and in a variety of leisure landscapes such as the beach or the mountains.

Reflection (on creative actions of self and other)	Students then gave an informal presentation on their work, explaining to the group why and how their digital images represented their hope. Several students, for example, shared that they located themselves in a fancy sports car because they hoped for financial success in their future. One student shared that she hoped Obama would become president and her dad would get out of jail. At this stage, we encouraged students to reflect on their own definitions of hope. This led to meta-reflections on the relationship between success and money, as well as the difference between desire and hope.
Creative action (with some reflection)	Students responded to questions about their work in particular and about the theme of hope in general. Reflecting on the group's feedback, students further edited their digital images to include a short voiceover or some language-based text to more explicitly name what hope meant to them.

When well-intentioned praxis is not enough

Despite my commitment to reflective and reflexive practice in the ERC, after the project ended I was able to see some of the more problematic implications of my approach to praxis in this project. My focus on inclusive pedagogical goals, such as locating students' lived experiences in the classroom and next to formally sanctioned histories, proved somewhat limited and thus limiting in our goals to participate in (re)making history. In many ways my approach to praxis (students' and my own) failed to engage youth around how power functions in and through the form and content of our project, as well as the form and content of history. We reflected quite a bit on responsible representation of our personal stories and what it means to show and tell our experiences for an outside audience. We also reflected on how students' lived experiences intersected with and diverged from those in history. Unfortunately, our conversations and reflections rarely addressed critical and systemic contexts, such as racism, sexism and other hidden curriculums that directly inform students' lived experiences and the histories they study.

Wendy Hesford (2009) draws on Henry Giroux (1992) to argue that critical pedagogies should "help students recognize the limits of their self-positioning and worldviews [...] and develop critical awareness of the power discourse instead of being subsumed by it" (60). In other words, teaching artist work that locates youth voices in the context of history is not enough; a critical approach to performance praxis requires that we explicitly develop students' (and our own) consciousness around the production of knowledge, specifically how making and performing history shapes our relationship to the past, present and future. While our digital storytelling project worked to value youth experiences and disrupt traditional power dynamics between teachers and students (as well as in the construction and transmission of history/knowledge), I rarely engaged students around how their/our/my own identity markers—such as race, class and gender—shape and are shaped by personal stories, histories and systems of power at large. The type and quality of reflection that I emphasized for students shaped a limited approach, view and critique of history. Our approach to praxis did not include reflections on how histories, official stories of the past/present, are made and reinforced, or how they ultimately shape our own understandings of ourselves and the world around us.

Critically engaged praxis

Critical pedagogue Joe Kincheloe (2004: 9) argues that "Anytime teachers develop a pedagogy, they are concurrently constructing a political vision." In other words, the process and products—the form and content—of our teaching-artist praxis shape what and whose stories count as official or valued knowledge. It also shapes how meaning and power is made or shared in the classroom. If I wish to truly change and expand who and what stories are represented in the whole of history, I must think about new ways of developing, archiving and distributing alternative histories performed in our creative spaces. I must work toward a critical performance praxis, a creative process of action and reflection that attends to the systems of power that shape the very institutions and values that we hope to shift.

Reflecting on this project and my unexamined ideas about praxis pushed me to further explore the relationship between critical contexts and personal reflection. My attention is now focused on how digital-storytelling praxis can critique, not simply represent or expand, our own and others' histories. I am becoming more attuned to how my own identity and privilege shapes my approach to praxis. I am also considering additional responsibilities that come with locating students' personal narratives in the context of history.

How else might I/we employ critical performance praxis to address why and how certain stories (their stories) get excluded from these histories in the first place?

In looking ahead, I want to imagine how critical engagements with history can help broaden the impact and distribution of alternative histories—those of youth and other marginalized populations. I want to rethink responsibly in my pedagogy and practice. I want to facilitate not just praxis, but critical performance praxis.

I hear the youths' voices in my head again. Hope, hope, hope.
This is just the beginning.

Christina Marín

ENACTING *LIDERAZGO*: WHERE DRAMA PRAXIS AND LATINO LEADERSHIP INTERSECT

In 2006, I was invited to lead a session for the United States Hispanic Leadership Institute (USHLI) titled Latino Theatre for Social Change. Located in Chicago, this educational leadership organization hosts a national conference offering young Latinos/as the opportunity to learn important skills including political organizing within their communities, interviewing for employment and applying for scholarships to help support their educations. The expectation for my session was the traditional, presentational form of theatre, using actors and a script to portray social justice issues affecting the Latino community.

I had recently directed José Casas's ethnodrama *14* in Phoenix, Arizona, and was preparing excerpts from the play for the NYU Forum on Ethnotheatre and Theatre for Social Justice, and thought this was a perfect fit for the target audience at USHLI. The play addresses the contentious binational immigration issues plaguing the US–Mexico border through monologues based on interviews and research. I directed a Latina student actress in several of the monologues and we traveled to Chicago to participate in the conference.

The session was very well received. Attendees sat in the audience and watched the play, applauded when it was over, and even engaged in a lively talkback about the social justice issues after the presentation. So why did I feel like something was missing? What was this session lacking? As the director of the piece, I had the opportunity to observe the audience as they watched and reacted to the play. They were engaged, yes, but their passive positions prevented them from having any impact in the moment. We could talk about the issues, but I wanted them to be more deeply involved in the action. I needed to reflect on what might work better and make a proposal to the conference organizers for the institute the following year. My own experience studying theatre served to feed my reflection and I turned to what had been most inspirational in my development as a Latina theatre educator.

During my doctoral studies, I was introduced to Augusto Boal's Theatre of the Oppressed techniques and discovered that this work was rooted in the liberatory, educational theories and practices of Paulo Freire. Boal developed the Theatre of the Oppressed techniques recognizing the potential in Freire's claim that men and women have the power to reflect on their world and take action to transform it. Through Theatre of the Oppressed we engage a praxical approach, employing theatre to reflect on the world in its present form and transform that which we wish to change. In my own words, praxis is the symbiotic relationship between the actions we engage in, followed by a critical and theoretical reflection on those actions through dialogue, culminating in the actions we pursue as a result of that reflection. This correlation between theory and practice gives us a heightened sense of our purpose in the world. Through praxis we become active agents in our own education and catalysts for social change.

I reflected on our experience in Chicago and realized that the Theatre of the Oppressed work I had engaged in during my graduate studies would be an even better fit for the conference attendees, because we could address the issues that they found important in their communities through an immersion in action. What better way for them to be able to benefit from the transformational insights I had gleaned from Freire and Boal's writings than to engage in these theories and practices in a dialogical framework? And, as luck would have it, I realized I wouldn't have to reinvent the wheel; I already had a model to work from. In 2002, I submitted a proposal to present a theatre workshop at the National Council of La Raza's (NCLR) Líderes Youth Leadership Summit in Miami Beach, Florida. The goals of the annual meeting were very similar to those of USHLI, including offering leadership and teamwork skills, discussing community engagement and empowerment, and networking with other Latinos/as from around the country. My session was titled "Can You Change the Image You See? Using Augusto Boal's Image Theatre to Create a Dialogue Among Latino Youth Regarding Issues of Identity." The workshop interrogated identity construction with Latino youth and became the cornerstone for my dissertation research.

As a Latina, I wanted to create an atmosphere in this session that would be inviting to the target audience. The various academic and professional conferences I had attended in the past seemed to be exclusionary and lacked the pluralistic demographic that I believe is important for young people of color entering higher education, and the work force, to see. I wanted the young Latinos/as at the Líderes Summit to feel welcomed in a way I never had at these other conferences. I also recognized that I had to get the crowd warmed up to play theatre games. So I plugged in my CD player and as the conference attendees filed into the room, I turned up the volume on the song *Latinos* by Proyecto Uno. The rhythms of this Dominican American *merenrap* group channeled merengue, rap, techno, dancehall reggae and hip-hop and as some of the participants filed into the rows of seats with confused looks, others resisted this passive stance and began subtly keeping time to the beat in the aisles. My goal was for these young people to bring their heartfelt, physical and emotional identities with them into the session, and it seemed to be working. In most (if not all) of the other sessions they had been attending, even at this conference, they were asked to sit facing a presenter at the front of the room, who often brought their best game through a PowerPoint presentation and shared his or her expertise in lecture format, just like in the traditional classroom. I wanted us to be able to break with tradition and do things our own way. I am inspired by Maxine Greene's suggestion that, "[our workshops ...] ought to resound with the voices of articulate young people in dialogues [that are] always incomplete because there is always more to be discovered and more to be said" (1995: 43). In order to break from the traditional, unidirectional pedagogy that many of these young people are used to, we had to open a space in which we could co-construct meanings through the work together.

We warmed up with several theatre games that got the young people up and out of their seats and moving about the room. Through Image Theatre techniques we sculpted our bodies to express the negative stereotypes society has layered over Latino/a identity in today's world. These young Latino leaders have no problem reading the world in which they live; they know many people expect them to drop out of school, join gangs, get pregnant, do drugs and land in early graves. But they have a different version of the world, one that they want to write in their own voice. As Paulo Freire and Donaldo Macedo reminds us, "On the one hand, students have to become literate about their histories, experiences and the culture of their immediate environments. On the other hand, they must also appropriate those codes and cultures of the dominant spheres so they can transcend their own environments" (1987: 47). I believe the Theatre of the Oppressed opens the door for these emerging Latinos/as leaders to navigate this complex terrain.

My role as facilitator of the work is to mediate an experience in which the participants take ownership of the process. Their ideas, their questions and their concerns are paramount. Image Theatre invites participants to use their bodies to express abstract concepts and realistic projections corporeally. They work collaboratively, in small groups, to sculpt visual images in silence that tell stories about the real world. At the Líderes Summit in Miami Beach, the participants presented images that depicted teenage pregnancy and the tensions that might arise in a family as a result, and gang violence, among others. After the images were presented to the rest of the group we engaged in a dialogue about what the participants saw. This reflects the form of literacy described by Freire and Macedo (1987) as a reading of the world, through which the participants in the workshop share what they perceive to be the messages portrayed through the image. As the discussion progressed, the participants realized that not everyone's interpretation matched, even though they were looking at the same phenomenon. This made the conversation infinitely more interesting. At that point, conjuring the title of the workshop, I asked the participants, "Can you change the image you see?" We then worked toward resculpting the existing images to reflect a world in which they were able to intentionally and successfully combat the oppressive structures portrayed in their stationary scenes: converting the seemingly static circumstances into dynamic moments suggestive of change. This interactive sequence of action, reflection and transformation is inherent in the collaborative nature of the Theatre of the Oppressed and reflects the liberatory praxis described by Freire. Through this session we used theatre as a pedagogical framework to reflect upon the hackneyed images society seems determined to imagine for us, and we reimagined a transformed future in which we are the authors of our own lives. Theatre was the tool that allowed me to illustrate the concept of praxis for these young leaders of the future.

In 2003, I returned to the Líderes Youth Leadership Summit, this time in Austin, Texas, with a session titled, "Will the Real Latinas Please Stand Up? Using Theatre for Social Change Techniques to Interrogate Forms of Social Oppression Experienced by Latinas." I saw the way the youth responded to the Image Theatre work in Florida and wanted to continue to develop these interactive forms to invite more Latinos/as to take ownership of their versions of the world. This workshop employed Forum Theatre anti-model scenarios and invited audience members to intervene in the negative situations being portrayed onstage in order to rewrite reality through diverse strategies and tactics. The first scenario, "Shades of White," depicted two cousins of Mexican heritage, one with a more traditional understanding of her Latina identity, and the other with a more progressive sense of herself. As the scene progresses the traditional Latina belittles her cousin for not speaking enough Spanish, not having enough curves and listening to *rock en Español* (Spanish Rock). The audience members who replaced the second cousin in this scene came back with responses centered on individuality, and the fact that there are many ways to express Latina identity. The second scene, "Who's to Blame?," depicted a mother who finds contraceptive pills and condoms in her teenage daughter's room. She is devastated and demands answers from her daughter.

In Forum Theatre, participants have the ability to intervene and rehearse different possible tactics to confront the oppressor in the scene and work toward social change. While some strategies may seem feasible for some of the participants, we must recognize that, much like the images we interpreted through diverse lenses, each strategy will be perceived differently. Some tactics will work for some people, and yet others may exacerbate the problem depicted in the scene. Each participant must decide for themselves, through an individual praxis, as we recognize that there is no definitive, formulaic solution to many of the oppressions we face in life.

One of the most eye-opening interventions performed in the second scene, "Who's to Blame?" was actually offered by a young man. I had to think on my feet and recognize the gender issues at play, heightened because of the cultural construction of *machismo* in the Latino community. My gut instinct told me to invite this young man up onstage to play out his strategic contribution in the role of the daughter. After the initial giggles subsided, this young man committed to his role and asked 'her' mother why 'her' older brother was allowed, and even encouraged, to prove his manhood by having multiple girlfriends and partners. Along with the majority of the audience, my jaw dropped. This participant showed us how the multiple layers of gender politics and double standards play out in our own families and communities. My understanding of the potential that the Theatre of the Oppressed offers us was heightened by this experience.

In 2007, when I was invited to return to USHLI and present the Latino Theatre for Social Change session, I reflected on my experiences with the young people in Miami and Austin, and proposed a bilingual, interactive theatre workshop rooted in the Theatre of the Oppressed techniques. For the past six years I have been facilitating these workshops at USHLI and I learn so much every time I am there. Through theatre activities and critical conversations, we unpack how the participants envision themselves as leaders in their communities and in the country. They have been my teachers as much (if not more) as I have been theirs. They challenge me as much as I challenge them. We work together in the limited time we have each year to address the numerous issues we are still facing today as Latinos/as.

Finally, in reflecting on my practice at these conferences, I recognize a huge challenge of my work within this context. Because each of these workshops lasts for only 75 minutes, I have been challenged to carefully gauge the time we spend on every exercise and on the praxis through dialogue we engage in after each activity. I am constantly making choices in the moment based on the responses offered by the group, the number of participants and even the gender balance in the room. I have found that different group dynamics are better suited to certain games and exercises and if one isn't working I have a myriad of alternatives from which to choose. Ultimately, my experiences facilitating Theatre of the Oppressed workshops at Latino Leadership conferences have taught me many important lessons and I continue to learn as I refine and remodel these sessions every year. I always prepare for the unexpected, but I bring my experience with me into the room. I always emphasize the fact that while we are engaged in each game or exercise the participants should be critically conscious of how the activity reflects circumstances and situations we face in the real world, and they must also respect that everyone in the room may not interpret the experience in the same way. I design the workshops to actively engage the hearts and minds of the participants, and remain open to every opportunity I have to learn more!

Peter B. Duffy

ESSENTIALIZING RESIDENCIES: COLLECTING TROPHIES OF THE OPPRESSED

Before coming to teach at the University of South Carolina, I was the Director of Education and Community Outreach for the Irondale Ensemble Project in Brooklyn, New York. Irondale is one of the country's oldest, continuously running, ensemble theatre companies. As the education director, I didn't get much time to teach in schools anymore and I missed it. So when I had the chance to work with a high-school English teacher in the South Bronx, I jumped at it. That twinge of excitement borne from working in the South Bronx reminded me of something that took me a long time to understand— we are not where we teach. It is a curious thing about being a Teaching Artist but the quality of our work is often judged by where we work, not always by what we do with young people. The impulse to work there belied an insight I gained years before at a conference. Two conference participants engaged in an odd, ego-driven game of one-upmanship. The conversation went something like this:

I work with kids in a youth detention center.

Nice, I work with men in a maximum security prison.

Cool, I work also with survivors of sexual assault.

Wow, that's really valuable. I work with orphaned Sudanese refugees.

These two went on for some time trying to demonstrate how valuable their work was by attaching it to negative stereotypes and pathologized communities. It was as if these two talented and well-meaning Teaching Artists validated their own work through displaying the trophies of the oppressed they've collected through years of solid practice. It occurred to me then that when the work becomes more about the practitioner's identity and less about creating partnership with individuals within a community, the impact of the work is lost.

The critical pedagogue and cultural educator, Paulo Freire, encouraged teachers to reflect on their teaching process in order to transform it. Freire called this transformative process *praxis* (Freire 1993: 68). Raines and Shadow illustrate the difference between teaching and reflective practice with the terms *reflective practice* and *routine action* (Raines and Shadow 1995: 271). Reflective practice quickly becomes routine action when Teaching Artists forget Maxine Greene's notion of "I am not yet" (Greene 1998: 253). We cannot *be* reflective practitioners; we are *becoming* reflective practitioners.

Early in my career, I was prone to forgetting this notion of becoming. I had all the right philosophy, read the right books, worked in the right 'oppressed neighborhoods' and trained as a Teaching Artist for one of the premiere theatre-in-education organizations in New York City. I had the complete resume to 'do good.' And yet, in spite of what should have helped me know better, my studied process was stuck in process mode and did not move to the deep reflection required to transform my practice.

The Bronx residency

The train ride from my apartment in Brooklyn to the Bronx's Longwood neighborhood took about an hour and 20 minutes. That time on the train was ideal to plan, prepare, rehearse, review and reflect. But my reflection was far removed from praxis because, when I was honest with myself, I was litigating the past. The time on the train became a time to replay what went well (for which I took credit) and what did not work (for which I assigned blame). There were several moments that could have made a difference, but because I thought about them at the level of routine action, the start of the residency did not go well.

Heading for my first day, I stood sandwiched in a subway car and reread the play the English teacher, Justin (pseudonym), and I were going to explore with his students. Justin chose William Wells Brown's play *The Escape: Or a Leap for Freedom*. The play mirrors Brown's experience of living under the tyranny of slavery, which was riddled with brutality, sexual violence and a complete disregard for family, religion and sovereignty over one's body, education and aspirations. The story is a pointed critique of the dehumanizing regime of slavery and of the hypocrisy that existed among slave owners in pre-Civil War America. Reading the characters' words in the play, I imagined the young men and women in the class hearing themselves in its words. I thought they would translate the unjust economic and social forces that oppressed the characters and recognize similar systems in their own contemporary contexts. I thought they would latch on to the themes of poverty, exploitation, a lack of access to education and to the strict mores around love. I thought they would be dying to confront these issues in their own lives. As the train rattled underneath oppressed neighborhoods, I heard the play's contemporary echoes all the louder. I was convinced that this play was the perfect piece to use in this, one of the nation's most economically disadvantaged neighborhoods. I felt my mind swell with dramatic possibilities, and from the very moment I learned of the project, I planned how I could help student disassemble their internalized oppressions through this play.

My plans, however, only took ten minutes in the classroom to unravel. The students were as eager to work on this play as I would be to dig my way to the center of the earth with a tablespoon. In retrospect, it is clear that I was too enamored of the opportunity to unpack these ideas with 'kids from the Bronx' to consider what that actually meant. I was preparing to work with students in order to 'learn 'em up' and to invite them to listen to a dialogical negotiation of meaning-making between the text and me. I was preparing to do the exact opposite of what Freire meant when he said teachers, "learning in their teaching is observed to the extent that, humble and open, teachers find themselves continually ready to rethink what has been thought and to revise their positions" (1998: 17). I was planning and developing liberating lessons to enact upon students in order to help them see just how oppressed they are.

To be sure, Longwood is a neighborhood that knows hardship and bears the scars of marginalization. And yet, the children playing in the elementary school yard don't play like marginalized children. They don't scream and run and jump and giggle like marginalized kids. The teenagers holding hands and sneaking a kiss before school don't slip into marginalized love. Despite this place's hardships, images of promise, glimpses of beauty and examples of generosity were as easy to find here as boarded-up buildings, broken windows and graffiti. The bricks of indifference, poverty, racism, substandard schools and unemployment create walls that constrain communities like Longwood. But all walls can be scaled.

I arrived about an hour early and walked through the neighborhood to see firsthand what the students had to endure by living here. Of course, during my walk, I essentialized the experiences of these *poor kids*. I resented the litter-strewn alleys I passed. I regretted the long line to the church's daily soup kitchen. I tut-tutted at the lack of fresh fruit and juice in the bodegas that only offered kids sugared sodas and snack cakes. I leapt to conclusions and judged the experiences of the students.

248

I entered the classroom that morning planning on using Image Theatre, a process in Augusto Boal's Theatre of the Oppressed that encourages participants to use their bodies to create still images of ideas, thoughts, emotions and/or stories (1992). I thought we should end our first day together by creating tableaux of their experiences in the neighborhood. This could make for an easier entry into personalizing the concepts in *The Escape.*

The classroom teacher, Justin, introduced me and informed the students that we'd be working together a couple of times a week on the play. We'd be using theatre as a process to inspire writing, get the play up on its feet and create a deeper understanding of the themes, issues and histories contained within its pages. The students were mostly engaged with their phone/personal devices, which were all the rage in 2008, called Sidekicks. They looked up only briefly to size up this 'Teaching Artist' in their room and then quickly returned their gazes to their phones. I had been a Teaching Artist for a long time by this point and I didn't expect rose-petal pathways strewn before me, but the utter disconnection was a bit of a surprise.

I asked the students to join me so that we could do a few name games and get-to-know-you exercises. There was a palpable reluctance in the room and I distinctly remember thinking if *they* only knew how committed *I* was to addressing these issues with them they'd be much more inclined to join in. The students knew immediately what took me a while to realize: I came to the classroom for me and not for them. Eventually pity moved three students out of their seats. The four of us stood there for a minute and then a student leader in the room badgered a couple of others and they begrudgingly joined in.

I wrote off their unwillingness to participate with what I interpreted as a lack of understanding. Convinced that they would *catch on*, I was eager to jump into *The Escape* with them. Even though I knew better, a silent part of me assumed that because the play was about slavery and racism, the students would be on board with charging through the play like General Sherman, leaving racism smoldering in our wake. The students did not warm up to the play. They read it because that was the expectation, but the play was not the transformative experience I imagined. (Someone was being transformed, but it was not the students.) What I thought was praxis was only routine action repeated and repeated. The repetition of a bad idea is not praxis. It is simply a repurposing of products that are not working. In order for transformation to happen, my own culpability had to be recognized. It was not enough that I wanted to 'do good.' I had to be in dialogue, which, according to Freire (1993: 69),

is the encounter between men [sic], mediated by the world, in order to name the world. Hence, dialogue cannot occur between those who want to name the world and those who do not wish this naming—between those who deny others the right to speak their word and those whose right to speak has been denied them.

Without dialogue, I was insisting on lessons that had little consequence and relation to their lives. Who knew that critical pedagogy (well, critical pedagogy done poorly) could be so oppressive? Even though I knew better, I was seduced by the gratification of feeding my ego. The need to collect the trophy of working in an alternative high-school in the South Bronx superseded my ability to work in fellowship, and not invite them to join mine.

I think I have enough distance on these experiences to be able to say that I was interested in this work because it had the potential to legitimize my identity as a Teaching Artist. Having successful experiences in 'challenging neighborhoods' raised the stature of my expertise and talent. It is one thing to say that I had a successful drama lesson in an affluent suburb of New York City, it's another thing to say that I was able to work with other populations like incarcerated youth, homeless families and high-school students at an alternative high-school in the South Bronx.

Reflection plus action

That hour and 20 minute train ride back and forth from my neighborhood to Longwood ended up being a meditation in reflective practice. Standing in the circle with about six students and seeing ten or so still seated unwilling to join me, I realized what I had done. I acquired an aerial view of the landscape, and didn't know it. The students in Longwood were about as eager to uncover their oppressions through the lens of slavery as I was to understand my own oppressions through the guise of the Irish potato famine. True, it is a thread woven into the tapestry of self, but it is only a thread.

There is no room for the ego in reflective practice. The ego is something that demands to be protected, nurtured and fed. If a Teaching Artist's practice is ego-driven then the reflection on the process will lead to essentialized conclusions. Because the residency started out poorly, my ego could have ascribed blame to the kids, or the school, or the neighborhood or any number of reasons. There have been times in my career when I confused reflective practice with scapegoating. Now, I endeavor to remember that I am becoming a reflective practitioner and that I cannot confuse compassion with essentializing. Compassion comes from fellowship. Essentializing comes from taking an hour and a half train ride to the residency and not being changed by the people of that neighborhood.

I still do a lot of work in the so-called marginalized communities, but I don't do it to change lives or to dismantle oppressions. I do it to listen. I do it to learn about my own teaching practice. I do it to learn how I can be present, challenging and vulnerable with students who are and are not like me. I still believe in the transformative power of critical pedagogy, but I believe more in the power of being present and honest with young people. I believe in admitting that learning and teaching are hard, and working co-intentionally with others is scary, emotionally tenuous and uncharted. In order to work with young people as a Teaching Artist with integrity and inquiry, I had to learn to map the community by following where students lead. Too many times I dragged students to where I thought the destination was. But that was an ego collecting trophies; that was not a Teaching Artist learning how to humanize my corner of the world.

PART 3

The Reflexive Practitioner

Chapter 8

Participatory Action Research

Research is a life project, not a one-time exploration—no matter how grand that exploration might be. The artist returns to the work to push further and deeper into that initial investigation.

(Jones 2008: 206)

HOW DO I BECOME A REFLEXIVE PRACTITIONER?

Teaching Artists often work alone, with limited time and support structures to conduct formal assessments of their work. However, as discussed in Chapter 6, assessment can be used by any practitioner at multiple times in their process. All Teaching Artists have their own living laboratory for participatory action research: "an enquiry by the self into the self, undertaken in company with others acting as research participants and critical learning partners" (McNiff and Whitehead 2002: 15).

Action research is a systematic inquiry into one's own practice and research. In action research the teacher uses their discoveries to shape further research about their own practice (Riel 2010). Participatory action research (PAR), as detailed by educational researchers Stephen Kemmis and Mervyn Wilkinson, invites the teacher to research personal practice, but it also asks the teacher to pay attention to how the larger systems, or places of work, shape what and how they do what they do and to share their findings with others (1998: 21–36). PAR is an opportunity for you to help yourself become a better practitioner and to improve the quality of teaching artist work in the field.

The PAR process has the potential to shift a residency, project or program into a purposeful learning experience for the Teaching Artist and her participants. Each step of the PAR process can be embedded in the natural preparation, flow and conclusion of the typical teaching-artist project. PAR also creates a way for the teaching-artist to consider each of the core concepts argued for in this text. Through our proposed adaptation of PAR, the Teaching Artist will:

- Identify the context and consider INTENTIONALITY: The *What, Where, Who*, and *Why*?

- Construct a question related to QUALITY and ARTISTIC PERSPECTIVE: *What do I want to know?*
- Gather answers to the proposed question through a qualitative ASSESSMENT tool: *How will I answer my question?*
- Reflect upon and synthesize what is discovered to change practice: *What do I think about it?*
- Apply new knowledge to future work to activate PRAXIS and begin to consider the next inquiry: *What will I do with what I learned?*

To begin this process you'll need a large piece of blank paper, something to write with and a few pages of blank paper for notes (a computer screen works great too). For additional inspiration, add in a fellow Teaching Artist or two as co-thinkers and have a PAR-ty.

STEP 1: IDENTIFY THE CONTEXT AND INTENTIONS

What factors shape the specific context that I want to consider?

The what

Pick a drama/theatre learning experience. Ideally, you should select a project or residency with multiple sessions so you have the opportunity to observe potential shifts in attitude, skill or knowledge during the length of the project. It is also useful to select a project that includes some familiar element so you have some sense of expectation about what might happen. For example, the project might:

- Be in a familiar location (e.g. school, afterschool program or professional theatre, youth theatre program)
- Follow a familiar process (e.g. adapting short fiction to stage, exploring the industrial revolution through a process drama or creating a teen improv troupe)
- Or involve a familiar population (e.g. urban teenagers, English Language Learners, third graders, young women, preschool students or LGBTQ teenagers at a drop-in center)

Once you've identified the project, make a detailed list of *what* you will do in your selected drama/theatre learning experience. What are all the steps in this project, from the meetings with stakeholders or partners or supervisors as part of your preparation through the full implementation of the project? As an example, we will explore a teaching artist project at an elementary school throughout this chapter.

Example

What **is my drama/theatre learning experience?**

Program name: Performing Identity

Program description: Six-session in-school residency program for fourth and fifth graders, co-facilitated by a classroom teacher from the school and a local Teaching Artist.

General list of activities:

1) Meet with teacher to co-plan project, set times, goals and final sharing date/time. Set expectations for work that needs to happen outside of teaching artist sessions.

2) Session 1: Introduce Living Newspaper form, introductory, ensemble theatre games and first research assignment—find an article about your community in the paper. Reflect on session.

3) Session 2: Review ensemble theatre games—focus on body, learn tableau, share article research and create tableau image with selected text. Teach critical response methods for sharing work. Reflect on session.

4) Session 3: Review ensemble theatre games—focus on listening, discuss how to interview, practice interviewing and give community interview assignment. Reflect on session.

5) Session 4: Review ensemble theatre games—focus on voice and diction, share community assignments, stage ensemble performance using community assignments and share with critical response. Reflect on session.

6) Session 5: Vocal and physical warm-up, look at all material created, structure final performance, assign tasks, have a group-working session and create prop list. Reflect on session.

7) Session 6: Vocal and physical warm-up, rehearse sections, give feedback notes and assign final rehearsal tasks for work with teacher. Reflect on session.

8) Parents/caregivers, teachers and other project stakeholders attend final performance.

The where

To work with intentionality, you need a complete picture of your context. Often we don't realize how many different places and people impact what and how we do what we do as Teaching Artists. PAR asks us to identify the larger systems that surround our work. The hope is that once we begin to see how our actions are impacted and shaped by others we can begin to use our discoveries to shape our world. One way to see the relationships in our work is to build a map that identifies where practice is taking place and who is involved in each level of location and interaction.

Take a look at your list of activities. Where does the bulk of the work with the participants happen? Take out a blank piece of paper and write the key location in the center of your paper and draw a shape around it (a circle, a square, a heart or whatever you want). This is the start of the map of your specific location. Next, write in the larger work environments located outside and around the immediate location. Assign each level of the system a new shape. Label all of the locations to show how they are interrelated. Be as expansive as possible at this stage: list all possible places that are connected or could be connected to this drama learning experience.

Example

Where does the project take place?

I am a Teaching Artist whose work primarily occurs in *classrooms in a school*. The classroom where I will do my project is located in a school that received money to bring Teaching Artists into the elementary grades to support theatre education that wasn't being taught by a certified theatre teacher. The school is part of a school district that has funding from a new district-wide arts initiative. The arts initiative is looking at the arts as a way to increase student engagement, attendance, and improve test scores. The district uses state and national standards of education in arts and nonarts content areas that shape what I can do in the classroom. My work includes an oral-history research component, where students collect and stage articles and interviews from the local neighborhood about community issues to perform for the school and families.

    The *where* map example shown next includes the school, district and community as additional outside locations, each with their own needs and goals, that potentially impact my practice in a school classroom in different ways.

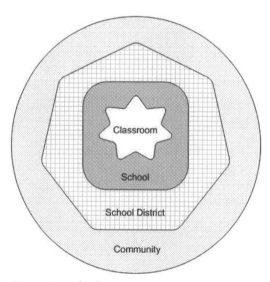

Figure 8: Example *where* map.

The who

Next, brainstorm who is in each layer of the picture. Who are the stakeholders—the people who impact, inform and participate in some way—in each of the 'where' locations listed? Look back at your list of activities. What people appear? Where are they located on your map? What additional people, not on your immediate list, shape what you do? Individual names or groups of people can be written in each location. It is important to be expansive. Include as many people and/or titles that are relevant to your work.

Example

Who **is involved in this project?**

The students in the classrooms where I work are primarily English Language Learners and almost all are students of color. There is a classroom teacher and one teacher aide in the classroom when I come to work. At the school level I sometimes work with curriculum-instruction personnel and/or school leadership like the assistant principal, principal and the president of the Parent Teacher Association who helps coordinate the project. I also work with the visual art teacher at the school who helps to design and paint backdrops for our performances. The school district's Fine Arts Director supervises the project. The classroom teacher coordinates interviews between students and older adults at a local community center as part of the project. The older adults are invited to our final performance. The students will perform their devised oral-history play for their parents, school and district leadership and the community. Funders from a local nonprofit who are sponsoring the project will also attend the performance.

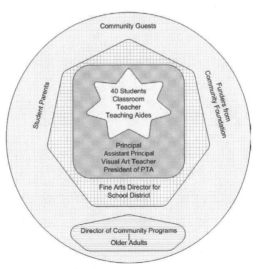

Figure 9: Example *who* map.

The why

It's time to link this specific project to your larger goals, assumptions and understandings about your practice or your personal intention. In this part of PAR we hope to chart out the relationship of your map to your larger goals. Let's imagine that our example Teaching Artist selected the core value of *meaningful work,* which she associates with relevant learning. She crafted her chart based on key activities that she needed to accomplish within the structure of her residency and wondered if further attention towards relevance might support her ability to meet participant, collaborator and community needs and intentions.

Example

Core Value: Relevance				
Where	*Who*	*What*	**If relevance is important, I could...**	**Why? Because I wonder if...**
1 Classroom	Students	Students will use interviews to create an original performance about their community to share with our community.	Have students interview each other as part of the larger research to be dramatized about the history of the community.	Students will be more engaged in the process when they can make personal connections to the topic (i.e. It's their story too!).
2 Classroom	Teacher	Teacher will be in the classroom supporting my project.	Focus on including English/ Language Arts standards that relate to biography and autobiography in my lesson.	The teacher will be more invested when they see the project meets a need from their mandated curriculum.
3 Community	Parents/ Caregivers	Parents and caregivers attend the final sharing at the school.	Include a talk back at the end of the performance where students can discuss the play-building process and answer questions from the audience.	Parents will understand and appreciate the rigor of the project more fully when they hear students describe the choices they made as artists in the process.

Now, it's your turn!

If you've worked your way through this text you should have a list of core values that you identified way back in Chapter 1. You can find this material on pages (21–22) as a reference.

- Select a core value that drives your practice.
- Think about a specific *where* in your chart and a *who* located inside this area and consider a specific practice or element of the project, a *what* from your project description that involves the *who* in the *where*. Or you can also start your thinking with a *what*: for example, a text or story you will explore or the way a certain drama skill is facilitated or how you choose to share artistic product during your process. Your *what* might even have to do with the larger relationship between your work as a Teaching Artist and other stakeholders within the school, community or arts organization. Once you've picked the *what*, then consider *who* is involved and *where* it happens. Wherever you start, begin with an element that most piques your interest related to the core value. Think about two or three possible examples of a related *where*, *who* and *what*.
- Now let's return to the *why*. Consider your selected core value. Consider how an emphasis on your core value might shift how you do the *what* you listed. Then reflect on the relationship between your core value and the result you would like to see because of this change. Why might this change happen? As a reminder, there is no one right answer; the focus is simply on *how* the Teaching Artist can use a core value to reflect on and improve their practice.

Your Example

My Core Value:				
Where	*Who*	*What*	If_____ is important, I could ...	Why? Because I wonder if ...

STEP 2: CONSTRUCT A QUESTION RELATED TO AN ASPECT OF QUALITY OR ARTISTIC PERSPECTIVE

How do I construct a research question?

The construction of the research question is key in this process. For this adapted version of PAR we have structured a research question template in a simple format that encourages the Teaching Artist researcher to tackle a reflective-practitioner study at a very basic level of inquiry. The question focuses on the *who* in the project involved in a specific *what*. It is purposefully open-ended and broad so that it can be used to gather information for future investigation. This question *does not* ask the Teaching Artist to prove that something causes a specific outcome or makes something happen. Instead the question is structured to simply ask, "What happened?" This observational approach is particularly useful for the Teaching Artist who wants to track the impact of a new approach based on his core values. The focus question requires the researcher to gather information to reflect on the impact of the new choice. This is also a productive way to begin to engage in a reflective practice, even if you aren't sure yet what to change or how to change your practice.

Question template

What is the experience of (*who*) in/during/within (*specific part of the lesson/ rehearsal/performance process)?*

All of the information necessary to construct this question is in the Core Value chart. Let's apply the question-template format to each of the example rows in our chart.

If your chart says:

Where	Who	What	If relevance is important, I could...	Why? Because I wonder if...
Classroom	Students	Students will use interviews to create an original performance about their community to share with our community.	Have students interview each other as part of the larger research to be dramatized about the history of the community.	Students will be more engaged in the process when they can make personal connections to the topic (i.e. It's their story too!).

Then your question might read:

> What is the experience of *students* during *the interview and staging of the interviews process*?

Goals: This question asks the Teaching Artist to observe and collect information (data) about students during the interview process.
   If your chart says:

Where	Who	What	If relevance is important, I could...	Why? Because I wonder if...
Classroom	Teacher	Teacher will be in the classroom supporting my project.	Focus on including English/Language Arts standards that relate to biography and autobiography in my lesson.	The teacher will be more invested when they see the project meets a need from their mandated curriculum.

Then your question might read:

> What is the experience of *the classroom teacher* during *the development of the project*?

Goals: This question asks the Teaching Artist to observe and collect information (data) about the classroom teacher during the development of the project.
   If your chart says:

Where	Who	What	If relevance is important, I could...	Why? Because I wonder if...
Community	Parents/ Caregivers	Parents and caregivers attend the final sharing at the school.	Include a talk back at the end of the performance where students can discuss the play-building process and answer questions from the audience.	Parents will understand the rigor of the project more fully when they can engage with students about the choices they made as artists in the process.

Then your question might read:

> What is the experience of *parents and caregivers* during *the final sharing*?

Goals: This question asks the Teaching Artist to observe and collect information (data) about the parents and caregivers during the final sharing.

Now, it's your turn!

Take some time to craft a few research questions for your project.

TEMPLATE	**What is the experience of** (*who*) **in/during/within** (*specific part of the lesson/rehearsal/performance process*)**?**
YOUR QUESTION	What is the experience of _____ in/during/within _____?
YOUR QUESTION	What is the experience of _____ in/during/within _____?
YOUR QUESTION	What is the experience of _____ in/during/within _____?

STEP 3: GATHER ANSWERS THROUGH A QUALITATIVE ASSESSMENT TOOL

How do I find an answer to my question?

Pick one question mentioned before that you would like to explore further. The next step is to consider how you will gather the information that answers the question. What sort of measurement options can be used to gather information/data? In this text we focus on qualitative research tools. Qualitative tools require us to consider:

- What is observable?
- Whom can we ask/what will someone tell us?
- What evidence can we gather from our artistic process?

Qualitative research can include *thick description,* which is a full, detailed description of what is happening or *a short written or verbal answer* to a question or a series of questions. It can also include objects from the process of making performance, or artistic reflection on the process, or the artistic product itself.

Qualitative research can be gathered:

- Through pre and/or post individual or focus group interviews where participants or stakeholders respond to a series of related questions.
- From an outside observer who typically completes a structured observational tool, created by the researcher.
- By the Teaching Artist through her own observation (through audio and/or visual means) to view afterwards with permission. Ethically, it is important to receive permission from parents/guardians as well as participants any time recordings are made and especially for research purposes.
- Through an analysis of arts-based artifacts that offer further insight into participants' level of skill, attitude or knowledge.

Let's imagine our example Teaching Artist selected the following research question:

> What is the experience of *the classroom teacher* during *the development of the project*?

To find the answer to this question, the Teaching Artist considers each of the available tools and determines which might help her understand the experience of the classroom teacher. Since our example Teaching Artist isn't able to have anyone observe the sessions, she only lists things she can accomplish on her own. She begins by naming the tool, then the form and who is involved, then makes notes of things that she feels she might want to pay attention to, particularly in reference to her core value and the change she hopes to make and study in the project. Finally she considers when the tool will need to be used so she is prepared and ready for action.

Data collection tool	How to use the tool	Advantages of tool	Challenges of tool
Observations	• TA facilitates/ reflects alone on experience during or after. • TA facilitates/ outside observer reflects on experience and shares data.	• TA experiences the moment with participant/s. • TA can record info as it occurs. • Outside observer is able to see the full picture of interaction.	• TA may miss important details, as it is difficult to facilitate and observe. • No one available to observe or not appropriate to have additional person in room.
Interviews	• Face-to-face— one-on-one interview. • Face-to-face— group interview, often called a focus group. • E-mail interview.	• Useful when participants can't be observed. • Participants can give further background about their experience or perspective. • Allows the researcher control over the questions.	• Information is filtered through interviewee. • Information does not come directly in the moment and is separated from the task. • The TA's presence may bias the information shared. • Participants' ability to accurately share information may be impacted by age or ability.
Arts-based artifacts	• Photographs of work-in-process. • Video of work-in-process. • Student writing in role. • Scripts. • The ideas are endless…	• Easy to gather quickly as part of work. • Can be shared with participants to include their perspective of their own work. • Focuses on the artistic process.	• Camera can interrupt flow or distract from task. • Can be challenging to interpret.

Examples of qualitative tools for Teaching Artist (TA) Participatory Action Research. Adapted from "Qualitative Data Collection Types, Options, Advantages, and Limitations" (Creswell 2000: 179–180).

Tool	Form	When is it gathered?	What should I try to include?
My observation	My field notes in personal journal.	After each planning session with the teacher and after each class session.	Specific phrases said by teacher; observations on body language and attitude about project relevance.
My interviews	Record conversation and e-mail documentation between me and teacher.	Before project; during project; after project.	Discussion about personal goals for project and other evidence of attitude about the project; notes about connections between arts and nonarts content skills; demonstration of new knowledge about students generated through project.
Arts-based artifact	All teacher contributions on project: reflection on script text; props or backdrops; participation in reflective activities with students.	Gathered throughout process.	A clear invitation and multiple opportunities to participate in and engage with the artistic process; time to reflect together on the process and any products.

What is the experience of *the classroom teacher* during *the development of the project*?

Now, it's your turn! Create your own list.

Tool	Form	When is it gathered?	What should I try to include?
My observations			
My interviews			
Arts-based artifact			

Research question

The example Teaching Artist chose to focus next on the specific language of the interview tool since it needed preparation ahead of time. She decided to administer pre- and post-interviews and a quick reflection session after each instructional day. She decided to use the quick reflection after each session to specifically track the progression of the teacher's attitude toward the project so she created a generic set of questions that could be asked each time they met as part of their reflection and planning process. Since she was interested in making the work relevant to the teacher, she realized she needed to ask questions that could help her document the teacher's attitude about and toward the project throughout the process. She realized that she needed to try to keep her questions open-ended to avoid 'leading' the teacher to certain answers. She also explained and received approval from the teacher for her research study. They both agreed to prioritize time for the interviews during the residency.

Example interview tool *to use to plan the project at the beginning of the process*

Date: Session #:   Location:

Question for teacher:

1. What do you hope to get out of this partnership project?
2. What do you hope your students will get out of this partnership project?
3. What would you like to see us accomplish at our first session?
4. What role would you like to play at the first session? How can I support you in this role?
5. What questions do you have for me about this project?

Example interview tool *to use after each session*

Date: Session #:   Location:

Question for teacher:

1. What do you think we accomplished today?
2. What did you notice about your students during the work today?
3. What would you like to see us accomplish at our next session?
4. What else would you like to share about this process so far?

Example interview tool *to use to reflect on the project at the end of the process*

Date: Session #:   Location:

Question for teacher:

1. What did you get out of this project?
2. What did your students get out of this project?
3. What do you feel we accomplished at the sharing?
4. What did you see as your role/contributions to this project?
5. How might you use what we did together on this project in the future?

Take some time to develop research tools that will help you get to the answers you need.

STEP 4: REFLECT ON AND SYNTHESIZE WHAT WAS FOUND

How do I analyze the data that I gathered?

Once you have completed your project and gathered your data, the next step is to consider what your information says about your work. In qualitative analysis we often spend a lot of time reading and rereading our data/information to look for common phrases or ideas that appear more than once. These common ideas or phrases relate back to our larger question or inquiry and help us understand what happened and what has changed over the course of our work.

Our example Teaching Artist might choose to group together all of the answers to one of her questions over the course of her six reflection interviews. Then she highlights language that relates to the quality and depth of teacher investment in the project with a focus on teacher attitude, knowledge and/or skills in relationship to the project. Following are some example excerpts from qualitative notes transcribed by the Teaching Artist, who tracked a single interview-question over six sessions. She highlighted key words and wrote a simple reflection on factors that seem to contribute to the teacher's investment in the project.

Example

Question: What do you think we accomplished today?		Notes on the quality and depth of teacher's investment in project
Session 1:	I think *you mostly helped* students understand what the project was going to be. They were confused about what type of play *you were going* to make with them. The games you played got them to understand how *actors need to focus*. They struggled with some of the games. They liked to come up with questions to ask their friends at lunch about what they like about the school.	Teacher isn't very invested. References the project as 'you' rather than 'us' or 'our.' Teacher uses the term 'focus' that we discussed and seems to recognize its importance. Teacher is positive but a little wary.
Session 2:	Today was a *good day*. They were talking about you coming all morning. *They got right to work and remembered all the rules* for the warm-up games. They played better today. Juan was very fast at the clap game and was *better behaved because you*	Positive about the session. Sees growth and improvement in students. Acknowledgment of positive behavior from student. Makes positive connection

	pointed out that he was a leader in that game. That was nice to see. Students were very *invested in sharing their research* about the school. I liked the *connection* between the interviews and thinking like a playwright. *I'm going to use that when we do creative writing next month.* "Think like how a playwright might tell the story through action and detail. That's good!"	to students investment in research. BIG SHIFT—teacher makes connection to her own practice and even quotes what I said: a sign of further buy-in to the project.
Session 4:	We got through so much today. *Students are very focused* on finalizing their scenes and monologues. *I gave them part of their sustained silent-reading time to finish their work and everyone was very on task. I collected a few of the school artifacts* that we discussed last time. I also found a picture of the school's founder. I can make it really big and we could add it to the final scene. Janice has really started to articulate clearly and shape her body into an older character. I've never seen her so engaged in class; she is going to be perfect in the part.	Positive behavior noted. Teacher is using her time toward the project. She sees it as worthwhile and engaging. Teacher has done outside work on the project and has more ownership in the project and the sharing. Teacher improvement in specific artistic skills (i.e voice and body) to discuss student success.

The Teaching Artist might conclude from this information that the biggest factor influencing the Teacher's investment was: time, her students improvement in theatre skills and level of engagement, and her perception that the Teaching Artist knew what she was doing. Also she seemed to appreciate when she was able to make connections between the work of the Teaching Artist and her other instructional tasks and needs. Most importantly, the research process itself seemed to increase investment for the teacher. The teacher agreed to the research study and therefore made an extra effort to meet and reflect on the work.

STEP 5: APPLY NEW KNOWLEDGE TO FUTURE WORK TO ACTIVATE PRAXIS AND BEGIN TO CONSIDER THE NEXT INQUIRY

How do I apply what I learned to my next project and investigation?

Now that you've drawn some conclusions based on the evidence that you gathered it is time to apply what was learned to upcoming practice. What did you discover and how can you make a 'better' choice based on what you learned? If you tried a new practice does the gathered information/data suggest that the new approach supports your core values? If so, how can this shift become a regular part of your daily practice? How can you share your findings with a colleague over coffee or at training or in an article for a professional journal or at a local, state or national conference?

If your participatory action research inquiry revealed that your strategy, skill or approach did not make the shift that you hoped, take time to consider why. Were there factors found in the larger system that impeded your ability to do what you hope to do? Is this issue beyond the scope of what you can accomplish within a drama/theatre learning experience or is what you hope to impact too difficult to accurately assess? Or did you realize that you are in need of further professional growth in a specific area? How can your research provide a recommendation about what type of further professional training or resources might best support your practice? Whatever the outcome, all information is useful information. This is the specific nature of research in comparison to evaluation. Your job is to investigate and reflect upon how and why, not if. By loosening the need to prove success, the Teaching Artists open their practice up to the larger ongoing journey of possibility and growth. Once the PAR cycle is complete, it is time to use the new information to begin a new action, with a greater sense of the world that shapes the action and your potential to shape the world. It is time to determine a new question, to begin the action and reflection cycle again.

Final Reflections

Education is not the filling of the pail, but the lighting of the fire.
(Unknown, though often attributed to William Butler Yeats)

It is the age of the Teaching Artist.
How do we embrace and fulfill our collective and personal potential?
How can we commit to deep engagement and reflection on, and within, our own work and our field as a whole?

The journey of reflection and reflexivity is expansive and enervating. It demands time, attention, effort, humility and risk. It is also wholly worthwhile. Reflective practice has the potential to make you a better, more engaged and ultimately more satisfied Teaching Artist. Reflection can support your return to practice on frustrating days and illuminate your calling on those days when you are at your best. This text suggests that the reflexive Teaching Artist reflects on the ways that intentionality, quality, artistic perspective, assessment and praxis can support better practice. This text argues for participatory action-research as a way for the Teaching Artist to better understand their practice and to feel empowered to shape their world.

As you reflect on your practice either through or outside this book, consider how you might invite your colleagues and students into the process. How can you share your collective discoveries with each other, your community and our field. Through the writing of this book, we, the authors, admit to some serious sea changes in our own work and beliefs. The discussions, disputes and détentes that paved our path through the collective narrative gave each of us new understanding and required us to acknowledge spaces where we could learn and expand. We truly hope that this book has inspired and will continue to inspire reflection on who and why you are a Teaching Artist.

It is the age of the Teaching Artist.
Come light the fire of reflexivity
And burn with possibility.

References

Ackroyd, J. (2000), "Applied theatre: Problems and possibilities," *Applied Theatre Researcher*, 1. http://www.griffith.edu.au/_data/assets/pdf_file/0004/81796/Ackroyd.pdf. Accessed January 20, 2013.

Akiyama, Y. (2011), LEAD Project Teacher Evaluation, Fall [online survey], January 11.

Alagappan, M. (2007), "Why we teach humane education." teachhumane.org/heart/about/. Accessed October 12, 2012.

Alrutz, M., Reitz-Yeager, T. and Brendel Horn, E. (Producers) (2008), *Hoping for a Better Future*. Informally published digital video from the Extended Research Classroom project. Orlando, Florida.

Anderson, L. W., Krathwohl, D. R., Airasian, P.W., Cruikshank, K.A., Mayer, R.E. and Pintrich, P.R. (2000), *A Taxonomy for Learning, Teaching, and Assessing: A Revision of Bloom's Taxonomy of Educational Objectives*. Boston, MA: Allyn and Bacon.

Anderson, M. E. and Risner, D. (2012), "A survey of teaching artists in dance and theater: Implications for preparation, curriculum, and professional degree programs," *Arts Education Policy Review*, 113, pp. 1–16.

Anzaldúa, G. (2007), *Borderlands/La Frontera: The new mestiza*. San Francisco, CA: Aunt Lute Books.

Argyris, C. and Schön, D. (1978), *Organizational Learning: A Theory of Action Perspective*. Reading, MA: Addison-Wesley.

Argyris, C. and Schön, D. (1974), *Theory in Practice: Increasing professional effectiveness*. San Francisco, CA: Jossey-Bass.

Beirne, M. and Knight, S. (2007), "From community theatre to critical management studies: A dramatic contribution to reflective learning?" *Management Learning*, 36(5), pp. 591–611.

Blei, M. (2012), "'Which way TYA?' A discussion with Tony Graham," *Incite/Insight*, 4(2), pp. 8–10.

Bloom, B. S., Engelhart, M. D., Furst, E. J., Hill, W. H. and Krathwohl, D. R. (1956), *Taxonomy of Educational Objectives: The Classification of Educational Goals; Handbook I: Cognitive Domain*. New York: Longmans.

Boal, A. (1992), *Games for Actors and Non-Actors*. New York: Routledge.

Boal, A. (1995), *The Rainbow of Desire*. New York: Routledge.

Bodrova, E. and Deborah J. L. (1996), *Tools of the Mind: The Vygotskian Approach to Early Childhood Education*. Englewood Cliffs: Prentice-Hall, Inc.

Bogart, A. and Landau, T. (2005), *The Viewpoints Book: A Practical Guide to Viewpoints and Composition.* New York: Theatre Communications Group.

Booth, E. (n.d.), *The Habits of Mind of Creative Engagement.* http://www.seanse .no/default.aspx?menu=151. Accessed October 23, 2012.

Booth, E. (2010), *The History of Teaching Artistry: Where We Come From, Are, and Are Heading.* https://docs.google.com/document/d/1sK3D2CIgJOdSJVX_ heV25iT-z_r6PAahjtTvdUGVGGE/edit?hl=en, Accessed May 20, 2012.

Booth, E. (2009), *The Music Teaching Artist's Bible: Becoming a Virtuoso Educator.* New York: Oxford University Press.

Boud, D., Keogh, R. and Walker, D. (eds) (1985), *Reflection: Turning Experience into Learning.* New York: Kogan Page Ltd.

Buechner, F. (1993), *Wishful Thinking: A Theological ABC.* San Francisco, CA: HarperCollins.

Carr, D. (2005), "On the contribution of literature and the arts to the educational cultivation of moral virtue, feeling, and emotion," *The Journal of Moral Education*, 34(2), pp. 148–149.

Carrier, M. and Pashler, H. (1992), "The influence of retrieval on retention," *Memory and Cognition*, 20, pp. 632–642.

Carroll, J. (1996), "Escaping the Information Abattoir: Critical and Transformative Research in Drama Classrooms." In P. Taylor (ed.), *Researching Drama and Arts Education: Paradigms and Possibilities.* London: Falmer Press, pp. 72–84.

Center for Digital Storytelling. "Stories". http://www.storycenter.org/stories/. Accessed June 2, 2011.

Chapa, S. (2011), "McAllen-based group holds valley's first 'gay prom,'" ValleyCentral.com, May 31. http://www.valleycentral.com/news/story .aspx?id=624496#.UGpdAxgfpCY. Accessed September 24, 2012.

Chi, M., de Leeuw, N., Chiu, M. and LaVancher, C. (1994), "Eliciting self-explanations improves understanding," *Cognitive Science*, 18, pp. 439–477.

Clark, H. P. (2003), "Ka maka hou Hawaii: The new face of the Hawaiian nation," *Third Text*, 17(3), pp. 273–279.

Clifford, S. and Herrmann, A. (1999), *Making a Leap: Theatre of Empowerment, a Practical Handbook for Creative Drama Work with Young People.* London: Jessica Kingsley Publishers.

Cohen-Cruz, J. (2005), *Local Acts: Community-Based Performance in the United States.* New Brunswick, NJ: Rutgers UP.

Conquergood, D. (2002), "Performance studies: Interventions and radical research," *The Drama Review*, 46, pp. 145–156.

Conquergood, D. (1985), "Performing as a moral act: Ethical dimensions of the ethnography of performance," *Literature in Performance*, 5, pp. 1–13.

Crace, J. (2007), "Jerome Bruner: The lesson of the story," *The Guardian*, March 26. www.guardian.co.uk/education/2007/mar/27/academicexperts. highereducationprofile. Accessed September 24, 2012.

Creswell, J. (2009), *Research Design: Qualitative, Quantitative, and Mixed Methods Approaches*. Thousand Oaks, CA: Sage.

Daichendt, G. J. (2013), "A brief, broad history of the teaching artist." In N. Jaffe, B. Barniskis and B. H. Cox (eds), *Teaching Artist Handbook*. Chicago: Columbia College Press, pp. 200–231.

Dawson, K. (2009), *Drama-Based Instruction Handbook*. Unpublished. Austin, TX: The University of Texas, p. 23.

Deasy, R. J. and Stevenson, L. M. (2005), *Third Space: When Learning Matters*. Washington, DC: Arts Education Partnership.

Delpit, L. (1995), *Other People's Children: Cultural Conflict in the Classroom*. New York: The New Press.

Derman-Sparks, L. (1995), "How well are we nurturing racial and ethnic diversity?" In D. Levine, R. Lowe, B. Peterson and R. Tenorio (eds), *Rethinking schools an agenda for social change*. New York: The New Press, pp. 17–22.

Dewey, J. (1933), *How We Think: A Restatement of the Relation of Reflective Thinking to the Educative Process* (Revised Edition). Boston: D. C. Health.

Dumbleton, M. (2007), *Cat*. Illustrations: Craig Smith. South Australia: Working Title Press. Denmark: Teater Refleksion. Accessed July 2009.

Egan, K. (2005), *An Imaginative Approach to Teaching*. San Francisco, CA: Jossey-Bass.

Frank, Y. (1939), *Pinocchio*. WPA Federal Theatre Project Production Script.

Freire, P. (1993), *Pedagogy of the Oppressed: 30th Anniversary Edition*. Trans. by M. Bergman Ramos. New York: Continuum.

Freire, P. (1998), *Teachers as Cultural Workers: Letters to Those who Dare to Teach*. Boulder: Westview.

Freire, P. and Macedo, D. (1987), *Literacy: Reading the Word and the World*. Westport, CT: Bergin & Garvey.

Fuchs, L. H. (1960), *Hawai'i Pono: A Social History*. New York: Harcourt, Brace & World, Inc.

Garrett, I. (2012), "Theatrical production's carbon footprint." In W. Arons and T. J. May (eds), *Readings in Performance and Ecology*. New York: Palgrave Macmillan, pp. 201–209.

Gay, G. (2010), *Culturally Responsive Teaching: Theory, Teaching and Practice*. New York: Teachers College Press.

Geertz, C. (2000), *Available Light: Anthropological Reflections on Philosophical Topics*. Princeton, NJ: Princeton UP.

Ginsberg, M. and Clift, R. (1990), "The hidden curriculum of preservice teacher education." In W. R. Houston (ed.), *Handbook of Research on Teacher Education*. New York: Macmillan, pp. 450–465.

Giroux, H. (1992), *Border Crossings: Cultural Workers and Politics of Education*. New York: Routledge.

Goldman, R. (2010), "Hawai'i's spirit guardians," *Nō Ka 'Oi Maui Magazine*, December. http://www.mauimagazine.net. Accessed July 15, 2012.

Grady, S. (2000), *Drama and Diversity: A Pluralistic Perspective for Educational Drama*. Portsmouth, NH: Heinemann.

Greene, M. (1995), *Releasing the Imagination: Essays on Education, the Arts and Social Change*. San Francisco, CA: Jossey-Bass.

Greene, M. (1998), "Toward beginnings." In W. Pinar (ed.), *The Passionate Mind of Maxine Greene: I Am…Not Yet.* New York: Routledge, pp. 253–254.

Greene, M. (2001), *Variation on a Blue Guitar: The Lincoln Center Institute Lectures on Aesthetic Education.* New York: Teachers College Press.

Griffin's Tale. (n.d.), "Home." http://www.griffinstale.org. Accessed April 4, 2013.

Hereniko, V. (1999), "Representations of cultural identities." In V. Hereniko and R. Wilson (eds), *Inside Out: Literature, Cultural Politics, and Identity in the New Pacific.* Lanham, MD: Rowman & Littlefield, pp. 137–166.

Herrera, S. (2010), *Biography-Driven Culturally Responsive Teaching.* New York: Teachers College Press.

Hesford, W. (2009), *Identities: Autobiographies and the politics of pedagogy.* Minneapolis, MN: University of Michigan Press.

Hetland, L., Winner, E., Veenema, S. and Sheridan, K. M. (2007), *Studio Thinking: The Real Benefits of Visual Arts Education.* New York: Teachers College Press.

Howard, V. (1991), "Useful imaginings." In R. A. Smith and A. Simpson (eds), *Aesthetics and Arts Education.* Chicago: University of Illinois Press, pp. 339–346.

Humphries, L. (2000), "Artistic process and elegant action." http://www.thinkingapplied.com/artistic_process_folder/artistic_process.htm#.US2XU6Wp0YA. Accessed February 19, 2013.

Improve Group, The (2012), 'Executive Summary, *Any Given Child Final Evaluation Report*, John F. Kennedy Center for the Performing Arts, July 10, pp. i.

Johnson, R. and Badley, G. (1996), "The competent reflective practitioner," *Innovation and Learning in Education: The International Journal for the Reflective Practitioner*, 2(1), pp. 4–10.

Johnston, C. (2009), *Improvisation Game: Discovering the Secrets of Spontaneous Performance.* London: Nick Hern Books.

Johnstone, K. ([2007] 1981), *Impro: Improvisation and the Theatre* (Revised Edition). London: Methuen.

Jones, J. and Olomo, O. (2009), "sista docta, REDUX." In M. Cahnmann-Taylor and R. Siegesmund (eds), *Arts-Based Research in Education: Foundations for Practice.* New York: Routledge, pp. 194–207.

Kaomea, J. (2005), "Indigenous studies in the elementary curriculum: A cautionary Hawaiian example," *Anthropology & Education Quarterly*, 36, pp. 24–42.

Kemmis, S. and Wilkinson, M. (1998), "Participatory action research and the study of practice." In B. Atweh, S. Kemmis and P. Weeks (eds), *Action Research in Practice: Partnerships for Social Justice in Education.* New York: Routledge, pp. 21–36.

Kincheloe, J. (2004), *Critical Pedagogy Primer.* New York: Peter Lang Primer.

King, N. R. (1981), *A Movement Approach to Acting.* Englewood Cliffs, NJ: Prentice-Hall Press.

Koppelman, K. (2011), *The Great Diversity Debate: Embracing Pluralism in School and Society.* New York: Teachers College Press.

Kozol, J. (1991), *Savage Inequities: Children in America's Schools.* New York: Crown Publishers.

Ladson-Billings, G. (1994), *The Dreamkeepers.* San Francisco, CA: Jossey-Bass.

Lambert, J. (2010), *Digital Storytelling: Capturing Lives, Creating Community* (3rd Edition). Berkley, CA: Life on the Water Inc.

Lambert, J. (2009), "Where it all started: The center for digital storytelling in California." In J. Hartley and K. McWilliam (eds), *Story Circle: Digital Storytelling Around the World.* Malden, MA: Wiley-Blackwell, pp. 79–90.

Lazarus, J. (2012), *Signs of Change: New Directions in Secondary Theatre Education.* Bristol, UK: Intellect.

Leider, R. J. (2010), *The Power of Purpose.* San Francisco, CA: Berrett Koehler Publishers, Inc.

Levy, J. (1997), "Theatre and moral education," *The Journal of Moral Education,* 31(3), pp. 65–75.

Linklater, K. (2006), *Freeing the Natural Voice* (Revised and Expanded Edition). New York: Drama Publishers.

Linn, R. L. and Gronlund, N. E. (1995), *Measurement and Assessment in Teaching* (7th Edition). Englewood Cliffs, NJ: Prentice Hall.

Lopez, B. (1990), *Crow and Weasel.* New York: North Point Press.

McIntyre, A. (2008), *Participatory Action Research.* Thousand Oaks, CA: Sage.

McKean, B. (2006), *A Teaching Artist at Work: Theatre with Young People in Educational Settings.* Portsmouth, NH: Heinemann.

McNiff, J. and Whitehead, J. (2002), *Action Research: Principals and Practice.* New York: RoutledgeFalmer.

Marquez, G. G. (2003), *Living to Tell the Tale.* New York: Vintage Books.

Mendler, A. (2000), *Motivating Students Who Don't Care: Successful Techniques for Educators.* Bloomington, IN: Solution Tree Press.

Mendler, A., Mendler, B. and Curwin, R. (2008), *Discipline with Dignity: New Challenges, New Solutions.* Alexandria, VA: Association for Supervision and Curriculum Development.

Mienczakowski, J. (1997), "Theatre of change," *Research in Drama Education,* 2(2), pp. 159–172.

Mitchell, C. (2011), *Doing Visual Research*. Los Angeles: Sage.

Moʻolelo Performing Arts Company (2007), *Green Moʻolelo*. http://moolelo.net/green/. Accessed April 6, 2013.

Moffitt, P. (2003), "The heart's intention," *Yoga Journal*, 176, pp. 67–70.

Neelands, J. (2006), "Re-imaging the reflective practitioner: Towards a philosophy of critical praxis." In J. Ackroyd (ed.), *Research Methodologies for Drama Education*. Stoke on Trent: Trentham, pp. 15–39.

Nicholson, H. (2005), *Applied Drama: The Gift of Theatre*. Basingstoke, UK: Palgrave Macmillan.

Nicholson, H. (2011), *Theatre, Education and Performance*. New York: Palgrave Macmillan.

Norris, J. (2009), *Playbuilding as Qualitative Research: A Participatory Arts-Based Approach*. Walnut Creek, CA: Left Coast Press.

Okamura, J. (1994), "Why there are no Asian Americans in Hawaiʻi: The continuing significance of local identity," *Social Process in Hawaiʻi*, 35, pp. 161–178.

Osorio, J. (2006), "On being Hawaiian," *Hūlili*, 3(1), pp. 19–26.

Osterman, K. and Kottkamp, R. B. (1993), *Reflective Practice for Educators*. Newbury Park, CA: Corwin Press.

Partnership for 21st Century Skills (2011), *Framework for 21st Century Learning*. http://www.p21.org. Accessed June 9, 2012.

Perkins, D. N. (1991), "What constructivism demands of the learner," *Educational Technology*, 31(9), pp. 19–21.

Perkins, T. (2010), "Christian compassion requires the truth about harms of homosexuality," *Washington Post*, October 11. http://onfaith.washingtonpost.com/onfaith/guestvoices/2010/10/christian_compassion_requires_the_truth_about_harms_of_homosexuality.html. Accessed September 28, 2012.

President's Committee on the Arts and the Humanities (2011), *Reinvesting in Arts Education: Winning America's Future through Creative Schools*. Washington, DC.

Pujic, I. (2012), E-mail conversation (Personal Communication), September 16.

Pukui, M. K., Haertig, E. W. and Lee, C. A. (1972), *Nana I ke kumu: Look to the Source, II*. Honolulu: Hui Hānai.

Rabkin, N. (2011), "Teaching artists and the future of education," *Teaching Artist Journal*, 10(1), pp. 5–14.

Rabkin, N., Reynolds, M.J., Hedberg, E.C. and Shelby, J. (2011), *Teaching Artists and the Future of Education: A Report on the Teaching Artist Research Project*. Chicago: NORC at the University of Chicago.

Race, P. (2005), *Making Learning Happen: A Guide for Post-Compulsory Education*. London: Sage.

Raines, P. and Shadiow, L. (1995), "Reflection and teaching: The challenge of thinking beyond the doing," *The Clearing House: A Journal of Educational Strategies, Issues and Ideas*, 68(5), pp. 271–274.

Reimer, J., Paolitto, D. P. and Hersh, R. H. (1983), *Promoting Moral Growth: From Piaget to Kohlberg* (2nd Edition), Oxford, UK: Longman.

Riel, M. (2010), *Understanding Action Research, Center for Collaborative Action Research*. Malibu: Pepperdine University. http://cadres.pepperdine.edu/ccar/define.html. Accessed September 1, 2010.

Rifkin, F. (2010), *The Ethics of Participatory Theatre in Higher Education: A Framework for Learning and Teaching*. Palatine, the Higher Education Academy, Lancaster: Lancaster University. http://78.158.56.101/archive/palatine/development-awards/1407/index.html. Accessed April 6, 2013.

Roadside Theater (1999), "Story circle guidelines." http://roadside.org/asset/story-circle-guidelines. Accessed April 10, 2013.

Rohd, M. (2008), *Devising New Civic Performance through Ensemble*. Workshop at Southeastern Theatre Conference, Chattanooga, TN, March.

Rohd, M. (1998), *Theatre for Community Conflict and Dialogue: The Hope is Vital Training Manual*. Portsmouth, NH: Heinemann.

Rohd, M. (2012), "The new work of building civic practice," HowlRound.com [Journal blog], July 8. http://journalism.howlround.com/the-new-work-of-building-civic-practice-by-michael-rohd/. Accessed October 3, 2012.

Rolfe, G., Freshwater, D. and Jasper, M. (eds) (2001), *Critical Reflection for Nursing and the Helping Professions*. Basingstoke, UK: Palgrave Macmillan.

Saldaña, J. (1998), "Ethical issues in an ethnographic performance text: The 'dramatic impact' of 'juicy stuff,'" *Research in Drama Education*, 3(2), pp. 181–196.

Saldaña, J. (2005), *Ethnodrama: An Anthology of Reality Theatre*. Walnut Creek: AltaMira.

Schaetti, B. F., Ramsey, S. and Watanabe, G. C. (2009), "From intercultural knowledge to intercultural competence: Developing an intercultural practice." In M. A. Moodian (ed.), *Contemporary Leadership and Intercultural Competence: Exploring the Cross-Cultural Dynamics within Organizations*. Thousand Oaks, CA: Sage, pp. 125–138.

Schön, D. A. (1987), *Educating the Reflective Practitioner: Toward a New Design for Teaching and Learning in the Professions*. San Francisco, CA: Jossey-Bass.

Schön, D. A. (1995), "Knowing-in-action: The new scholarship requires a new epistemology," *Change*, November/December, pp. 27–34.

Seidel, S., Tishman, S., Winner, E., Hetland, L. and Palmer, P. (2009), *Qualities of Quality: Understanding Excellence in Arts Education*. Cambridge, MA: Project Zero, Harvard School of Education.

Shakespeare, W. (1992), *Macbeth*. In P. Werstine and B. A. Mowat (eds), Folger Shakespeare Library. New York: Washington Square Press.

Silverman, D. (2007), *A Very Short, Fairly Interesting, and Reasonably Cheap Book about Qualitative Research*. London: Sage.

Stanford University Communications (n.d.), "Stanford University Common Data Set 2010–2011." http://ucomm.stanford.edu/cds/2010. Accessed April 4, 2013.

Stanislavski, C. ([1988] 1936), *An Actor Prepares*. London: Methuen.

Taylor, P. (1996), "Rebellion, reflective turning and arts education research." In P. Taylor (ed.), *Researching Drama and Arts Education: Paradigms and Possibilities*. London: Falmer Press, pp. 1–22.

Tharp, T. (2003), *The Creative Habit: Learn It and Use It for Life*. New York: Simon and Schuster.

http://www.thorsten.org/wiki/index.php?title=Triple_Loop_Learning. Accessed January 8, 2013.

UNESCO (2006), *Road Map for Arts Education*, The World Conference on Arts Education: Building Creative Capacities for the 21st Century, Lisbon, March 6–9.

UNESCO (2010), *Seoul Agenda: Goals for the Development of Arts Education*, The Second World Conference on Arts Education, Seoul, May 25–28.

Vygotsky, L. (1978), *Mind in Society: The Development of Higher Psychological Processes*. In M. Cole, V. John-Steiner, S. Scribner and E. Souberman (eds). Cambridge, MA: Harvard University Press.

Wenger, E. (1998), *Communities of Practice: Learning, Meaning, and Identity*. Cambridge: Cambridge University Press.

Wheatley, M. (2009), *Turning to One Another: Simple Conversations to Restore Hope to the Future*. San Francisco, CA: Berrett-Koehler.

Wiggins, G. and McTighe, J. (2006), *Understanding by Design* (2nd Edition). Alexandria, VA: Association for Supervision and Curriculum Development.

Williams, C. (2011), "New census data: Minnesota Somali population grows," *Star Tribune*, http://www.startribune.com/132670583.html, October 27. Accessed August 1, 2012.

Zeder, S. and Hancock, J. (2005), *Spaces of Creation: The Creative Process of Playwriting*. Portsmouth, NH: Heinemann.

Biographies

Kathryn Dawson is an Assistant Professor in the Department of Theatre and Dance at The University of Texas at Austin and serves as the Director of the Drama for Schools program. Her areas of research include arts integration, museum theatre, teaching artist praxis and arts-based educational research. She is the former coordinator of the Science Comes Alive interactive theatre program at the California Science Center. Katie also worked as a full-time classroom teacher and as a theatre-arts specialist in Los Angeles. As a Teaching Artist, Katie facilitates programming in schools, professional theatres and community settings in diverse places across the United States and Australia. She has given multiple keynote presentations and training workshops at national and international conferences on drama-based instruction, arts integration, museum theatre, community-engagement, and teaching-artist pedagogy and practice. She published a play, created two children's television shows, and her scholarship appears in national and international research journals. Katie was named the 2005 Winifred Ward Scholar by the American Alliance of Theatre and Education (AATE) and received their Creative Drama Award in 2013. Most recently, the University of Texas System named Katie a Regents' Outstanding Teaching Award winner.

An ardent and outspoken Teaching Artist, **Daniel A. Kelin, II** is the long-serving Honolulu Theatre for Youth Director of Drama Education. He was President of the American Alliance for Theatre and Education from 2011 to 2013. A 2009 Fulbright-Nehru Research Scholar in India, he worked with several theatres across that country. Theatre for Young Audiences/ USA awarded him an Ann Shaw Fellowship to collaborate with the Aazhi Children's Theatre in Pondicherry, India. He was a Teaching Artist Fellow with Montalvo Arts Center, California and an Aurand Harris Playwriting Fellow with the Children's Theatre Foundation of America. On the teaching artist roster of the John F. Kennedy Center for Performing Arts, Dan also served as Director of Theatre Training for both Crossroads Theatre for Youth in American Samoa and a Marshall Islands youth organization. He has performed Beijing Opera in China, danced in several Pacific Islands, worked with theatres in North and South India and created several plays for very young audiences. Published in journals such as *Teaching Tolerance, Multicultural Review, Teaching Artist Journal,* NCTE's *Talking Points,* NCSS's *Social Studies and the Young Learner, Indian Folklore Journal, Parabola, Early Childhood Education Journal* and *Highlights for Children,* he has three books to his name and is a contributing author to many others.

Heli Aaltonen, Ph.D., is Associate Professor in Drama and Theatre Studies at the Department of Art and Media Studies, Norwegian University of Science and Technology, Trondheim. Heli's mother tongue is Finnish, her everyday life is multilingual, and she is very experienced in international collaboration. She is an applied-theatre and performance researcher, performing storyteller and theatre/drama educator with a specialization in intercultural child and youth-theatre practices and ecocritical storytelling. She organizes international practices and has written her doctoral thesis in the context of a nongovernmental organization, European Drama Encounters, EDERED. Her thesis, *Intercultural Bridges in Teenagers' Theatrical Events: Performing Self and Constructing Cultural Identity through a Creative Drama Process,* was published in 2006. In 2010–2011 she was an artistic leader of multilingual Nordic Voices project, where the art educational focus was to celebrate oral storytelling and encourage adults and children to share stories with each other.

Megan Alrutz is an Assistant Professor of Applied Theatre and Community Engagement in the Department of Theatre and Dance at The University of Texas at Austin. She teaches courses in applied theatre, digital storytelling and theatre for social justice, and mentors MFA students in the Drama and Theatre for Youth and Communities program. Megan's creative and scholarly interests focus on theatre with and for youth—including applied theatre and digital storytelling, arts and media integration, directing and dramaturgy. She currently co-directs the Performing Justice Project (PJP), a community-based applied-performance program that addresses gender and racial justice. Her research has been published in *RiDE, Youth Theatre Journal, Teaching Artist Journal, Journal of Community Engagement and Scholarship* and *TYA Today.* Megan is co-editor of *Playing with Theory in Theatre Practice* (Palgrave Macmillan 2011) and is completing her book, *Digital Storytelling, Applied Theatre, & Youth: Performing Possibility* (Routledge).

Lisa M. Barker is an Assistant Professor of Secondary Education at The State University of New York at New Paltz. She received her Ph.D. in Curriculum and Teacher Education from Stanford University and her MA in Educational Theatre from New York University. The 2011 Winifred

Ward Scholar, she researches how improvisational theatre-training can influence teacher practice, and she facilitates workshops on improvisation, creativity and leadership for a range of international corporate clients. She taught with the Stanford Teacher Education Program and the Center to Support Excellence in Teaching, performed with the Stanford Improvisors and children's theatre companies such as Barrel of Monkeys and the Story Pirates, and founded Stanford's first children's repertory theatre company. She served as Director of Education for Adventure Stage Chicago and Manager of the Creative Arts Team's Kaplan Center for Educational Drama, where she helped launch the first MA in Applied Theatre in the United States.

Kim Bowers-Rheay-Baran is a Resident Teaching Artist for the Alliance Theatre Institute for Educators and Teaching Artists, Wolf Trap Teaching Artist, singer, actress and certified Montessori teacher. Her Alliance Institute work includes teaching on Wolf Trap drama strategies at Georgia State University, leading the Dramaturgy by Students program, integrating drama and the Core Curriculum in Kindergarten through fifth-grade classrooms in greater Atlanta, Georgia. Kim served on the teams of two Arts Model Dissemination Grants. Kim was the Creative Arts director and elementary teacher for a Montessori school in Fayetteville, GA and Assistant Educational Director for the Center for Puppetry Arts in Atlanta. Her performance highlights include Aldonza in *Man of La Mancha*, Tessie Tura in *Gypsy*, *Side by Side by Sondheim*, Mary Magdalene in *Jesus Christ Superstar*, *Candide* at the Alliance Theatre. Her national tours include Nimue in *Camelot* starring Robert Goulet, Sarah in *Quilters* and *Hello Dolly* starring Madeline Kahn.

Ryan Conarro makes his home in Juneau, Alaska. He's a Teaching Artist with the Alaska State Council on the Arts Artists in Schools residency program. He's enjoyed working in rural Alaska villages since his first year in the state as a journalist for Nome's KNOM Radio. He's served as an educator with the Lower Kuskokwim District arts-integration program in 14 village schools, and with the Alaska Department of Education's rural support team. Ryan provides professional development in arts integration through the Alaska Arts Education Consortium and the University of Alaska education programs. Ryan is a company member of Juneau's Perseverance Theatre and New York's Theater Mitu. He's directed two Alaskan operas, including *Arctic Magic Flute*, a statewide tour of his original adaptation of Mozart's classic. He earned a BFA in Theatre and English from New York University and an MFA in Interdisciplinary Arts from Goddard College.

Michelle Dahlenburg is an applied-theatre practitioner, theatre-maker and oral historian in Austin, Texas. She creates workshops, sound installations and performance pieces situated at the intersection of art and community, civic, and social change. She is the co-Artistic Director of Conspire Theatre, which facilitates theatre programs for women during and post-incarceration. She is also the Program Associate for HATCH: Inspired Social Change, and teaches Drama-Based Instruction at Texas State University. Michelle has been a Teaching Artist for a variety of organizations, including the Paramount Theatre, Texas Folklife, Creative Action, Still Point Theater Collective, American Theatre Company and others. Michelle has an MFA in the Drama and Theatre for Youth and Communities program from The University of Texas at Austin.

Peter B. Duffy heads the Master of Arts in Teaching program in theatre education at the University of South Carolina. There he teaches courses in applied theatre, dramatic literature for youth, creative drama, methods of teaching drama and children's theatre. Prior to USC, Peter was the Director of Education and Community Outreach at the Irondale Ensemble in Brooklyn, New York where he developed curricula and trained Teaching Artists and teachers in drama as pedagogy and performance assessments. Additionally, Peter taught middle and high-school German, English and drama for a decade. He also worked as a Teaching Artist in New York City schools. His research interests include storying experimental neuroscientific research through drama practices in the classroom, arts as reflective practice, culturally responsive pedagogy, Theatre of the Oppressed and youth, critical ethnography, and the arts as qualitative research methodologies. Peter is a proud member of AATE, IDEA and WAAE.

Andrew Garrod is Professor Emeritus of Education at Dartmouth College where he served as Chair of the Education Department and Director of Teacher Education. He was a public high-school teacher in New Brunswick, Canada for 16 years, where his Shakespearean productions with high school students won national and provincial awards. In addition to conducting research in aspects of moral reasoning and faith development in Bosnia and Herzegovina for the last 12 years, Andrew has directed several multiethnic, multilingual Shakespearean productions in Mostar to increase possibilities of reconciliation among children of the former warring ethnic groups. With Youth Bridge Global, a nonprofit co-founded with David Yorio to bridge cultural divides with drama and art, he and his associates have mounted eight bilingual Shakespearean productions at a Marshall Islands high school. In 2013, Andrew and his team directed a trilingual student production of *Romeo and Juliet* in Rwanda.

Marsha Gildin, a master Teaching Artist with Elders Share the Arts (ESTA), has taught drama, puppetry and intergenerational arts to students of all ages and different abilities in school and community-based settings since 1974. Her passion for connecting generations, cultures and communities through personal story and performance arts is far-reaching. She has led ESTA's intergenerational History Alive! theatre program in Flushing, New York since 1997. In 2008, Marsha co-facilitated region-wide intergenerational trainings through the Shin Kong Life Foundation in Taipei and, in 2009, traveled to the tsunami-affected region of Tamil Nadu, India to evaluate the impact of a psychosocial, arts-based, intergenerational, community regeneration curriculum designed by the Mumbai-based Dreamcatchers Foundation. Marsha received ESTA's 2012 Meritorious Service Award for creativity, leadership and outstanding contributions to the lives of older people. She served on faculty at CUNY Queens College Graduate School of Education, teaching arts-infused curriculum design and multiple-intelligences learning theory.

Tamara Goldbogen is currently a Program Manager at the Children's Museum of Pittsburgh. She recently spent six years at the University of Pittsburgh teaching theatre for youth and serving as Director of the Departmental Touring Outreach program. Her other work includes Children's Theatre Company in Minneapolis, Spoleto Festival USA, University of Hawaii, and she is the Founding Director of South Carolina Young Playwrights. She serves on the boards of Pittsburgh International Children's Theatre and Theatre for Young Audiences/USA. Tamara leads a study-abroad program that follows the ASSITEJ World Congress and Performing Arts Festival around the world. She holds an MFA in Drama and Theatre for Youth from The University of Texas at Austin.

Jo Beth Gonzalez holds an MFA in Directing from the University of Minnesota and a Ph.D. in Theatre from Bowling Green State University. A veteran of secondary theatre education, she teaches at Bowling Green High School in Bowling Green, Ohio. She is the author of *Temporary Stages: Departing from Tradition in High School Theatre Education* (Heinemann 2006) and *Temporary Stages II: Critically Oriented Drama Education* (Intellect 2013). She is the recipient of the 2002 Wilson National Mentor's Award to a High School Drama Teacher from the Children's Theatre Foundation of America. Jo Beth serves on the boards of the Children's Theatre Foundation of America and the American Alliance for Theatre and Education.

Nicole Gurgel is an Austin-based performance practitioner, educator and activist. She has worked as a performer, dramaturg, director, facilitator, Teaching Artist and administrator with communities and arts organizations in Minneapolis, Minnesota; Chennai, India; Roanoke, Virginia; Austin and McAllen, Texas. A 2012 graduate of The University of Texas at Austin, Nicole holds an MFA in Performance as Public Practice.

Amanda Hashagen is the founder and CEO of CreativeWorks, an educational arts nonprofit whose mission is to engage teens through applied theatre and digital media programs. Her work has focused on collaborating with marginalized groups throughout the world to use theatre and digital media as a means to explore and address issues that are important to them. Amanda was the Middle and High School Program Director at Theatre Action Project (TAP) in Austin, Texas. She served as an Assistant Director for the Circle Playhouse in Toronto, Canada. Amanda was a lead Teaching Artist for the Theatre In Prisons and Probation Center (TIPP) in Manchester, UK. Amanda obtained an MPhil in Drama from the University of Manchester. Her research focused on the use of Theatre for Development to achieve gender equity in Uganda. She has an MA in Applied Theatre from the University of Manchester, UK. She has BA degrees in English and Theatre from Benedictine College.

Michelle Hayford is an Associate Professor of Theatre and Assistant Director of the Center for the Arts at Florida Gulf Coast University. She writes and directs the Constellation series of applied-theatre works in collaboration with nonprofit partners and FGCU theatre students. Her previous plays include *Suit My Heart* and *Dog Wish*. She is committed to theatre for social change, interdisciplinary inquiry and bringing theory into practice through performance. Her research interests include applied theatre, ethnodrama, performativity in everyday life, identity, gender, and embodied ways of knowing. She developed the applied-theatre curriculum at FGCU. Michelle holds a Ph.D. in Performance Studies from Northwestern University. She thanks her *Suit My Heart* ensemble for the journey recounted in these pages: Nate Bartman, Jared Benner, Jacalyn Brunell, Rashad Davis, Michael Denkler, Janna Dewey, Florinda Diego-Juan, Steven Goldberg-Pannone, Ashley Graziano, Andrea Heighes-Revilla, Artkeda Hunt, Ben Kirchman, Kaitlyn Richey, Armando Rivera, Veda Roberts and Shane Serena.

As a classroom teacher in both suburban and urban schools, **Tracy Kane** has taught grades six through twelve and directed countless theatre productions. Prior to becoming a public-school teacher, she held education positions at professional theatres including Hartford Stage, Honolulu Theatre for Youth and American Place Theatre in New York City. For teachers, she has conducted workshops at Hartford Stage, the University of Hawaii and Farmington Public Schools. Her article, "A Surprising Starting Point: Toni Morrison as the Impetus for Classroom Drama", appeared in *Stage of the Art*, a journal published by the American Alliance for Theatre and Education. She has led workshops at national and state conferences including AATE and Connecticut Alliance for Arts Education. Her education includes a BA in Drama from Vassar College and an MA in Educational Theatre from New York University. Currently, she is working toward her Sixth-Year Certificate in Educational Leadership.

Stephanie Knight is an independent artist-researcher and works at the University of Glasgow, Scotland. Stephanie is an internationally published researcher, practitioner and writer in applied theatre and applied arts, specializing in social justice and human rights, international collaboration and reconciliation. She is a collaborative researcher in applied theatre and organizational development, international leadership and management. Stephanie has extensive experience in lecturing and education and in developing pedagogical and research methodologies with applied theatre and arts practitioners, at undergraduate and postgraduate levels. Stephanie has been the director of an arts organization, as well as the director of large-scale arts and education projects and international conferences. She is one of the judges for the Amnesty International Freedom of Expression Award, for outstanding theatre with a strong human rights message, which is awarded each year at the Edinburgh Festival Fringe. Stephanie is the Principal Editor of the international *Journal of Arts & Communities*.

Kati Koerner is Lincoln Center Theater's (LCT) Director of Education and Co-Chair of the New York City Arts in Education Roundtable, a service organization for the arts-education community. Prior to LCT, Kati taught high-school drama in Boston and served as Education Partnerships Coordinator at The Children's Theatre Company in Minneapolis. She was a member of the writing committee that created the *Blueprint for Teaching & Learning in the Arts: Theater* for the New York City Department of Education. For Theater Communications Group, she moderates a series of teleconferences for education directors and served as a member of their Theatre Education Assessment Models (TEAM) working group. Kati has worked extensively as a director, translator and Teaching Artist in the United States, England and Germany. In 2011, she received the American Alliance for Theatre and Education's Lin Wright Special Recognition Award.

Bridget Kiger Lee studies the effects of active learning and instructional strategies on educational outcomes. In particular, she examines how drama-based pedagogy impacts various achievement and psychological outcomes for teachers and students. She has presented her findings at the Southeast Center for Education in the Arts as well as the Arts and Learning SIG for AERA, AATE, Society for Personality and Social Psychology, and Society of Research on Adolescence, among others. Bridget's work can be found in the *Review of Educational Research, Teaching and Teacher Education,* and the *Teaching Artist Journal.* Currently, Bridget is a Post Doctorate Researcher at Ohio State University with Stand Up for Shakespeare—a collaboration between Columbus city schools and the Royal Shakespeare Company. Bridget has been a middle-school teacher, a Teaching Artist, an education director of a theatre and a teacher trainer. She received her MFA in Drama and Theatre for Youth and Communities and her Ph.D. in Educational Psychology from The University of Texas at Austin.

Gillian McNally is the Head of Community Engagement and Programs for Youth for the School of Theatre and Dance at the University of Northern Colorado. She co-directs programs for graduate and undergraduate-level teachers in theatre education. Gillian specializes in the connection between the arts, youth and community. She has presented papers on this topic in Australia, Mexico and Denmark. Currently, she serves as Vice-President for Theatre for Young Audiences USA. Gillian is the recipient of the Alliance for Colorado Theatre's 2011 Higher Education Theatre Educator of the Year Award.

Christina Marín, Ph.D., is an Assistant Professor of Performing Arts in the Program of Theatre Education at Emerson College in Boston, Massachusetts. She teaches Theatre of the Oppressed, drama as education, human rights in theatre, contemporary issues in education, and qualitative research. She is an international Theatre of the Oppressed practitioner who has conducted workshops and delivered conference papers in Singapore, Colombia, Turkey, South Africa, as well as in cities all around the United States. She is published in journals such as *Gender Forum, STAGE of the Art* and *Youth Theatre Journal,* and in the edited collections *Children under Construction: Critical Essays on Play as Curriculum* (Peter Lang 2010), and *Youth and Theatre of the Oppressed* (Palgrave Macmillan 2010).

Gary Minyard has been involved in nearly 250 theatrical projects ranging from directing professional productions at major theaters to devising small plays with elementary school children. As a Teaching Artist, he has helped students write, act, swordfight, sing, dance and do a host of other performance activities. He graduated with an MFA in Theatre for Youth and Directing from Arizona State University in 2007. Gary also studied at the University of Houston and trained at the L'Ecole Internationale de Théâtre Jacques Lecoq in Paris. He has recently been elected President-Elect of the American Alliance for Theatre in Education. He is a co-founder of the Eastern Pennsylvania Arts Alliance, an active member of Theatre for Young Audiences, the Society of American Fight Directors, and Directors, Communications Group. He has toured as an actor, director and Teaching Artist through 48 of 50 US states (plus one territory!) with several professional theatre companies.

Sarah Myers is an Assistant Professor at Augsburg College in Minneapolis. She holds a Ph.D. in Performance as Public Practice from The University of Texas at Austin, where she also earned her MFA in Playwriting and Drama and Theatre for Youth. Before moving to Minneapolis, Sarah was a company member with Austin-based Rude Mechanicals and co-director of Rude Mechs' Grrl Action program. As a playwright and performer, her work has been featured at the Wild Project (New York); the Blue Theater, the Off Center, Hyde Park Theatre (Austin); Columbia College's Center for Book & Paper Arts (Chicago); and the Bonderman National Playwriting Symposium (Indianapolis). Since 2011, she has been working with Twin Cities artists to adapt classic plays for performance with local community members in historic homes, villages, and other sites throughout rural Minnesota.

Karina Naumer, MFA, is an educational-theatre consultant based in New York City, specializing in early childhood theatre-education and theatre with English Language Learners. Karina conducts professional-development workshops, summer courses and in-school residencies for Lincoln Center Theater's Learning English and Drama Project and develops and teaches arts-based early childhood programming for HEART: Humane Education Advocates Reaching Teachers, a humane education company. Nationally she has developed and taught professional development courses and workshops for the Alliance Theatre Company, Childsplay and Wolf Trap Institute for Early Learning though the Arts, among others. For 13 years, Karina was the founder and Director of the Creative Arts Team/New York City Wolf Trap Program: Early Learning through the Arts. In 2001, she was awarded the American Alliance for Theatre and Education's Creative Drama Award for excellence in the field. She currently serves on the AATE Board as Programming Director, National.

Jennifer Ridgway is the Director of Education and Outreach at Fulton Theatre in Lancaster, Pennsylvania. Jennifer serves on the Neighborhood

Bridges National Advisory Board for the Children's Theatre Company of Minneapolis. She received her MA in Theatre for Young People from the University of North Carolina, Greensboro in May 2009. As a graduate candidate, she was nominated as a Winifred Ward Scholar, received the Kay Brown Barrett Theatre for Youth Scholar, and was named the International Performing Arts for Youth Scholar. Working in the DC Metropolitan area, Jennifer was affiliated with the Kennedy Center, Imagination Stage, Arena Stage, InterAct Story Theatre, Wolf Trap Institute for Early Learning through the Arts, Adventure Theatre, the Smithsonian Institution's Discovery Theatre, Kaiser Permanente Educational Theatre Programs, among others. As co-founder and company member of Euphoria Theater Company, Jennifer brought literacy-based drama programs to the DC Arts and Humanities Education Collaborative.

Roxanne Schroeder-Arce currently serves as an Assistant Professor of Theatre Education at the Department of Theatre and Dance, The University of Texas at Austin. She previously served as an Assistant Professor at Emerson College in Boston, Massachusetts and at California State University Fresno. Roxanne received her MFA in Drama and Theatre for Youth from UT Austin and her BS degree in Theatre and teaching credential from Emerson College. She taught high-school theatre in Texas for six years. She also served as Artistic and Education Director of Teatro Humanidad in Austin for several years. Roxanne has published three bilingual plays that have been produced throughout the United States. Her research interests include cultural and ethnic representation in theatre, culturally responsive pedagogy with pre-service theatre educators, and US Latino/a youth identity. Her scholarly works have been published in a variety of theatre-education journals, including *Youth Theatre Journal, Teaching Theatre Journal* and *TYA Today*.

Carol T. (Jones) Schwartz founded and directed the Alliance Theatre Institute for Educators and Teaching Artists in Atlanta. In her 30-year tenure she initiated programs including Dramaturgy by Students and GA Wolf Trap. Carol has been a recreation therapist, special-needs teacher, director/composer for children's theatre groups in NC and GA, and a Teaching Artist. Carol served on the boards of TYA/USA and AATE and on taskforces for NAEP and the National Standards in Theatre. She earned an MS in Recreation Administration (UNC); an M.Ed. in Special Ed. (Coppin State) and a specialist degree in Arts Integration (Plymouth State, New Hampshire) She received the AATE Barbara Salisbury Award in 2006 for contribution to the field of theatre and education. Carol lives with husband, Arnie, in Denver,

New York where she volunteers as a consultant with Open Eye theatre. She hosts a movie music show on Wiox Radio 91.3 FM in Roxbury, New York.

Jamie Simpson Steele, Ph.D., is an Assistant Professor at the College of Education, University of Hawai'i at Mānoa where she prepares teacher candidates to integrate the arts throughout the curriculum. As a Teaching Artist, she continues to explore the development of new curriculum and contribute to professional-development opportunities for Teaching Artists and in-service teachers. Her research interests address issues of social justice, performances of culture, arts integration and performance as research methodology. Jamie collaborates with leading arts organizations, such as Honolulu Theatre for Youth, Hawai'i Arts Alliance, and Maui Arts and Culture Center, in order to better understand and sustain the arts in schools throughout the state of Hawai'i.

Cory Wilkerson is a Theatre Artist and arts consultant specializing in theatre for youth and applied theatre. Her recent career focus has been on standards-based arts education and arts assessment. Cory was appointed Pennsylvania's Theatre representative to the Council of Chief State Schools State Collaborative on Assessment and Student Standards, National Arts Assessment Institute, and went on to become a consultant in arts assessment and standards-based curriculum for the Pennsylvania Department of Education. Currently she works as part-time Project Director for the State Education Agency for Directors of Arts Education, serving with their partners at the National Coalition for Core Arts Standards. In her diverse career, Cory has been a director, performer, Teaching Artist, classroom teacher and arts administrator. She is proud to be a recipient of a Pennsylvania State Legislature Certificate of Achievement for her work with children and youth.

Index